THE ETHICS OF PERSUASION

CLASSICAL MEMORIES/MODERN IDENTITIES
Paul Allen Miller and Richard H. Armstrong, Series Editors

THE ETHICS OF PERSUASION

Derrida's Rhetorical Legacies

∼

BROOKE ROLLINS

THE OHIO STATE UNIVERSITY PRESS
COLUMBUS

Copyright © 2020 by The Ohio State University.
All rights reserved.

Library of Congress Cataloging-in-Publication Data
Names: Rollins, Brooke, author.
Title: The ethics of persuasion : Derrida's rhetorical legacies / Brooke Rollins.
Other titles: Classical memories/modern identities.
Description: Columbus : The Ohio State University Press, [2020] | Series: Classical memories/modern identities | Includes bibliographical references and index. | Summary: "Through Derridean deconstructive readings of some of the rhetorical tradition's most esteemed texts on persuasion by Gorgias, Lysias, Isocrates, and Plato, the book suggests that an ethics emerges from even the most forceful instances of persuasion"—Provided by publisher.
Identifiers: LCCN 2019048248 | ISBN 9780814214244 (cloth) | ISBN 081421424X (cloth) | ISBN 9780814277874 (ebook) | ISBN 081427787X (ebook)
Subjects: LCSH: Derrida, Jacques. | Persuasion (Rhetoric) | Ethics. | Rhetoric, Ancient—Philosophy. | Deconstruction. | Classical literature—History and criticism.
Classification: LCC PN175 .R65 2020 | DDC 808—dc23
LC record available at https://lccn.loc.gov/2019048248

Other identifiers: ISBN 9780814255834 (paper) | ISBN 0814255833 (paper)

Cover design by Angela Moody
Text design by Juliet Williams
Type set in Adobe Minion Pro

For Lee and Cooper Bauknight

CONTENTS

Acknowledgments		ix
INTRODUCTION(S)		1
CHAPTER 1	Derrida's Rhetorical Ethics	25
CHAPTER 2	Gorgias's Pre-Performative Address	47
CHAPTER 3	Lysias's Ghost	65
CHAPTER 4	Isocrates's Promise	101
CHAPTER 5	Plato's Friendship	135
CHAPTER 6	Derrida's Farewell	161
EPILOGUE		177
Works Cited		183
Index		195

ACKNOWLEDGMENTS

I feel lucky to have had the support of a wonderful editorial team at The Ohio State University Press. I am so grateful to series editors Paul Allen Miller and Richard Armstrong for seeing in *The Ethics of Persuasion* the potential to contribute to the Classical Memories/Modern Identities series and for championing the project every step of the way. My acquisitions editor, Ana Jimenez-Moreno, provided wise and supportive guidance throughout the publication process, and I owe a debt of gratitude to the anonymous reviewers who provided their time and insight through multiple stages of review. Your comments have shaped my thinking and made the argument better.

I am grateful for John Muckelbauer's guidance, friendship, and continued support. Thank you for being a wonderful teacher and generous reader and for convincing me that publications are, most of all, markers of our learning. So much of this one I learned thanks to you.

This book has benefitted from the substantive and incisive feedback from a number of generous colleagues: Michael Bernard-Donals, Diane Davis, Christy Friend, Byron Hawk, Barbara Heifferon, Kyle Jensen, Steve Lynn, Elsie Michie, Allen Miller, and Thomas Rickert. Allen, no words can adequately convey how incredibly grateful I am for your intellectual generosity and your unwavering commitment to this book. Diane, I cannot thank you enough for your unflagging support of me and this project. You are a constant inspiration. Elsie, you are a dream reader. One of your comments on an early draft gave me the idea to make the chapter on Lysias about hospitality. It ended up being my favorite, and it was the most fun to write.

I'm grateful for the wonderfully supportive community at Lehigh University and for my colleagues who regularly take the time to read and comment on my work: Kate Crassons, Beth Dolan, Lyndon Dominique, Suzanne Edwards, Mary Foltz, Scott Gordon, Dawn Keetley, Michael Kramp, Barry Kroll, Jenna Lay, Ed Lotto, Seth Moglen, Barbara Pavlock, Amardeep Singh, Stephanie Watts, Bob Watts, and Ed Whitley. Thank you for advocating for me and for providing a vibrant intellectual space in which to work. I am grateful to have received generous financial support from Lehigh University's Faculty Research Grant and the Paul J. Franz Fellowship. Among other things, this support enabled me to secure the assistance of the wonderful Ashlee Simon, who made invaluable contributions during manuscript preparation.

Thank you to my dear friends Lisa Bailey, Mark Brantner, and Eme Crawford, whose friendship, support, and humor have sustained me from the earliest days of writing this book. And thank you Maggie Callahan-Mabus, Kevin Casper, Erin Cromer, and Katie DeLuca, former students (and now wonderful friends) who continue to teach me so much.

I am so grateful for the lifetime of love and encouragement of my parents, Robert and Sherry Barnhart and Robert and Carole Rollins, and my grandmother Doris Kohli. Thank you for all that you've given me—too much to name—and for your unwavering faith that I could do this.

Lee and Cooper Bauknight, you two are my world. Thank you for making this possible.

An early version of a now entirely revised version of Chapter 2 appeared as "Persuasion's Ethical Force: Levinas, Gorgias and the Call to the Other" in *JAC: A Journal of Rhetoric, Culture, & Politics* vol. 29, issue 3 (2009), and an early version of Chapter 6 appeared as "The Ethics of Epideictic Rhetoric: Addressing the Problem of Presence through Jacques Derrida's Funeral Orations" in *Rhetoric Society Quarterly* vol. 35, issue 1 (2005). I am grateful for the permission to revise and reprint.

INTRODUCTION(S)

~

> There are two kinds of Introduction: the Direct Opening, in Greek called the Prooimion, and the Subtle Approach, called the Ephodos. [...] Between the Subtle Approach and the Direct Opening there is the following difference. The Direct Opening should be such that by [...] straightforward methods [...] we immediately make the hearer well-disposed or attentive or receptive; whereas the Subtle Approach should be such that we effect all these results covertly, through dissimulation [...].
>
> —*Rhetoric to Herennius*, 1.4.6–1.7.11

> The staging of a title, a first sentence, an epigraph, a pretext, a preface, a single germ, will never make a beginning. It was indefinitely dispersed.
>
> —Jacques Derrida, *Dissemination*, 43

PROOIMION: THE DIRECT OPENING

Writers of the early rhetorical handbooks knew well the power of an introduction to transform the disposition of an audience: Pitched just the right way, it could soften the skeptic or capture the imagination of the most disinterested bystander. Both the classical Greek *Rhetoric to Alexander* and the Roman *Rhetoric to Herennius* (80s BCE), for example, attest to the power of opening with just the right gambit, and each handbook discusses the introduction's ability to foster in the audience a receptivity to the argument to come. While these texts suggest that there are myriad ways to effectively open a speech, depending on the circumstances, the *Alexander* explains that the introduction is, in its most basic form, a *prooimion*: "a declaration of the subject in a summary manner [...] in order that [the audience] may know with what the speech is concerned and may follow the argument" (1436a).[1] Because this book focuses on texts from the classical rhetorical tradition that, like the *Alexander*, attempt to theorize, teach, and/or practice the art of persuasion, it seems fitting to follow this formula and state, first of all, my central argument: that

---

1. Line numbers for *Rhetoric to Alexander* refer to the text included in *The Complete Works of Aristotle, The Revised Oxford Translation, Vol. 2*, edited by Jonathan Barnes, Princeton UP, 1984.

even the most forceful instances of persuasion can be shown to demonstrate that we are not sovereign speakers and audience members who by turns wield and stand guard against linguistic techniques of rule. Our persuasive endeavors, rather, are made possible by an ethical encounter in which self-presence is interrupted and through which expressive identity is radically challenged. I make this argument by drawing on the work of Jacques Derrida, whose claims allow me to identify and theorize the ethical dimensions of persuasive activity, particularly as they emerge in the work of the classical thinkers Gorgias, Lysias, Isocrates, and Plato, each of whom offers a still-influential perspective on the theory, practice, and pedagogy of the art of persuasion. *The Ethics of Persuasion* reads some of rhetoric's most esteemed historical texts through this Derridean lens in order to tease out from within them an ethical imperative that traditionally has been subsumed by a focus on rhetoric's persuasive utility. I should note, as well, that what began as a Derridean reading of rhetorical thought became more complicated when the classical discourses themselves illuminated anew some of the powerfully rhetorical dimensions of Derrida's philosophical work. Thus, while Derrida enables us to reimagine the persuasive arts, long known for their utilitarian focus on the force of language, this same tradition provides a supple vocabulary for highlighting the important rhetorical elements of deconstruction.

But first, a brief discussion of this book's central term: ethics. When I use this term, I refer to a particular sense of ethics that I take from Derrida's work and that refers, not to a moral ground or to predetermined conceptions of the good, but to the ongoing interruption of being by otherness. Challenging prescriptive notions of ethics, which assume a rational, self-present, and autonomous subject who chooses to act (or not) in accordance with accepted moral codes, Derrida suggests that ethical acts cannot be attributed to a subject who has caused them. There is no being, in other words, making ethical choices and decisions prior to her relations with others. Instead, ethics emerges in the event of an expropriating encounter with otherness in which self-identity is unsettled. As Derrida suggested in a 1991 interview with Jean Luc Nancy, the ethical subject is not "the figure of mastery of self, of adequation to self, center and origin of the world" (Cadava, Connor, and Nancy 103), but rather "a singularity that dislocates or divides itself in gathering itself together to answer to the other, whose call somehow precedes its own identification with itself" (100). In this way, the priority of the other over and above the selfsame subject resists what Derrida calls "the lure of the I"—a powerful tendency he describes as "dreaming of an operation of ideal and idealizing mastery, transforming hetero-affection into auto-affection, heteronomy into autonomy" (*Margins* 297). What it means to answer to the call of the other before the advent of subjectivity, in other words, is that the other cannot be cast out of the safe home of one's identity. Ethics thus rests on a subject perpetually haunted by the other's trace.

As that which is beyond the "order of the calculable" (*Psyche Vo1. 1* 39), "otherness" and the "other" are impossible terms to define, but Derrida makes clear that there is nothing so important as seeking out, asking after, and responding to the other in order to be transformed by the encounter. "The interest of deconstruction," he argues, "is a certain experience of the impossible: that is [. . .] of the other" (15). This experience of the impossible emerges differentially across Derrida's oeuvre, and within his writings the other has gone by an array of names: event, *pharmakon, khôra, hôte,* and specter, to name but a few. In each case, the figure of the other is an "unanticipatable alterity [. . .] for which no horizon of expectation as yet seems ready, in place, available" (39), and so it is utterly beyond my grasp, my mastery, and my abilities of comprehension. Encountering this other reveals not a dialectical separation between a self and an other, but an interruptive and constitutive relation in which the self is simultaneously invented and dispersed. The encounter with the other, in other words, reveals that the "relation to self [. . .] can only be *différance,* that is to say alterity, or trace" (Cadava, Connor, and Nancy 100). What results in the experience of the impossible, in other words, is a responsibility to the other that precedes and frustrates self-identification. And it is precisely in this unsettling moment of encountering the other as other that ethics begins. As Simon Critchley explains it, the ethics that emerges from Derrida's work is not "based upon the recognition of the other, which is always self-recognition, but would rather begin with the expropriation of the self in the face of the other's approach" (*Ethics, Politics, Subjectivity* 14). Grounded in this Derridean perspective, one of my aims is to seek out "certain experiences of the impossible" within the classical rhetorical tradition and to show the ways that the largely instrumental art of persuasion involves a transformative encounter with otherness in which the subject is at stake.

The exigency for such a project is rooted in the classical rhetorical tradition's penchant for instrumentality, in particular its essential role in the quest for social and political power in the context of a burgeoning Athenian democracy. Composed in part of treatises that theorize the persuasive features of expression, real and dramatized speeches from Athenian legal and political settings, and handbooks—such as the *Alexander* and *Herennius* noted above— that recommend tactical approaches for speaking to various audiences, classical rhetoric is a highly practical discipline. Opposed to philosophy from the time of Plato, rhetoric is defined, for good or for ill, as a utilitarian art. Concerned with persuasion and public opinion, rhetoric (and the texts and histories that make up its classical tradition) is involved in the highly sophisticated but sometimes guileful production of linguistic rule. Jean-Pierre Vernant vividly characterizes this forceful, even potentially dangerous power of persuasive rhetoric: "The system of the *polis* implied [. . .] the extraordinary preeminence of speech over all other instruments of power. Speech became the political tool par excellence, the key to all authority in the state, the means of commanding and dominating others" (49). John Muckelbauer has characterized this dimension of rhetoric as "asignifying," noting that, with its focus on persuasion, rhetoric concerns itself not so much with what things *mean* but rather with *how to produce persuasive effects*. "Rather than attempting to identically reproduce the proposition as a meaning in the mind of the audience," he argues, "persuasive rhetoric attempts to make the proposition compelling, to give it a certain force" (*The Future* 17). In other words, Muckelbauer adds, "if I am trying to persuade the polis, I am primarily concerned with getting them to *do* something and not primarily interested in getting them to understand something" (18).

The *Alexander* and the *Herennius,* those early handbooks, strongly emphasize these action- and effect-oriented characteristics: The focus of these texts, and the countless others like them that have been lost to history, was on rhetorical technique, on individual sections of speeches and their arrangement, on commonplaces, and on appeals to audience members' emotions (Kennedy *A New History* 30–33, "Earliest" 293–306). The advice they proffered was characterized by how a given rhetorical strategy might affect an audience rather than what information should be included in any particular speech. In this way, persuasion is involved in the production of what J. L. Austin calls perlocutionary force, which, as I discuss in Chapter 1, refers to what happens in the mysterious space between speech act and effect. The lesson we can take from rhetoric's emphasis on asignification is that meaning or content *sometimes* plays a part in creating persuasive force, but not always, and not necessarily in a primary fashion. In the *Alexander,* the chief focus is on putting audience members in a receptive state by providing them with a map of sorts, one that clearly marks the destination and provides a route for arriving there. The most basic way of setting out this route *happens* to occur by way of providing an account of what lies ahead, but the emphasis is on the act of preparing the audience in a favorable way, not on the message itself; thus, representative meaning becomes an instrument used to enact the more important end of making hearers receptive. The *Herennius* even more explicitly prioritizes persuasive force over meaning when it distinguishes between two types of introductions, one direct (the *prooimion*) and the other subtle (the *ephodos*), noting that in some cases a covert treatment of the central claims puts audience members in an amenable state and makes them more likely to come around to the speaker's way of thinking. Thus, while signified content sometimes performs the persuasive function of readying the audience, at other times it has the opposite effect. In these latter cases, the speaker is well advised to take another tack, one that involves withholding the central claim (*Herennius* 1.6.9). In both the *Alexander* and the *Herennius*, then, the discussions of how best to compose introductions subordinate meaning to force, and in these cases meaning is valuable not in and of itself, but because it has the capacity to affect an audience.

These practically oriented texts were often criticized for this very reason: because they paid too much attention to how to appeal to external audiences and not enough to the production of substantive content. Aristotle, for example, notes that authors of the early rhetorical handbooks "give most of their attention to matters external to the subject; for verbal attack and pity and anger and such emotions of the mind [. . .] do not relate to fact but are appeals to the juryman. As a result, if all trials were conducted as they are in some present-day states and especially in those well-governed [the handbook writers] would have nothing to say" (*On Rhetoric* 1.1.3–4).[2] Relatively unconcerned with the content of any particular speech, the rhetorical handbooks assist their readers in identifying, categorizing, and producing different types of forces. This a uniquely rhetorical perspective, and because of it, rhetoric—classical rhetoric in particular—has earned the reputation as an instrumentalist body of theory, practice, and pedagogy that is put to work for specific ends. While persuasion may be useful for fostering social cohesion and for helping communities decide how to proceed in uncertain political situations, its perennial threat is that it deals in appearances rather than truths. Unmoored from meaning and focused on effecting some predetermined end, persuasion would seem to be at best free of ethical value and at worst prone to mercenary self-interest. While several important thinkers from the classical tradition argue that there can and should be an ethical component to artful persuasion, the received wisdom is that ethics is something that must be added on—a supplement to an art and practice that is constituted by its capacity for manipulation. Over the course of *The Ethics of Persuasion*, I challenge this received wisdom by demonstrating the ways that the preoriginary, interruptive ethics I've begun to describe with Derrida infiltrates persuasion essentially. What my readings of ancient rhetorical texts reveal is that when the trace of the other interrupts identity, persuasive instrumentalism implodes.

---

2. Section numbers for Aristotle's *Rhetoric* refer to the George A. Kennedy translation: *On Rhetoric: A Theory of Civic Discourse*, Oxford UP, 2007.

Drawing on Derrida's claim that the encounter with the other initiates an ultimately ethical expropriation of the self, I argue that four classical rhetorical locations—two dealing with persuasion's artful and expert practice and two focused on the pedagogy of persuasion—involve participants in the transformative encounter with otherness. Although the "unanticipatable alterity," to borrow Derrida's term, emerges differently in the highly instrumental persuasive address of Gorgias (Chapter 2), the ghostwritten speeches of Lysias (Chapter 3), the famed rhetorical *paideia* of Isocrates (Chapter 4), the pedagogical displays of Socrates in Plato's *Lysis* (Chapter 5), and Derrida's own funeral speeches (Chapter 6), in each case persuasion's instrumental force is undermined. In each of these rhetorical locations, I argue, persuasion is less "commanding and dominating," to recall Vernant's formulation, than it is disruptive and unsettling. We encounter no controlling, autonomous speaking subjects here, but beings constituted (and so interrupted) in an encounter with difference. What was once figured as a scene of domination is thus recast as a nontotalizable encounter in which responsibility, negotiation, and decision are owed to the other.

Such analyses are useful and necessary, I want to suggest, because rhetoric's disciplinary orientation toward influence—its primary focus on moving others, on bringing others around to the orator's way of thinking, and on inducing them to act according to the speaker's desires—frames persuasion as little more than a communicative transaction in which none of the participants is fundamentally affected. If, for example, as in the legal settings alluded to by our handbook writers, the speaker persuades his audience to acquit him of murder charges or to find him eligible for a pension from the state, then it would seem that he has presented his case shrewdly and appealed successfully to the audience that has the power to decide his fate.[3] And while the audience members have been won over by this presumably astute presentation, they have had the chance and, importantly, the *choice* to come to their own conclusions and grant the speaker what he sought. On either side of this equation, then, it would seem that both the speaker and the hearer maintain their presence-to-self and that they are uncompromised in the encounter with persuasion's force. In Chapter 1, I explore our propensity for this fantasy by

---

3. I use masculine pronouns here and elsewhere in the book when I refer to the individuals involved in ancient rhetorical political, legal, and educational practices. I do so not to ignore or simply accept the exclusionary nature of this tradition, but to avoid covering over it. My central claim actually bears on this issue: The alterity ethics that I argue infiltrates several classical rhetorical examples ultimately interrupts the determination of identity, which is itself the basis for social, political, legal, and economic exclusion. This point is not to suggest that such exclusions were and are not powerful and real (quite the contrary), but to show that they are premised on categories that are neither essential nor complete.

revisiting Derrida's transformative inheritance of the Austinian performative utterance.[4] Derrida, as we will see, comes to understand performativity as an ethical relation prior to Austin's primary concern: the distinction between what words mean and what they can be made to do. From my point of view, this debate is important because its thoroughgoing attention to the asignifying force of language helps highlight and articulate the rhetorical sensibility of Derridean ethics. Whatever his objections to Austin, what becomes clear is that the *structure* of Austin's speech situation (though not its metaphysical assumptions) provides Derrida with a useful way to talk about one's constitutive responsibility to the other. (As I argue in Chapter 1, Derrida often uses rhetorical terminology to explain the ethical components of deconstruction.) This larger point—that ethics has a rhetorical structure—is one Diane Davis has developed in a number of texts over the course of the last ten years, and her work has been influential for my own thinking. *Inessential Solidarity: Rhetoric and Foreigner Relations* (2010), for example, figures one's capacity to be persuaded as a *primordial* ethical relation. That is, before any artful speechmaking—before any attempts to use language to initiate action in the world—there will have been an ongoing entanglement with the trace or with *différance,* and it is this entanglement that enables responsibility. "If rhetorical practices work by managing to have an effect on others," Davis writes, "then an always prior openness to the other's affection is its first requirement: the 'art' of rhetoric can be effective only among affectable existents, who are by definition something other than distinct individuals or self-determining agents" (3). For Davis, the term *rhetorical* does not apply simply to the artful production of linguistic rule, but to the "fundamental addressivity and responsivity" that take place at both the level of the letter and the level of "life itself" ("Rhetoricity" 432). She calls this a "preliminary rhetoricitiy" (435) that goes "all the way down" (436) to the structure of the cell. Drawing on Davis's insights, as well as Derrida's claims that illimitable force transforms what we have traditionally called "communication" into an interruptive encounter with difference, I argue that persuasion contains an important ethical dimension that has yet to be inherited.

---

4. When I refer to this account of the persuasive scenario as a "fantasy," I am thinking of Barbara A. Biesecker's influential argument in "Rethinking the Rhetorical Situation from within the Thematic of *Différance*" (1989). She argues there that "Derridean deconstruction begins by considering the way in which all texts are inhabited by an internally divided non-originary 'origin' called *différance.* The divisiveness of that 'originating' moment is, so to speak, covered over or [. . .] finessed into a unity by [. . .] writing and [. . .] speaking. [. . .] *Différance* underwrites all discursive practices and thus exposes all beginning points, all primordial axioms and all founding principles as constructions—impositions, traces of a will to knowledge" (120).

There has been an important body of work in the field of rhetoric and writing that brings Derrida's thought to bear on the history of rhetoric (as well as work that does the same for thinking about persuasive action more specifically). In 1979, Sharon Crowley initiated the discipline of rhetoric and composition's interest in Derrida with "Of Gorgias and Grammatology," an essay in which she draws on Derrida's critique of the metaphysics of presence to make a case for ushering out the then-predominant and impoverished pedagogical practice of "current-traditional rhetoric" (279).[5] Linking Derrida's poststructuralist approach to Gorgias's "pre-metaphysical" opinions on the relationship between speech and thought, Crowley made an early assertion about Derrida's relevance for rethinking both the classical rhetorical tradition and contemporary writing instruction (279). Following this essay, a surge of scholarship (from roughly 1985–1989) by Crowley, Gregory L. Ulmer, G. Douglas Atkins and Michael L. Johnson, Barbara A. Biesecker, and Jasper Neel, among others, constituted what we might loosely call the first generation of rhetoric's engagement with Derrida. Drawing on the terms elaborated in Derrida's early work, these thinkers used the concepts of *différance*, *arche*-writing, and grammatology to radicalize assumptions about the writing process, to rethink the elements of the rhetorical situation, and to develop pedagogical approaches that stressed invention and performance over the representation of knowledge.

More recently, scholars in the discipline have gravitated towards Derrida's later work to explore and articulate rhetoric's post- and extra-human dimensions (see, for example, Michelle Ballif, Davis, Natasha Seegert, and Lynn Worsham), to expand rhetoric's scope and function within the complex ecologies of the networked age (Brown), and, as I attempt here, to make a case for rhetoric's explicitly ethical aspects and effects. In *Inessential Solidarity*, Davis draws on Derrida's work on hospitality to make a case for the fundamentally rhetorical nature of what it means to be preoriginarily exposed to otherness and to argue that this "constitutive persuadability" is what provides the opening for justice (121). Taking this focus on the relation to the other into the extra-human realm, Ballif argues that rhetorical practice should be retheorized "while acknowledging the address, the addressor, and the addressee as being essentially *haunted*" ("Regarding" 466). "This," she adds, "is what renders rhetoric an *ethical* rather than an *epistemological* enterprise" (466). In addition to drawing on Derridean hauntology to argue that rhetoric's ethical

---

5. As Crowley notes, current-traditional rhetoric is "the system of rhetoric that replaced the vigorous classical theory of rhetoric sometime in the nineteenth century" (279). Its pedagogical implementation played out to the detriment of writing students everywhere, who were forced to "concern themselves almost exclusively with prescriptions about arrangement and style, ignoring invention altogether" (279).

injunction is to address the living dead other—"to lend an ear to the ghostly whisperings of that which (continues to) haunt rhetoric"—Ballif uses Derrida's *Specters of Marx* to retheorize historiography as an ethical practice that "demands listening to, learning from, [and] conversing with those inhabitants of [the] border" ("Historiography" 140). Rather than gaining a better understanding of such unfamiliar ghosts, the historiographer herself is at stake, transformed in the encounter with the radically unknowable other.

What I attempt in *The Ethics of Persuasion* is to illuminate some instances of what Ballif might call classical rhetoric's "ghostly whisperings." By highlighting the uncontrollable and radically unknowable forces that escape classical rhetoric's traditional system of communication, I attempt to show that even the most highly utilitarian persuasive scenes involve an encounter with alterity and thus an ongoing interruption of being by otherness. Whether this phenomenon is intended or not (which I would not claim to know), what we find is that some of the most traditionally humanistic rhetorics (such as Isocrates's famed *logôn paideia*, which offered the moral education of the whole orator) require a prior ontological disturbance. By using this approach, I attempt to link Derrida's early thinking on *arche*-writing and performativity, which I contend in Chapter 1 is uniquely rhetorical, to his later work, which, as some have argued, takes up more explicitly ethical themes. Despite this still fairly common diagnosis, Derrida has denied that his work took an ethical *turn*, suggesting instead that ethics was always central to his project: "[T]here never was in the 1980s or 1990s, as has sometimes been claimed, a *political turn* or *ethical turn* in 'deconstruction' [. . .]. The thinking of the political has always been a thinking of différance and the thinking of différance always a thinking *of* the political" (*Rogues* 39). And, I would add, a thinking of the ethical. Derrida's early engagements with Austin refigure communication itself as the performative response to the unknowable to come. In this radically retheorized model, force is not merely asignifying (involved in the utilitarian production of a consequence) but constitutive of difference itself. What this suggests in turn is that perlocutionary acts are—strictly speaking—impossible.

For Derrida, one privileged location for highlighting the necessity of contending with "emergence or the event" is the ancient landscape of Western metaphysics. Through his complex deconstructive explications of ancient Greek thinkers, Derrida outlines and dramatizes the philosophical and ethical concepts central to his own thinking. To note a few familiar examples, he offered an account of the supplement via his analysis of Plato, of hospitality via Sophocles, and of friendship via Aristotle. The Greek philosophical tradition, in short, is an essential component of Derrida's work, and, as Paul Allen Miller has noted, he conceives of it "as the intimate other who is also always already part of the same, both different from and yet formative of our identity, and hence able to serve as a means of refashioning it" (*Postmodern Spiritual* 11). And Miriam Leonard argues that for Derrida "an engagement in antiquity was fully constitutive of a new vision of philosophy—a philosophy grounded in a radical rereading of the foundational texts" ("Introduction: 'Today'" 2). My hope is that *The Ethics of Persuasion* participates in a similar project—that it allows us to inherit some of the field of rhetoric's most highly determined texts differently. Derrida's interest, furthermore, in demonstrating how the law of contamination underwrites all of Western metaphysics is no doubt central to his longstanding affinity for the work of ancient Greek theorists. As he explains in the essay "'We Other Greeks'":

> It is not only the non-Greek that attracted me in/to (*chez*) the Greek (it's a question of knowing in short what *chez* means), not only the other of the Greek (the Egyptian, the Barbarian, or whoever is determined by the Greek as *his* other, and so is excluded-included, posed as opposable), but the wholly other of the Greek, of his language and his *logos*, this figure of a wholly other that is unfigurable by him. This wholly other haunts every one of the essays I have devoted to 'Greek' things and it often irrupts within them: under different names, for perhaps it has no proper name. (25)

In my analyses of the classical rhetorical tradition in the coming chapters, I try to make it clear that the "wholly other of the Greek" interrupts traditional narratives about persuasion's instrumental and utilitarian force. Drawing on Derrida's theoretical insights as well as his style of reading, I will show that the origin of Western rhetoric (which we have had no choice but to inherit, to take up, and to contend with) is far less stable, less utilitarian, and perhaps even less Greek than we might be inclined to think. Bringing Derrida's thought to bear in this way on a specifically Athenian rhetorical tradition allows us to rethink and transform that tradition from within. Despite my appreciation for and theoretical indebtedness to recent calls, like Ballif's and Davis's, to theorize rhetoric beyond the realm of the human, we simply do not have the option of leaving classical rhetoric's strongly humanistic impulses behind altogether. We can, however look for the ways that classical rhetorical practices, theories, and pedagogies of persuasion are other to themselves—and the ways that they undermine their own humanism from within.

This approach also affords the opportunity to look to some of the specifically rhetorical aspects of Derrida's own work. As Michael Naas has argued, deconstruction is perhaps best described as the simultaneous affirmation and transformation of the tradition (*Taking*). Thus, when Derrida reads philosophical texts, Naas argues, he does so not only (or even primarily) to make representative claims about the inner workings of their content. Rather, he uses language in a highly performative manner, often playing with the very styles and conventions that define the traditions in question. Muckelbauer advances a more extreme version of this assessment by arguing that Derrida's writing style "actively subtracts its own substantive claims" (*Thinking*). "The purpose behind this endeavor," he argues, "is to highlight or foreground the conceptual/discursive movement through which those claims emerge—the 'how' or 'style' of thinking rather than the 'what' of the content" (*Thinking*). While the sophistication (and by many accounts, unjustifiable difficulty) of Derrida's style has been commented upon often, it has not been given a full rhetorical accounting. What I argue is that when Derrida installs identifiable rhetorical figures and forms in the heart of his more properly philosophical work, he shows us the way these formulaic features function to interrupt the communicative loop. In other words, he seemed to find within the classical tradition of persuasion powerful tools for interrupting metaphysical prejudice. Thus, what I attempt in *The Ethics of Persuasion* is to bring together two traditions—Derrida and classical rhetoric—in order to add to the ongoing conversations about the ethics of each.

To this end, I have in this book two primary goals: First, I want to add to the discussion about the rhetorical qualities of Derrida's ethics, which I characterize as aporetic and connect to the purpose and function of the rhetorical figure of aporia. Second, I want to use Derrida's aporetic ethics to rethink the rhetorical tradition. In Chapter 1, I argue that Derrida's interest in performativity allows us to reconceive of rhetoric's orientation toward influence as a profoundly ethical and relational inclination. His inheritance and transformation of Austin's speech act theory, I argue, shows us that while persuasion is involved in the production of perlocutionary force, the perlocutionary act is interrupted from the start by a pre-performative and ongoing affirmation of alterity. In Derrida's reception of Austin's concept of the performative, that is, presence to self is perpetually interrupted by the other and by difference, issuing an other-before-me ethical imperative. Following this account of the powerful interruptive force of persuasive communication, I examine—in Chapters 2 and 3—two renowned rhetorical artists, practitioners of rhetoric whose work is simultaneously celebrated and condemned for its deployment of powerful rhetorical force. My readings (of Gorgias and Lysias, respectively) suggest that, even in the midst of seemingly calculated instances of linguistic rule, the masterful speech artist (as well as the person to whom the speech is addressed) can be shown to be interrupted, invented, and transformed in an encounter with alterity.

Chapter 2 focuses on Gorgias's *Encomium of Helen,* a speech that is many things: lyrical; playful; performative (it does to us the very thing that Paris is said to have done to Helen); and, finally, associated for all time with the powerful instrumental capacities of persuasion. Here, Gorgias famously celebrates persuasion for its ability to overwhelm audience members' critical capacities, and his claims for speech's power support the broader cultural view of the sophist as a figure bent on molding audiences to his own design. But the speech is also ethical in the sense that I have elaborated thus far. It makes the case that who we are is given to us only when we respond to the other's unwilled address. This is what Gorgias suggests to us about Helen and what he does to us as his audience, more than two millennia after he wrote the speech. I argue that Gorgias portrays Helen as engaged at the pre-performative level, prior to the formation of her will. I read the speech as a presubjective drama in which Helen's performative power is committed in advance to the others who address her. She never *is,* she is only ever *in relation* to otherness. And this is the same kind of subjectivity that Derrida theorizes for all of us: Our presence is always haunted by our response to a radically unknowable other. We never *are,* we are only ever *in response.* Thus, we have in the *Encomium* compelling evidence that a constitutive ethics interrupts even the most celebratory—and infamous—accounts of persuasion's instrumental force.

In Chapter 3, turning from one well-known advocate of persuasion's instrumental force to another, I conjure Lysias, the classical rhetorical tradition's most famous ghost(writer)—and by some accounts, its most famous purveyor of "unethical rhetoric." That this prolific and, as some have argued, promiscuous logographer is an easy target is exactly the point: Lysias has long served as a poster child for those who claim that rhetoric has no concern for truth, is a means to an often-selfish end, and appeals to our lesser angels to achieve these ends. As a rhetorical gun-for-hire known to write speeches for just about anyone so long as he was paid, Lysias certainly invited criticism. Plato, for one, depicts him as an unscrupulous hack, ascribing to him in the *Phaedrus* an underdeveloped speech in which Lysias turns love on its head in trying to persuade a young man to sleep with him. In this chapter, I do not argue against these criticisms of Lysias. Instead I offer a counterreading that reinterprets the qualities that have been deemed problematic or worse and that shows how they are contaminated by a radical otherness that interrupts subjectivity itself. Because of his liminal position as an Athenian metic, because of the way he is depicted by Plato, and because of his powerful association with *ethopoeia* (the practice of developing vivid and authentic-seeming individual characteristics for others), Lysias, I argue, is a spectral figure in the Derridean sense. An outsider who by turns inhabited the positions of guest, host, hostage and ghost, Lysias stalks the borders of presence and absence and ultimately settles, disruptively, inside the Athenian democracy that, in the end, could not contain him.

While Chapters 2 and 3 identify and make a case for the ethics essential to even the most seemingly calculated forms of persuasive force, Chapters 4 and 5 focus on rhetorical pedagogy, specifically on the very different ways that Isocrates and Plato formulate this process. Although they fundamentally disagree on the scope and purpose of formalized learning as it emerges in the fourth century BCE, both men figure learning not as the masterful reduction of difference to the realm of the same, but as a radical transformation of the subject that is initiated by an encounter with alterity. The renowned rhetoric teacher Isocrates, as I note in Chapter 4, is traditionally seen as the paragon of conservative moral pedagogy. Drawing on Derrida's concepts of the promise and the decision, I refigure Isocrates's famed rhetorical *paidea* not simply as training in civic virtue but as fundamental preparation for what Derrida calls the future to come. Through rereadings of *Antidosis, Against the Sophists, To Demonicus,* and *Panegyricus,* among other Isocratean treatises, I argue that Isocrates's concern for virtue is shot through with—and ultimately interrupted by—alterity. This is the case because, in these texts, self-presence, or what we experience as self-presence, is internally structured by the anticipation of a radically unknowable future (which Isocrates discusses in terms of *kairos*). My argument here is important for two reasons: First, it casts Isocrates in a new and, ultimately for scholars of rhetoric, more productive light. In this reading, he becomes more than a believer in the capacity of rhetorical pedagogy to develop civic virtue and in the subsequent contribution this virtuous eloquence makes to the community at large. Rather, Isocrates becomes a thinker of the radically unknowable (wholly other) future and its untimely transformative effects on us. More specifically, despite his reputation as a quaint conservative moralist, Isocrates suggests that self-presence is always disrupted by the future to come. And, second, my rereading of Isocrates has broader and perhaps more immediate implications for higher education itself. It shows that any kind of moral education, including liberal arts programs in general and composition classes in particular, is structured by uncontainable risk because there is no possibility of guaranteeing virtue in the face of the radically unknowable future.

In Chapter 5, I turn to Plato's *Lysis,* which, while absent from the pantheon of the philosopher's rhetorically themed dialogues (such as *Gorgias, Protagoras, Phaedrus,* or *Sophist*), presents an ostensible topic—friendship—that hinges on and must be understood in relation to its explicit and highly dramatized instances of persuasion. Although most of the dialogue's content is devoted to questions concerning how to acquire friends, what, if anything, friends share in common, and whether friendship is reciprocal, these conversations are framed as playing out within Socrates's highly calculated and sometimes comically staged persuasive demonstrations. More specifically, Socrates undertakes a conversation with Lysis (one of the primary interlocutors in the dialogue) in order to demonstrate to a lovesick Hippothales (who has an important role at the outset of the dialogue, but who fades to the background and becomes an observer much like Plato's readers do) how to snare the affections of a desirable boy. Socrates punctuates this conversation on friendly love by reminding Plato's reading audience that his address to Lysis is a persuasive model for Hippothales. And this structure is replicated when Socrates turns his attention to Menexenus at the request of Lysis, who seeks a Socratic comeuppance for his argumentatively inclined friend. Once again, Socrates addresses one audience for the benefit of another that looks on. What I make of all of this is that the *Lysis*'s serial-persuasive form—when considered alongside the interlocutors' ultimate inability to define a friend—disperses the perlocutionary force of Socrates's persuasive attempts. Although it is clear that Socrates knows his various audiences and targets them like a master marksman, the structure of the dialogue suggests that the instrumental force of persuasion will always be frustrated in advance by *différance*.

In Chapter 6, I turn my rhetorical/analytical lens from the work of classical thinkers and practitioners of persuasion to Derrida's own most identifiably rhetorical work, the funerary texts written for some of the leading intellectuals of his generation. In this way, I cast Derrida as a modern inheritor of the classical tradition his work has helped me reimagine. Having delivered funeral speeches for many friends, Derrida remains, I believe, one of our most sensitive and accomplished epideictic orators. My analysis in this chapter accounts for Derrida's inheritance of the particularly Athenian genre of the funeral oration (famously discussed and sampled in Thucydides's *History of the Peloponnesian War*, among other classical locations) by showing that for Derrida, it is necessary to attempt to leave friends—those we would seem to know so well—to their otherness. He uses these speeches, in part, to demonstrate the importance of refraining from using friends for one's own end (to discuss a friend in order to make oneself feel better, for example, as we so often do in the wake of incomprehensible loss). He shows that the only way to do justice to the friend is to attempt a (never fully realizable) nonappropriative rapport by pushing highly prescribed rhetorical conventions to their limit. In this case, it is the repetition of the highly prescribed rhetorical form of aporia that interrupts the otherwise appropriative discourse of mourning. Derrida's speeches often dramatize his larger philosophical point that who "I am" is given only when the other settles inside "me," disruptively. The highly prescribed rhetorical form and its associated figures settle within Derrida's funerary lamentations, and in so doing, they ensure that his addresses for his dead friends do not venture into unseemly appropriation.

Having described my primary rhetorical locations and overall argumentative trajectory, I want to offer the following qualification, which I take to be central to my conceptual approach in this book: The classical rhetorical tradition—not to mention the question of what counts as the rhetorical tradition—is expansive, diffuse, and much contested, and I do not claim to represent the whole of it here. While the thinkers I analyze in these chapters are recognizably canonical (falling within the fifth and fourth centuries BCE), I would argue that one of the most compelling things about the texts that make up the rhetorical tradition is that they question whether such a notion is rigorously possible. I should note, furthermore, that while I emphasize instances of rhetorical action that feature persuasion in some way, I do not mean to suggest that persuasion is the only thing that makes up the rhetorical tradition (in the necessarily provisional sense I have in mind when I use this term). I view persuasion, rather, as one significant element of that larger tradition, which also has quite a bit to say about pedagogy, relationality, the production and reception of knowledge, and the nature of selfhood. What I have found, in fact, is that there is no way to talk about persuasion without connecting it to these and other related concerns.

What the classical thinkers featured in *The Ethics of Persuasion* do have in common is a practical, pedagogical, or theoretical contribution to our larger understanding of the *art* of persuasion. That is, each contributes to our thinking of what it means to address another, the ethical potential that underlies this address, as well as the ontological risks involved in the moment when we attempt to exert a persuasive force. In some cases, to make the necessary presence of ethics all the more striking, I have chosen rhetorical instances that would seem to be the most utilitarian, and at times, the most appropriative—as in the case of the logographer Lysias, who reportedly donned the mask of many an unsavory character in order to persuade, or the case of Pericles's funeral oration, in which the eloquent general used the death of Athenian citizens to propagandize his war. Although these chapters come together to make a claim about the ethics of persuasive action, my hope is that they amount to more than their propositional content. I imagine them as staging singular moments of ultimately transformative encounter between

Derrida and the rhetorical tradition. This is in part because no one has shown us more clearly than Derrida himself that intellectual traditions—even ancient ones—are always yet to come, that they are not reducible to some overarching claim about their content. The only way to effect this coming is by way of a close but inventive reading that attempts to remain faithful to the text under examination even as it produces something new within it. Ultimately, what I learned while pursuing persuasion's other is that rhetoric's ethics can never be presented as such. If that is the case, then this introduction, this *direct opening*, to return to the typology of force provided for us by the *Rhetoric to Herennius*, has attempted this very presentation. It has attempted to reduce singular moments of encounter to an easily digestible form, and thus it seems to demand a different kind of treatment of its primary theme.

EPHODOS: THE SUBTLE APPROACH

Beginning with Derrida's understanding of ethics as structured by the ongoing interruption of being by otherness, I argue that the seemingly utilitarian act of persuasion in fact involves an interruptive encounter with the event. Despite all of the calculated attempts (such as those featured in the *Alexander* and the *Herennius*) to figure out in advance an audience's emotional state, its general receptiveness to the argument at hand, and its likely range of responses to carefully chosen persuasive approaches, classical rhetoric itself suggests that the audience remains entirely beyond our comprehension and control, so much so that the very concepts of "speaker" and "audience" are put into question. I articulate this claim, in part, by drawing on Derrida's idea that subjects are never fully present to themselves, that they are instead interrupted from the very beginning by an alterity that breaks apart unity and sovereignty. This nonpresence, furthermore, applies not just to human others, but to others writ large: texts, traditions, propositions, and the list goes on. Thus, in bringing together two seemingly discrete traditions, Derrida and classical rhetoric, I attempt to do more than read one through the other. In fact, I would argue that neither is static enough to simply serve as a lens. By staging these moments of encounter, rather, I attempt to show that these traditions simultaneously illuminate and transform each other. What this kind of reading effects, I hope, is a performative movement in concert with one of my central concerns: that the other cannot be defined or identified according to positive terms, and that this impossibility is precisely the point. The other is wholly other, it cannot be reduced to an ontological form, and as such it presents itself in a disruptive manner. It resists being summarized by (or for) those who would like to possess it. To encounter the other, then, is to come undone; it is to be compromised in the face of what is unrecognizable rather than to be maintained in a moment of masterful comprehension. Thus it would seem that the very idea of a direct opening, one that lays out in advance the propositional content of what is to come, attempts to short-circuit the encounter with alterity. It attempts to determine that other whose identity is yet to be determined and to make present the work that is still on its way.

For our purposes here, one significant complication of the direct opening is that it reduces the writing in the chapters to come to a signified content, one that is ultimately tied to the author's intention-to-mean. Two logical inconsistencies would seem to arise from this complication. First, an argument about persuasion as the encounter with the unknowable event is reduced to a set of content claims, and second, an argument about the impossibility of subjects possessing full mastery over rhetorical scenes (by virtue of their nonpresence) seems to assume this very mastery. The underlying assumption of this second point is that my authorial subject position exists prior to and apart from the text and that it is uncompromised in the introductory explanation of the argument (and in the production of the argument itself). Given my larger interest here in rhetoric's disruptive claims to asignifying force and alterity, then, the direct opening appears to be a conceptually problematic rhetorical form in that it presents the work to come prior to that moment of encounter that I've argued invents and transforms both the work and its reader.

Derrida has long held an appreciation for the significance of rhetorical forms and the unique way these interface with their audiences. Because the introduction and its associated prefatory texts deal in "presentation," he deems them a particularly complicated collection of affiliated genres. "The *pre* of the preface," he argues in *Dissemination,* "makes the future present, represents it, draws it closer, breathes it in, and in going ahead of it puts it ahead" (7). Thus "the *pre* reduces the future to the form of manifest presence," and so the work of the introduction is at once an "essential and ludicrous operation" (7). While genres like the introduction, the preface, the prelude, and the prolegomenon take on slightly different rhetorical forms, their structural function is to give over to the reader (in advance of her reading) a condensed version—a mainly *propositional* version—of the work to come.[6] By making the future present,

---

6. In his extended reading of introductory texts in the "Outwork" section of *Dissemination,* Derrida explains that different types of prefatory remarks have slightly different primary functions. The preface, for example, typically varies from edition to edition and takes into account the historical circumstances of the book's production, while the introduction more often attempts to present a general concept and so is more closely linked to the content-based arguments found within the text. According to this distinction, what you are reading right now is an introduction, although by breaking this form into the two distinct types named

the direct opening, in particular, reduces the text to a static signified content that can be easily digested by its reader. It ignores the text's performative force and attempts to undermine, indeed, to cancel out both the text's disruptive potential and its capacity to be transformed in the moment of reception. No longer other, the work to come is safely delivered to the reader's interpretive grid and transformed into the other-for-me. Such a giving over, furthermore, attempts to affirm reader, writer, and text each in its self-sufficient unity: "From the viewpoint of the fore-ward," Derrida suggests, "the text exists as something written—a past—which, under the false appearance of a present, a hidden omnipotent author (in full mastery of his product) is presenting to the reader as his future" (*Dissemination* 7). Such a presentation essentially relieves the reader of responsibility: Having already foreseen what is yet to come, the reader "might just as well dispense with reading the rest" (7). Responsibility is thus undermined in two senses: Not only is the reader excused from reading the writing to which the direct opening refers, but she is also allowed to avoid the disruptive encounter with the text as other.

Because it attempts to reduce the other, because it assumes the unity of an author and insists on her intention to mean, and because it allows the reader to avoid a disruptive encounter with the work to come, the direct opening (with its reduction of the "future to the form of manifest presence" [7]) would seem to undercut the performative movements I characterized above as irreducible to signified content. And yet Derrida (and Aristotle, as we'll see) ultimately suggests that the introduction (even an introduction as highly propositional as the direct opening) effects far more than a short circuit of the reader's encounter with alterity. Even as it attempts to foreclose the encounter with the text-as-other (and cut away the myriad other interpretive possibilities for that text), the direct opening has its own powerfully disruptive force. This is why Derrida refers to the work of the introduction as simultaneously "essential *and* ludicrous" (7, emphasis added). While the direct opening tries to arrest the disruptive performative movements that put us in relation with alterity, and while it attempts to make the wholly other visible to (and an

---

in the *Rhetoric to Herennius*, I hope to demonstrate that there is no single, uncomplicated preliminary expression of propositional content. While Derrida notes the differences in these beginning forms, he explains that their conceptual difficulties are analogous by virtue of their problematic external relation to the text (17–18). In this discussion, Derrida doesn't explicitly take up the *prooimion* or the direct opening to which I refer, but I see no reason to exclude this particular type of introduction from Derrida's claims about "outworks" in general. In fact, I would go further to suggest that the handbook tradition offers Derrida a finer and more nuanced array of introductory forms that ultimately illuminate the claims about presence so central to his work. The handbook tradition, that is, deals with introductions in such a way as to suggest that there is no way to simply make present signified content.

object for) the reader who has yet to encounter it, it never finally succeeds in these endeavors. This is because, while the introduction is an attendant discourse meant to prop up and affirm the unity of the work that is already written, its very presence suggests that that work cannot stand on its own. On the level of content, the direct opening says, "Here, in the form of a distilled proposition, is what you will read." It insists on the unity of this propositional content and positions it as a presence that can come to be possessed. The reader may or may not ultimately be persuaded of these claims, but the direct opening argues without equivocation that they are there. What this content claim effects, however, is something else altogether. The very need to insist on the unified presence of the work to come (which is figured as *primary* and logically and temporally *prior to* the introduction, even though it is not the first thing the reader reads) suggests that the propositional content is somehow structurally incomplete. The need to announce in advance what is to come suggests, in Derrida's words, that the primary text is in "fear of remaining unreadable," and that it is unable to "present or teach itself on its own" (*Dissemination* 38). And so the primary discourse—the one that seemed to have authorized the introduction in the first place—is rendered uncertain (even fearful) by the very text that makes the case for its certainty. For all its seeming insistence on the unproblematic presence of the work to come, then, the direct opening nonetheless challenges this presence and in so doing exerts a disruptive force, both on the text to which it refers and the one who will ultimately read it.

Such attention to the threatening nature of the introduction is not unique to Derrida. Aristotle treats this form reluctantly and with suspicion precisely because it seems to threaten the conceptual primacy of the speech it precedes. While the *Alexander* and the *Herennius* emphasize the importance of the direct opening for putting one's audience in the proper frame of mind, Aristotle prefers to focus instead on the integrity of a proposition and its proof and grants only secondary attention to the composition and function of a speech's introduction (*Rhetoric* 3.13–14).[7] When in the *Rhetoric* he does take up this topic, Aristotle argues that the direct opening is not a necessary part of a speech ("If the subject is clear or short, there is no need of a prooemion" [3.14.6]), although he concedes that it is often useful for making one's purpose

---

7. When handbook writers focus on the individual parts of a speech, Aristotle claims, they "make ridiculous divisions" because the elements on which they so often focus—the diegesis, the prooemion, the antiparabole, and the epilogue, for example—are not structurally necessary. In many speeches, he explains, these parts do not appear at all. Aristotle, then, deems the handbook writers' formal focus frivolous and lacking in the intellectual heft of his own primary attention to the enthymeme (3.13–14).

clear: "He who gives, as it were, the beginning into the hand [of the hearer] allows him, by holding on, to follow the speech" (3.14.6). In a brief moment of agreement with the anonymous writers of the *Alexander* and *Herennius*, Aristotle acknowledges that the benefit of the direct opening is that it functions as a kind of map or key that guides the hearer's encounter with the more substantive claims to follow. A flattened-out image of what is yet to come, the direct opening indicates where the hearer is headed and lays out the path ultimately needed to arrive there. While it might not be a structural necessity, then, it nonetheless possesses a powerful rhetorical force that helps move the hearer in a right direction.

From Aristotle's point of view, the direct opening's primary benefit—its ability to provide "a sample of the argument in order that [the audience] may know what the speech is about" (3.14.6)—is the very thing that makes it a deeply problematic, indeed, threatening rhetorical form. A signal for what lies ahead, the direct opening figures for Aristotle as an excessive genre. It is an ancillary discourse, beyond the realm of what is truly at stake and required because of the intellectual and moral deficits of those hearers in need of a guide. Although he is willing to discuss how the direct opening might make an unreceptive audience more open and attentive, he insists that "one should not forget that all such things are outside the real argument: they are addressed to a hearer who is morally weak and giving ear to what is extrinsic to the subject" (3.14.8). Thus, the direct opening is external to the "real argument" in two important ways. First, it is a false double of the primary claim. A mere "sample," to borrow Aristotle's phrasing, it provides an abbreviated preview of an argument that will be fully justified in the speech's body. And the argument, for Aristotle, belongs to the body: "There would be no need of a prooemion except for setting out the headings of the argument in order that the body [of the speech] may have a 'head'" (3.14.8). It is a depthless image, a mere snapshot of the fully rendered argument that has not yet had the chance to appear. Second, the direct opening (as a false double of the central text) is structured not simply by the argument itself, but by (and toward) the audience who needs its help. The introduction may help guide the hearer as he undertakes the rhetorical journey to come, and it may make him more receptive to something he might otherwise not care to hear, but these benefits derive from the introduction's having been cut away from the speech's central claim and sutured onto a morally and intellectually needy audience. No longer simply an abbreviated double of the speech (which is already something of a problem for Aristotle), the direct opening is structured by its attention to the outside. Although it may seem at first an attendant discourse, the direct opening's hidden danger is that it actually cares nothing at all for the body of the speech. Neither simply inside nor outside of the speech to which it refers, the direct opening has a contaminating presence. It is the simulacrum of the speech and it threatens the logical and conceptual priority of the "original" primary text.

There is no internal connection, in other words, between the direct opening and the speech's central proposition and proof. As the false double of these, the introduction is an *extra* text in two senses of that word: it is both outside of and in addition to the primary text. At once derived from and then subsequently added to the body of the speech, the direct opening is also constituted by its future hearer. Its movement toward the audience (along with its constitutive extra-ness) highlights the fact that the argument itself is unable to maintain a masterful position over its attendant discourse. Although he seems loath to admit it, Aristotle concludes his chapter on the direct opening by noting that the structurally unnecessary form is nonetheless often needed "for ornament, since the speech seems carelessly done if it does not have one" (3.14.11). Thus, the direct opening, which in the first place appears as a supporting discourse—derived from and then added to the central text for the benefit of the audience who needs it—takes on a surprisingly threatening power. The primary text—the body of the speech itself—comes to depend on the direct opening to appear carefully designed and fully rendered. In need of the head that announces and explains its existence, the body is compromised and threatened, as if capable of being devoured by the hollow copy it once authorized. The very existence of the direct opening demonstrates that the body of the speech cannot stand, as it were, on its own two feet.

For all those reasons, the direct opening, in the sense provided for it by Aristotle and the handbook writers (as a straightforward expression of the speech's propositional content) and by me (as a straightforward expression of the book's propositional content), never quite accomplishes its primary goal. While at the propositional level it insists on the clear and simple presence of the content that has yet to be encountered, it nonetheless demonstrates that the work to come is an uncontainable dispersion. In the same moment it says, "Here, in the form of a distilled proposition, is what you will read," it pierces the unity and self-sufficiency of this very reading. The direct opening, that is, produces an effect—an interruption—that cannot be reduced to meaning, and this disruptive force affects not only the work to come, but also the reader to whom it is addressed. Just as the unity of the primary text wavers in the face of the direct opening, so too does the unity of the reader because she is put in relation with a performative rhetorical force that is entirely beyond the interpretive realm. This otherwise utilitarian rhetorical form, even though it is tied to signified meaning and involved in an attempt to make the reader susceptible to the claims to follow, produces a force incapable of being fully mastered, and as such it puts the reader in relation with an unintelligible alterity, something wholly other. Because the reader is faced with what is beyond the horizon of meaning, her interpretive mechanisms are disrupted and along with them her fantasies of mastery and self-sufficiency. Eluding our interpretive grasp, the performative force produced by the direct opening disrupts nothing less than the assured self-presence that would seem to be safely external to the text we have yet to encounter.

Thus, in the direct opening we have an instance of the ethics of persuasion I have been discussing from the start. In one sense, the direct opening is a highly determined rhetorical form meant to serve a persuasive end. By providing in advance the content that will be encountered later, it helps the reader see where she is headed with the hope that, because she will have been able to follow the lines of argument, she will prove more likely to be persuaded in the end. (For the anonymous handbook writers, remember, and for Aristotle too, the significance of understanding in advance what would come later had less to do with meaning per se than with the persuasive effects of grasping this meaning.) But in the midst of this calculated persuasive action, a disruptive force is also produced, one that puts into question not only the unified presence of the signified content on which it insists, but also the unified presence of the ones who read, write, and speak it. In the same moment the direct opening makes familiar and recognizable the other that has yet to be encountered, it exerts a force that remains entirely other, one that cannot be transformed into the other-for-me.

EX(ORDIUM) POST FACTO

Whether the opening is subtle or direct, a *prooimion* or an *ephodos*, it is *ex post facto*, formulated after the event of the writing to which it refers. Coming from after the action, it "returns" to the front of the line and attaches itself there as if that were its place all along. So positioned, its job is to make present the work to come. But as I have suggested, identifying the introduction's proper location and its initial point of reference isn't quite so simple. One of the hallmarks of the introduction is that it is created for (and thus structured in advance by) the audience that has yet to encounter the so-called primary discourse. Because it bears neither an external nor an internal relation to this primary text, the introduction has no particular place. It is perhaps best described as *in motion*, and its retroactive movement, which is engineered by the need to put the audience in relation to its future, generates powerful ripples that disturb the unity not only of the text to be read but also of the reader herself.

The introduction, in other words, disperses. But it is also itself a dispersion—it is always moving in multiple directions. As we have seen, the *Rhetoric to Herennius* tells us that there are two categories of introduction: the direct opening that "straightaway" prepares the audience to listen (1.4.6) and the subtle approach that operates "covertly, through dissimulation" (1.7.11). And within these categories, there are infinite possibilities for any particular introduction, driven, for example, by the nature of the speaker's cause, be it "honourable, discreditable, doubtful, [or] petty" (1.3.5), and by the character and needs of the audience. These are examples of the multiple moving parts that make up any persuasive action. But the introduction, as I have tried to show in my two versions above, also is itself a multiplicity of forces. No more a unified whole than the text to which it refers, the introduction signifies and asignifies simultaneously. It makes reference to signified content and thus is involved in a hermeneutic operation. At the same time, even in its most propositional instance, it produces disruptive forces that cannot be reduced to meaning. Thus, I would argue that even the direct opening operates covertly, like the subtle approach, because it disguises the fact that it disrupts the presence of the text and the reader by piercing the full presence of what lies ahead in the very moment of insisting on it. The reason for staging twin introductions, as I've done here, is to demonstrate this point, to show that even the most utilitarian rhetorical form exerts a disruptive force that makes presence waver, even as it ostensibly positions that "present" self in relation to its future.

The introduction is not a unity—just as the text is not and the reader is not. When we are put in relation to something that cannot be reduced to meaning or otherwise comprehended, we are disrupted, our interpretive mechanisms are thrown off their hinges. This is what happens when we encounter the multiplicity that is the introduction, despite its ostensibly orienting function. In the moment of trying to make us receptive to a message, perhaps by telling us exactly what that message will be (and thus undermining the very presence of that message), the introduction exerts a force that cannot be contained. Thus, despite the utilitarian bent of the introduction—its design to prime the pump for the argument to come—it provides an opportunity to learn from the other, to be unsettled in the moment of its arrival.

And this relation to otherness, I argue, is the ethics of persuasion that has been undertheorized for more than two millennia. This inattention to ethics is due in part to rhetoric's emphasis on the production of persuasive force over and above representational content. The rhetorical handbooks, for example, have from their inception been dismissed by a variety of critics as frivolous for their focus on emotion, ornamentation, and form rather than on logical argument. Aristotle, for one, writes that the handbooks, in prescribing "the introduction [*prooemion*] or the narration [*diegesis*] and each of the other parts [. . .] concern themselves only with how they may put the judge in a certain frame of mind, while they explain nothing about artistic proofs [. . .]" (*Rhetoric* 1.1.9). This criticism of the handbooks—as utilitarian, calculating, and unconcerned with truth or substance—has become the criticism of rhetoric itself. Unconcerned with truth or meaning, rhetoric is that insubstantial yet forceful form against which audiences must stand guard. As Cicero has famously argued, strong faculties of persuasion must be *supplemented by* "integrity and supreme wisdom" lest rhetorical training amount to placing "weapons into the hands of madmen" (*De Oratore* 3.14). That Cicero—a strong proponent of rhetoric and of broad-based rhetorical pedagogy—believes integrity and wisdom must be *added to* persuasive talents would seem to suggest that there is no ethics of note that reside *within* persuasion itself. Yet that is precisely the claim I make in this book: That even the most forceful instances of persuasion are constituted by an ethics of otherness or alterity. I argue that just as we can see a powerful ethics emerging from the handbooks in general and from their attention to the form of the introduction in particular, so can we read rhetoric writ large as what Derrida might call a "completely other structure" (*Dissemination* 35), a discourse that thematizes and, perhaps more importantly, produces the disruption of self-presence. Classical rhetoric, in other words, whatever its instrumental capacities and intentions, always involves an essential relation to alterity.

CHAPTER 1

Derrida's Rhetorical Ethics

> For [some critics], the word deconstruction is simply a negative
> project which undermines everything and does not leave anything
> in place; and we have to reject this. I have [. . .] insisted on the
> contrary and on the fact that deconstruction is mainly affirmation,
> affirmation. [. . .] Affirmation does not mean reconstruction, it
> does not mean position, something positive; it means constant
> reference to a yes. Yes, I speak to you, I address you, I listen to you.
> [. . .] I am a little wary of the word ethics [. . .]. Nevertheless, if you
> call this an ethics of affirmation, it implies that you are attentive to
> otherness, to the alterity of the other, to something new and other.
>
> —Jacques Derrida, "'Talking Liberties':
> Interview with Alan Montefiore," 180

In a 1992 interview with his friend, the British philosopher Alan Montefiore, Derrida voices the complicated place of ethics within his broader philosophical agenda. While he is quick to denounce those commentators—both admiring and disapproving—who understand deconstruction as an abandonment of meaning and context and thus a nihilistic assault on the metaphysics of presence, he is also unwilling to unproblematically declare deconstruction an ethical vocation. To do so, he suggests, would be a no less egregious abdication of responsibility. Despite a strong desire to refute those who believe themselves "to have found in Deconstruction [. . .] a modern form of immorality, of amorality, or of irresponsibility" (*On the Name* 15), Derrida argues it would be even worse to endorse or encourage "a community of complacent deconstructionists, reassured and reconciled with the world in ethical certainty, good conscience, satisfaction of service rendered, and the consciousness of duty accomplished" (17). All of which is to say that it is no simple task to deem deconstruction an enterprise that is, clearly, entirely, and on its own, *ethical*. Given the intricacies of this subject, which I will explore further in the pages to come, the aim of this chapter is to articulate a working definition of ethics within the context of Derrida's thought for the purposes of clearly presenting the theoretical lens I use throughout the book. In one sense, my goal here is to define the ethics of *The Ethics of Persuasion* (although, as we will see, the concept necessarily resists definitional certainty). To do this, I will identify and explain what I take to be the primary characteristics of Derrida's idea of ethics, which I draw from his writings and place within the context of critical interpretations by several of his key commentators. In the end, I hope to add to the ongoing conversation, outlined in the introduction, that draws out and develops the rhetorical significance of this (non)concept. Specifically, I explain that when he generalizes J. L. Austin's notion of the performative utterance by positing the performative structure of every event (including the event of being itself), Derrida articulates an ethics whose essential structure mirrors that of persuasive speech. I make this aspect of the argument by revisiting Derrida's famed commentary on speech act theory, particularly his long-standing engagement with Austin's idea of the performative utterance. What I suggest in this analysis is that Derrida's unique account of performativity—which involves a radical rethinking of what it means to address someone in a speech situation and which first arises in the context of his response to Austin—underwrites his continued analyses of more identifiably ethical concepts such as hospitality, responsibility, and friendship. I develop this claim to accomplish two things: first, to add to the ongoing project of articulating the rhetorical elements of Derrida's ethical contributions and, second, to demonstrate that our most highly invested, canonical rhetorical texts can and must be inherited differently.

As Derrida suggests to Montefiore in the epigraph to this chapter, if there is such a thing as a deconstructive ethics of affirmation, it comes by way of an encounter with otherness that might best be described in the terms of an address. The closest he comes to characterizing the ethical dimension of deconstruction is by deploying phrases that have to do with *speaking*, with *listening*, and with *being attentive* to the other—all significant components of the classical rhetorical paradigm of persuasion. To be clear, Derrida is not talking about effectively targeting and appealing to an audience member in the manner of the rhetorical handbooks I described in the introduction; one of the primary takeaways from his response to Austin is that the traditional model of communication is a fantasy meant to prop up the full presence of meaning. But Derrida does use rhetorical terminology when he describes deconstruction as a turn towards the other, and he hints that this style of engagement contains an ethical imperative. The guiding premise of my book is that this ethical imperative enables and encourages us to confront the metaphysical prejudice so often associated with our classical models of persuasion. What *speaking to*, *addressing*, and *listening to* each involves in this case is a certain *rapprochement* with an ultimately unassimilable other, and thus the address itself is absolutely necessary for the possibility of ethics. This is the case because the address maintains an important nonappropriative separation between "self" (a term this proposition puts under erasure, as we will see) and other. It maintains what Derrida calls in *Of Grammatology* the "minute difference [. . . and] spacing" between the other and the same, which dislocates self-identification and opens in turn an ongoing responsibility to the other (234). What is thus affirmed here is an ethics that can be thought of only in relation to an other who is impossible to contain and, as Derrida's claims about iterability or the emergence of the mark make clear, always still to come. Such an ethics, if it were indeed an ethics, would involve an ongoing negotiation with the other.

Despite his hesitancy to refer to the affirmative dimension of deconstruction as ethical, Derrida does insist that his style of philosophical engagement involves "in itself, a positive response to an alterity which necessarily calls, summons, or motivates it" (Kearney *Debates* 149). Offered in response to Richard Kearney, who asked Derrida in a 1981 interview if deconstruction could "ever surmount its role of iconoclastic negation" (149), Derrida once again frames affirmation in rhetorical terms by thematizing deconstruction as a response: "Deconstruction is [. . .] vocation," he says, "—a response to a call" (149). Such metaphorics call attention to and prioritize the voice, the summons, or the call of the other who both remains at a distance and constitutes being by way of interrupting it from within. "It is in this rapport with the other," he adds, "that affirmation expresses itself" (149). Once again, I do not mean to suggest that Derrida is referring to simple speech acts—to specific instances in which one subject calls out to another in order to produce a desired action. But I do believe that the nonsubjective rapport to which he refers shares the primary structure of such a rhetorical act and that this is one crucial avenue through which we might access the affirmative ethics in question.

One final caveat: Deconstruction is involved in the destabilization and transformation of metaphysical concepts; or, perhaps better put, it demonstrates the way that metaphysical concepts deconstruct themselves. Ethics is one such concept, and one that Derrida has insisted must remain open, undecidable: "What is the ethicity of ethics? The morality of morality? What is responsibility?" he asks in "Passions: An Oblique Offering," a response essay in which he considers the complexity and impossibilities of what it means to respond (*On the Name* 16). "These questions are always urgent," he insists. "In a certain way they must remain urgent and unanswered" (16). To be clear, then, Derrida never espouses an ethics or suggests that such a concept would be immune to deconstruction. As Geoffrey Bennington has argued, "'Ethics' cannot fail to be a theme and an object of deconstruction [. . .]. Deconstruction deconstructs ethics, or shows up ethics deconstructing (itself)" (*Interrupting* 34). And yet, he adds, "*some* sense of ethics or the ethical, something archi-ethical, perhaps, survives the deconstruction or emerges as its origin or resource" (34). For me what survives is the strong sense that the work of inheriting the rhetorical tradition is never finished and that there is always the possibility of drawing out—from within that very tradition—the ethical events that interrupt our settled narratives.

A number of critics have argued that the manner in which Derrida addresses the other in his philosophical writing is, in itself, ethical. Robert Bernasconi, for one, suggests that deconstruction's unique ethical style is borne of its penchant for prioritizing the thinkers it engages, and for allowing those thinkers to speak through it without being judged:

> The saying of the said, its writerly saying, is [. . .] found in deconstruction—whenever it finds a 'voice' of its own. But we find the ethical enactment above all in the way deconstruction ultimately refuses to adopt the standpoint of critique, renouncing the passing of judgments on its own behalf in its own voice. ("Deconstruction and the Possibility" 136)

Michael Naas also indicates that Derrida's most significant ethical contribution can be found not in the constative arguments that emerge from his texts, but in the performative quality of his engagement with other thinkers and traditions. In particular, Naas figures Derrida's philosophical approach as a form of welcoming, and he suggests an important doubling up of the ethical within Derrida's work.[1] Recalling Derrida's claim that absolute or unconditional hospitality is indissociable from conditional hospitality, Naas argues that "Derrida always attempted to welcome the 'elsewhere' in an *unconditional* way, but he did so always from within a context or text that was specific, marked by a particular epoch and language—in a word, within a context that was always *conditioned*" (*Derrida From Now* 29). Naas then concludes that "it is in this sense that we might see hospitality not simply as a delimitable theme within the corpus of Derrida but as the very 'activity' of Derrida's work" (29). I have always been struck by the artistry and rhetorical power of Derrida's writing, and so I am persuaded by claims such as these that credit so much signifi-

---

1. See also Bennington, who suggests a similar doubling up of ethical style and content in Derrida's writing: "Derrida's work does not just reflect, in a way we might want to call ethical, on the relation to the traditionality of thought *in general,* but also, on occasion, within that *milieu,* reflects on the traditionality of ethical concepts in particular" (*Interrupting* 39).

cance to its "activity."[2] I would like to press the point a bit further, however, by stressing the affective nature of Derrida's style of engagement and by noting the rhetorical status of this asignifying force. Both Bernasconi and Naas stress what Derrida's language *does* over and above what it *means,* and, like Derrida before him, Naas makes use of a verbal address (a phrase that produces, rather than refers to, a state of affairs) to characterize this work.

Claims like these reflect the profound transformation of the response to Derrida's work inside the academy over the course of the past five decades. Early receptions (in the late 1960s and early 1970s, particularly in the United States) framed the philosopher's thought as profoundly relativistic and skeptical and often cast Derrida as a value-free nihilist who espoused textual indeterminacy and boundless free play.[3] Now, however, roughly twenty-five years after Derrida began writing about the themes of justice, the gift, friendship, and responsibility, it is far more common to characterize his thought as having undergone an "ethical turn." Despite his claims to the contrary,[4] many identify in Derrida's thinking a certain evolution or maturation—indeed, a marked change of course—that could be pinpointed on a biographical timeline. Often attributed to the blowback he felt after the events of 1987—the year of both the Heidegger affair (felt largely in Europe) and the de Man affair (felt largely in the United States)[5]—Derrida's so-called "ethical turn" signals a progressivist

---

2. Naas's *Taking on the Tradition: Jacques Derrida and the Legacies of Deconstruction* (2003) thoroughly pursues this argument and calls attention to the importance of Derrida's writing style and strategy: "The way Derrida says things, the way his texts are performative, is inseparable from *what* he says and the claims he makes. My contention is ultimately that only by taking into account the performativity of Derrida's language will we really be able to understand his claims" (xxi).

3. See, for example, Richard Rorty's "Philosophy as a Kind of Writing: An Essay on Derrida" (1978), John R. Searle's "Reiterating the Differences: A Reply to Derrida" (1977), and Jasper Neel's *Plato, Derrida, and Writing* (1998).

4. See, for example, Derrida's "Force of Law: The 'Mystical Foundation of Authority'": "There are no doubt many reasons why the majority of texts hastily defined as 'deconstructionist'—for example, mine—*seem,* I do say *seem,* not to foreground the theme of justice (as theme, precisely), or the theme of ethics or politics. Naturally, this is only *apparently* so" (7). See also *Rogues: Two Essays on Reason* (39), which is quoted in the introduction.

5. Simon Critchley's comments in a *Los Angeles Review of Books* interview illuminate this point: "There are two poles of Derrida's work: a Heideggerian pole and Levinasian pole, and those two poles of attraction have been constant throughout his work. After the late '80s, the Levinasian pole of attraction gets stronger, and his work moves further and further in that direction. There's no doubt in my mind that that's because of what fell out of the Heidegger affair and the de Man affair" (Butman). Derrida biographer Benoît Peters also argues that the revelations of Heidegger's and de Man's Nazi sympathies, followed by the querulous responses to Derrida in the aftermath of these revelations, led Derrida to think more explicitly about ethical and political issues in his own writing: "The two years [1987–1988] of ceaseless combat which Derrida had just experienced did [. . .] mark a kind of break. The following period would

transformation during which deconstruction became a form of socially aware inquiry.[6] While I recognize the seductiveness of this narrative, I am convinced that Derrida's early work (particularly the work on performativity, as I will explain) has a significant ethical component that gives strength and energy to those later interventions better known for their explicitly ethical themes.[7]

The most influential text for initiating and shaping this ethics-oriented reception of Derrida remains Simon Critchley's *The Ethics of Deconstruction: Derrida and Levinas* (originally published in 1992, with subsequent editions in 1999 and 2014). While Critchley was not the only commentator to link Derrida to Levinas on the topic of ethics around this time, *The Ethics of Deconstruction* is the text most prominently identified with this development, and it makes the most forceful argument for the singular importance of the affiliation.[8] Here, Critchley makes the innovative (and, at the time of its initial publication, largely counterintuitive) claim that "the pattern of reading produced in the deconstruction of [. . .] philosophical texts has an ethical structure: deconstruction 'is' ethical; or [. . .] deconstruction takes place (*a lieu*) ethically" (2). The ethics that Critchley identifies in Derrida's thought is defined by way of reference to Levinas, who, in *Totality and Infinity*, defines ethics as the "calling into question of my spontaneity by the presence of the Other" (43). Identifying in Derrida a certain Levinasian duty to or responsibility for the "irreducible particularity of [. . .] the singular other, prior to procedures of universalization and legislation" (*The Ethics* 18), Critchley emphasizes the pre-ontological, nonvoluntary character of Derrida's ethics. In particular, he

---

be characterized by the emergence of an apparently more mellow Derrida. As if in response to these accusations, ethical and political questions would soon move to the centre of the stage" (401).

6. This is a widely accepted narrative, but for two specific examples, see Michel Rosenfeld's "Derrida's Ethical Turn and America: Looking Back from the Crossroads of Global Terrorism and the Enlightenment" and Joshua Gunn's "Mourning Humanism, or, the Idiom of Haunting." Robert Doran's *The Ethics of Theory: Philosophy, History, Literature* offers an excellent overview and analysis of the critical reception of Derrida following the events of 1987.

7. On this point I agree with Nicole Anderson, who argues that "the ethical is a focus of Derrida's work from his earliest writings on language, to his work on hospitality, justice, responsibility, politics, and beyond" (3).

8. Christopher Norris's *Derrida* (1987), for example, also helped inaugurate a new thinking of the ethical in Derrida's writing. In it, Norris claims that "there is an ethical dimension to Derrida's writings which has yet to be grasped by most of his commentators" (228). Even before the publication of Critchley's book on this topic, Norris defines the ethical thread in Derrida's thought by way of reference to Levinas, whose work identifies the other of the Western philosophical tradition (228–37). Bernasconi's "Deconstruction and the Possibility of Ethics" (1987) and "The Trace of Levinas in Derrida" (1988), David Wood's "Beyond Deconstruction?" (1987), and Richard Kearney's "Derrida's Ethical Re-Turn" (1993) also explore the important ethical affiliations between Levinas and Derrida.

argues that Derridean deconstruction is characterized by a doubled or "*clôtural*" reading that locates the other of philosophy from within a repetition of the dominant interpretation of philosophy. Arguing that Derrida pursues alterities within texts and traditions, Critchley posits an ethical significance that can be clearly articulated only in relation to Levinas. Both thinkers, he says, interrupt the totality of the ontological tradition, and in so doing, they threaten its primacy.

What followed the publication of Critchley's book (as well as the work of those commentators, noted above, who affiliated Derrida with Levinas around the same time period) was a growing chorus of commentators who developed the idea of a far more ethicized Derrida than was initially thought. While many writers have disagreed with the extent to which Critchley aligned Derrida with Levinas, and still others rejected Critchley's secondary claim that "deconstruction fails to navigate the treacherous passage from ethics to politics" (189),[9] a new wave of scholarship began to expand and redefine the place and notion of ethics in Derrida's work. Bennington (*Legislations*, 1994 and *Interrupting*, 2000) and Kearney ("Derrida's Ethical," 1993) stressed the ethical dimensions of Derrida's accounts of reading and writing, noting that these practices entail an irreducible responsiveness to alterity, and Christina Howells (*Derrida: Deconstruction*, 1999) sketched the transforming relational ethics inherent in Derrida's deconstructed account of the human subject. Rodolphe Gasché (*Inventions*, 1994) noted the (at that time largely overlooked) affirmative aspects of deconstruction by highlighting the priority Derrida grants to the unknowable to come. And, drawing on Derrida's accounts of performativity and contextual reinscription, Jeffrey T. Nealon (*Alterity*, 1998) and Matthias Fritsch (*Promise of Memory*, 2005) articulated the futural character of Derrida's ethics. This future-oriented formulation, their work suggests, necessitates a responsive negotiation with alterity that, as Nealon puts it, resists the ontologizing logic of "the theme, the concept, and the same" (117). Clearly, then, the thinker once best known for dismantling people's deeply held beliefs and for espousing indeterminate textual free play has been roundly reconsidered.

Martin Hägglund's influential *Radical Atheism: Derrida and the Time of Life* (2008) is a notable exception to this trend. He contends that thinkers such as Critchley, Caputo, and Bernasconi (among others) have gone too far

---

9. See, for example, Richard Beardsworth's *Derrida and the Political* (1996), Christina Howells' *Derrida: Deconstruction from Phenomenology to Ethics* (1999), Geoffrey Bennington's *Interrupting Derrida* (2000), Marko Zlomislic's *Jacques Derrida's Aporetic Ethics* (2007), and Nicole Anderson's *Derrida: Ethics Under Erasure* (2012). And Critchley himself later softened his thinking on this issue. In the second edition of *The Ethics of Deconstruction (1999)*, he notes that "based on a reading of Derrida's work since 1992, I am more positive about the political possibilities of deconstruction" (xii).

in their claims about Derrida's ethical agenda. Warning against overly religious or moralistic readings of deconstruction, Hägglund argues that there is no transcendental other in Derrida's work to whom we owe a nonviolent response, but instead a disruptive temporal tracing or an autoimmunity that ensures, he says, that "there must be openness to whatever or whoever comes" (31). The "failure to understand the status of this 'must,'" Hägglund maintains, has perpetuated a far too normative account of Derrida's ethics (31). Writing against the grain of those who would align Derrida too closely with Levinas, Hägglund argues that "the idea of a primary peace is incompatible with deconstructive thinking" (76). While I find many aspects of his analysis persuasive and insightful, I simply do not agree with Hägglund's insistence that we must disjoin Derrida from Levinas, not least because the Levinasian framework is helpful for articulating the significance of both Derrida's attempts to unsettle the dominant philosophical tradition and his insistence that ethics has no recourse to recognition that, as Kelly Oliver has noted, is exclusively "conferred by the very groups and institutions responsible for withholding it in the first place" ("Rethinking Response" 620).

Further, we can find throughout Derrida's work a strong affinity for what he identified even in "Violence and Metaphysics" as Levinas's "Ethics of Ethics"—the idea that "Levinas does not seek to propose laws or moral rules, does not seek to determine *a* morality, but rather the essence of the ethical relation in general" (111). He takes care to note, remember, that "this is not an objection" (111). Derrida does insist, of course, that we must engage in an ongoing negotiation between this ethics of ethics—the unconditional priority of the other over the self—and the conditional principles that govern the often-conflicting responses that are demanded of us in the here and now.[10] But he also insists that it is important to attend to the conditions of (im)possibility that necessarily haunt any assumed presence. Conceptually prior to identity, ethics is thus figured as an excessive or hyperbolic structure that *enables* responsibility. Derrida stressed the importance—even the urgency—of attending to what is before and beyond applied ethics in a 1991 interview with François Ewald:

> There is in fact no philosophy and no philosophy of philosophy that could be called deconstruction and that would deduce from itself a "moral component." But that does not mean that deconstructive experience is not a responsibility, even an ethico-political responsibility, or does not exercise or deploy any responsibility in itself. By questioning philosophy about its treat-

---

10. This is a problematic Levinas himself addresses in *Otherwise Than Being or Beyond Essence* when he discusses justice and the entrance of the third party, whose arrival contradicts my responsibility to the other (157).

ment of ethics, politics, the concept of responsibility, deconstruction orders itself [...] on an exigency, which I believe is more *inflexible,* of response and responsibility. Without this exigency, in my view no ethico-political question has any chance of being opened up or awakened today. (*Points* 364)

This is an aporetic approach to ethics that highlights once more the rhetorical dimensions of Derrida's ethics. An ancient Greek term referring to a "perplexing difficulty" or an "impasse," *aporia* refers to paradoxical premises, specifically to the conditions that make an idea simultaneously possible and impossible. In the context of deconstruction, aporetic determinations refer to conditions of emergence, such as the aporetic conditions that give rise to Derrida's complicated articulations of the gift, of hospitality, and of forgiveness (none of these being strictly possible, as he has often insisted). Thus, what it means to understand ethics as aporetic, as François Raffoul argues, is to "problematize the ethicality of ethics, as opposed to presupposing its senses" (284). In this way, the rhetorical figure of aporia—an expression of doubt in which the speaker deliberates with herself or her audience about where to begin in order to appropriately address an issue—is also illuminating.

Because it concerns itself with "questioning philosophy," Derridean ethics in the aporetic sense I refer to here takes place before and beyond the choice-making, rule-following approaches associated with normative or applied ethics, but it nonetheless requires an urgent accounting of what Nealon has called the "alterity within any supposed constitution of sameness" (*Alterity* 116). What is at stake in this accounting is nothing less than the status of the ethical subject itself, which is no longer understood as a causal agent but as an effect of *différance*. As Howells has argued, "It is his understanding of the subject as effect which lies at the root of Derrida's aporetic conception of ethics" (135). What this means is that while Derrida's approach to ethics is unable to provide moral directives, it proposes a form of responsibility that is inaugurated when the self is disrupted (also invented) in an encounter with alterity. One particularly illuminating example of this aporetic ethics can be seen in the idea of the decision, which, as Derrida has explained in "Force of Law" and *Politics of Friendship,* requires both a rigorous attempt to gather all of the information relevant to the situation and an absolute leap away from knowledge into the realm of the incalculable. This, Derrida says, is "the aporia we have to face constantly" (Kearney and Dooley 73). He insists, however, that "aporia is not simply paralysis, but the aporia or the non-way is the condition of walking: if there was no aporia we wouldn't walk, we wouldn't find our way; path-breaking implies aporia. This impossibility to find one's way is the condition of ethics" (73). To put this another way, any ethics that provided in advance a program or a clear path for how to proceed would not be an ethics at all. What is so important about this aporetic structure, I would argue, is that it opens the space for decision, responsibility, and negotiation. It initiates the impossible task of what Derrida calls "eating well" in which one maintains "respect for the other at the very moment when, in experience [. . .] one must begin to identify with the other who is to be assimilated, interiorized, understood ideally" (Cadava, Connor, and Nancy 115).

When I use the term *ethics* in *The Ethics of Persuasion,* then, I refer to this aporetic sense of ethics that interrupts ontological formulations and that draws from Derrida's suggestion that ethics emerges in the affirmative encounter with alterity. This understanding of ethics does not espouse universal principles in an attempt to regulate behavior, and it cannot provide a moral code that would ultimately assure an ethical subject that she has behaved well. Instead, this ethics "signals," as Derrida puts it, "in the direction of [. . .] an imperative injunction to which one must finally respond *without norm,* without a presently presentable normativity or normality, without anything that would finally be the object of knowledge, belonging to an order of being or value" (*Points* 362). Because it operates beyond the horizon of knowledge and before the determination of prescriptive values, this Derridean sense of ethics interrupts or, as Nicole Anderson argues, puts "under erasure" (11) the classical metaphysical understanding of ethical responsibility. There is no self-present subject who takes responsibility, Derrida explains, "for oneself, *in one's own name* and *before the other*" (*On the Name* 10). Instead, ethical responsibility is "what one must take for another, in his place, in the name of the other or of *oneself as other*" (10–11, emphasis added). In this way, ethics in Derrida is premised on a subject always already interrupted by alterity, on an "'I' that is structured by the alterity within it" (Derrida and Ferraris 84). Priority is thus granted to the other before any formulation of self, and so ethics is not simply a matter of consciously embracing difference. Instead the ethical subject is profoundly disrupted—constituted by an alterity that cannot be recuperated, mastered, or ontologized.

As I mentioned in the opening pages of this chapter, Derrida hesitates to name the aporetic formulation I have just described "ethics." Once again, we can see the link to the rhetorical figure of aporia, which typically functions in order to express doubt. He notes in *A Taste for the Secret,* for example, that the 'I,' "itself in a state of self-deconstruction, [. . .] is the possibility of the ethical but it is not simply the ethical" (Derrida and Ferraris 84). If alterity is the subject's *condition* of (im)possibility, in other words, it is not as though "I" have graciously decided to make room for the other. This dislocating encounter with the other is the case, and so in itself it does not warrant satisfaction for ethical services rendered. However, while acknowledging this distinction between the "ethical" and the "possibility of the ethical," I would stress the significant ethical implications that follow from the disrupted subject Derrida describes. In particular, this account of the interrupted subject demonstrates that self-sufficiency, self-identity, and purity are *fictions* and that all attempts to establish and maintain such fictions necessarily involve violence and exclusion.

We can find a powerful example of this phenomenon in "Plato's Pharmacy," Derrida's early essay about the ethics of reading, a piece well known for its virtuoso style of scholarly engagement. Here, Derrida offers both an incredibly close and seemingly infinitely dispersed reading of Plato's *Phaedrus* by zeroing in on (and prying wide open) the myth of the invention of writing that Socrates describes to Phaedrus near the end of their dialogue about love, seduction, and rhetoric. In this well-known passage, Socrates details an ancient mythical scene: The Egyptian demigod Theuth offers writing—which he touts as an aid to memory—to the god-king Thamus, who ultimately rejects Theuth's invention, deeming it a *pharmakon*. Such an external crutch would be better described, the king suggests, as an aid for forgetting. In his analysis of this passage, Derrida recasts the *pharmakon* as a differential supplement that is not external to memory but is in fact essential to it, and he extends this claim to the thematic economy of Western metaphysics writ large. Derrida's reading of Plato's text ultimately shows that speech, thought, and being itself are always contaminated, made possible (and thus impossible) only by way of an ongoing infiltration of alterity. If Plato frames writing as an external force that threatens the purity of internal consciousness, Derrida counters with the argument that "the outside is already *within* the work of memory" (*Dissemination* 109).

More is at stake here, however, than the sweeping philosophical claim that "the disappearance of any original presence, [. . .] is *at once* the condition of possibility *and* the condition of impossibility of truth" (168). Profound ethical ramifications issue from this aporetic determination, which, despite the focus on conditions of emergence, always bears on "real life" issues—very often on matters of life and death. We see this quite clearly when, within his broader discussion of the *pharmakon* as the concept that enables the opposition between inside and outside, Derrida describes a disturbing ancient Athenian purification rite. Citing historical research on ancient religious practices by James George Frazer and Jane Ellen Harrison, Derrida recounts that, in yearly ceremonies that occurred up through the fifth century, scapegoats known as *pharmakoi* were burned alive in a ritual attempt to relieve the city of plague, famine, or drought. As representative figures for whatever external force had entered in to cause harm, the *pharmakoi* were sacrificed in the name of recovering the unity and purity of the afflicted city. Noting that the purpose of the ritual was to "violently exclud[e] from [the city's] territory the representative of an external threat or aggression" (133), Derrida emphasizes that the *pharmakoi* were, from the start, part and parcel of the city itself. "The representative of the outside," he says, once again commenting on the significance of historical reporting by Frazer and Harrison, "is nonetheless *constituted*, regularly granted its place by the community, chosen, kept, fed, etc., in the very heart of the inside. These parasites were as a matter of course domesticated by the living organism that housed them at its expense" (133). In other words, there was never any "external" threat that had secretly entered into the city and so needed to be cast out, but instead, an always-already "contaminated" body politic. More than an ancient historical curiosity, this example illustrates that there can be no self-identity (just as there can be no group identity or cultural identity) without difference-to-self. This is an ethical determination, I would argue, because it reveals the desire for purity and full presence to be a murderous imagining—one that can be achieved only through violence and exclusion. One need only look to the 2017 white nationalist rally in Charlottesville, Virginia, for example, or to the marked increase of Immigration and Customs Enforcement arrests under the Trump administration to confirm that the fantasy of a purity lost—accompanied by a deep desire to "recover" that fantasy—is alive and well and that it continues to motivate violence and exclusion. In these cases, and in every case like them, a group of vulnerable individuals is designated as the external threat that needs to be eliminated or cast out. Derrida's insights about the contamination of identity shed light on both the futility and the horror of such logic, and they posit an essential relation to the other than can never be untangled.

Difference-to-self, to put this another way, is *not* a failure to be overcome. Quite to the contrary, the other's interruptive presence is the basis for all ethical responsibility. Contamination in this sense is not a reason for identifying the other and violently casting him out, but instead it is the very thing that allows us to answer to the other. Because this answerability occurs before any determination of and identification with self, what results is a divergence from traditional accounts of ethics that are premised on agency:

> Even before the question of responsibility was posed, [. . .] we are caught up, one and another, in a [. . .] curving of the relation to the other: prior to all organized *socius*, all *politeia*, all determined 'government,' *before* all 'law.' [. . .] We are already caught up, we are caught out, in a certain responsibility [. . .]. This responsibility that assigns freedom to us *without leaving it with*

us, as it were—we see it coming from the other. It is assigned to us by the other, from the place of the other, well before any hope of reappropriation allows us the assumption of responsibility—allowing us, as we say, to assume responsibility, *in the name, in one's own name,* in the space of *autonomy*. (*Politics of Friendship* 231–32)

Ethical responsibility, in other words, is not something we can assume for ourselves or masterfully take in hand. It is not a matter of an autonomous agent choosing to follow a universal principle and remaining unchanged in this process. Instead, ethical "freedom" comes only by way of the other. It begins with a profoundly disrupted subject whose identity is constituted by an alterity that can never be recuperated. Despite the move away from an agentive account of ethics, it is important to note that one's ethical responsibility is not weakened by virtue of being "caught up" in the relation to the other. By contrast, ethical obligation begins in the unsettling moment of *rapprochement* with the unassimilable other. Always in the midst of an unending, restless responsibility to and negotiation with the other, the ethical subject must respond without norm to what Howells refers to as "the impossible infinity of its object" (155).

In the end, the ethics we can glean from Derrida's work takes place not in the realm of universals, but in ongoing performative responses to a series of impossible-to-anticipate alterities. Each time, what we call the subject is enabled, interrupted, and transformed in an encounter with an other that cannot be reduced to an object of knowledge. Because it consists in the nonassimilating activity of response and responsibility, ethics is borne of the address. In this way, as Diane Davis has argued, ethics is profoundly *rhetorical*. She characterizes this sense of ethics as a "prelusive" scene enabled by an "undeclinable engagement with an alterity that addresses 'me' by announcing itself without coming clean and to which 'I' can only respond" ("Rhetoricity" 436). The possibility of ethics, in other words, is opened in the *rapprochement* with the other. Once again, the address I refer to here is conceptually prior to the persuasive scene described by Aristotle (in 1.2.1–1.2.20 of the *Rhetoric*), in which a speaker communicates with an audience member in order to direct social action. But it is an address nonetheless, and these two forms of address share an essential structure that I believe illuminates both the ethics of persuasion and the rhetorical elements of Derrida's aporetic ethics. In the coming section, I attempt to sharpen this claim by reexamining Derrida's inheritance of Austin's account of speech act theory. Revisiting this well-known academic exchange will enable me to explain precisely how an ethics of response and responsibility allows us to recast the traditional persuasive scene. Despite classical rhetoric's utilitarian focus on the force of language, that is, Derrida's aporetic ethical perspective provides an avenue for rethinking persuasion as a transformative negotiation with the other that precedes agentive accounts of perlocutionary force.

DERRIDA'S INHERITANCE OF SPEECH ACT THEORY: THE RHETORIC & ETHICS OF PERFORMATIVITY

> The Sophists [...] haunt our present debate,
> as more than one sign shall indicate.
> —Jacques Derrida, "Limited Inc a b c," 42

Early in his career, Derrida took a friendly interest in Austin's account of speech acts precisely because it attended to language's asignifying force rather than its representational capacity. Austin de-emphasized, in other words, the semantic aspects of language in favor of the performative ones. And his notion of the performative utterance—a phrase that enacts rather than refers to its object—appeared to Derrida to loosen language from the tyrannical grip of meaning: To utter a phrase such as "I promise," by Austin's reckoning, is to do it, not to refer to any signified content that exists before or beyond the locution, and so the performative was not confined to the "horizon of an intelligibility and truth of meaning" that Derrida complained dominated traditional philosophical notions of communication ("Signature" 310). Communication in this traditional sense presumes that an ideal thought content governs what we speak and write. In this model, the activities of speaking and writing are mere means of transport, neutral compartments that carry meaning from one place to the next *after* its emergence as an idea or thought. Taken in this sense (and Derrida argues that it is nearly always taken in this sense), communication merely "vehiculates a representation as an ideal content (which will be called meaning)" (314). What Derrida so appreciated about Austin's work, by contrast, was that it understood communication as more than the transmission of meaning and that it called attention to language's capacity to communicate "an original movement [. . .], an operation, and the production of an effect" (321). Austin's notion of the performative, that is, took into account the ways we could "communicate a force by the impetus of a mark" (321) and so it provided a unique vocabulary for "the value of force, [. . . the] difference of force" (322). He doesn't put it this way exactly, but what Derrida finds so compelling about Austin's work are its *rhetorical* dimensions—its attention to what language can do over and above what it means.

As if taking this cue from Derrida, Reed Way Dasenbrock ("J. L. Austin and the Articulation," 1987), Andrew Munro ("Reading Austin," 2013), and Barbara Cassin (*Sophistical Practice*, 2014) have noted the strongly rhetorical resonances of Austin's *How to Do Things with Words*, each of them highlighting the sophistic quality of Austin's attention to speech acts and noting the significance of the perlocutionary speech act for rhetorical studies. A speech act that produces "certain consequential effects upon the feelings, thoughts, or actions of the audience, or of the speaker, or of other persons" (Austin 101), the perlocutionary speech act is for Austin a way to characterize the activity of persuasion (103). Distinguished from the illocutionary speech act in that there is a temporal delay between speech act and effect, the perlocutionary speech act is precisely the domain of rhetoric. Furthermore, Austin's conclusion that *all* utterances are performative—even those that at first appear to be constative—certainly seems to follow from the claims of those classical rhetoricians who made a study of the power of language and its capacity to shape and reshape the world. Given the elegance with which Austin exemplifies the fine distinctions among a collection of speech acts, furthermore, and the wit and charm on full display in the lectures that constitute *How to Do Things with Words*, it is difficult to overstate the rhetorical acumen and disposition of that classic text. What is perhaps less obvious, however, is how often it wanders into ethical territory and how thoroughly the encounter with ethical questions nudges Austin's linguistic diagnoses and classifications into new realms. While his preferred ethos may be that of the light-hearted cultural observer, he cannot help but call attention to the ethical significance of performative speech acts, particularly the way these situate us both in relation to others and to ourselves. For instance, in the larger context of his discussion of his "doctrine of the *Infelicities*" (14), Austin notes that "a great many of the acts which *fall within the province of Ethics* [. . .] have the general character, in whole or part, of conventional or ritual acts" (19–20, emphasis added). While this is primarily an aside about the vulnerability of explicit performatives to various misfires and abuses, the comment highlights Austin's openness to the ambiguity of the nature of what he calls the "utterance-origin"—a term that that suggests far more certainty about its status than Austin ultimately seems to. Because felicitous performatives require both sincerity and the appropriate enactment of accepted conventions, at one and the same time, they also ensure that the source of the utterance has been interrupted by outside forces in an essential way. By Austin's own logic, as Shoshanna Felman has demonstrated, the most personal and deeply felt "'I' do" is a citation—a re-citation recited by countless numbers who have come before.

It was precisely this rhetorical and ethical promise that drew Derrida's attention and interest beginning in the early 1970s when he first posed a number of well-documented critical questions to Austin. In what would be the beginning of a long-standing intellectual engagement with the ordinary language philosopher, Derrida famously criticized *How to Do Things with Words* for its insistence on an ultimately untenable notion of context (one that was, as he said, "exhaustively determinable" ["Signature" 322]). Despite the strong challenge, however, "Signature Event Context" also initiated what would be an ongoing collaboration of sorts between Austin and Derrida, one that informed and was indeed essential to Derrida's conceptualization of the aporetic ethics I described above. In that early essay, Derrida made note of his plans to elaborate on his notion of iterability by taking "help from—but in order to go beyond it, too—the problematic of the *performative*" (321). Nearly fifty years after that initial pronouncement, the sentiment remains an apt description of Austin's profound influence on essential aspects of Derrida's thinking. This influence, of course, is marked by *différance* in the sense that Derrida radically reimagines Austin's notion of the performative: He comes to understand performativity as a condition prior to the distinction between what words say and what they do. And yet Derrida returns to the "problematic of the *performative*," as his readers know, time and time again, especially in those instances (such as in *Specters of Marx*) when he attempts to describe the necessity of affirming the unrecognizable other who simultaneously constitutes and disrupts being. This is no simple adoption and application of Austin's concept, of course, but rather a radical transformation. While Austin posits the performative structure of all utterances, Derrida pushes even further by positing the performative structure of every event, including the event of being itself. In other words, he takes up Austin's idea, transforms it, and nearly turns it inside out. Right where Austin uncomfortably senses the precariousness of the utterance-origin, Derrida intensifies the ethical stakes.

This complex inheritance suggests that there is no dissociating Derrida's early work on performativity from his later claims about the ongoing necessity of responding to the other whose irruptive presence opens the space of negotiation. The path to Derrida's ethics, in other words, goes not by way of a "turn," but straight through performative force.[11] He may be Austin's most

---

11. Several commentators have observed the importance of the performative for Derrida's ethics. J. Hillis Miller, for example, has noted the singular importance of Derrida's encounter with Austin, arguing that his distinctive "exappropriation" of Austin's performative utterance "is an essential aspect of Derrida's ideas about the secret, literature, friendship, hospitality, perjury, decision, sovereignty, politics, responsibility, justice, death, temporality, religion, and so on" (*For Derrida* 152). See also Anderson, who notes the significance of the performative for Derrida's thinking of the "call or promise to the future and thus to the other to come that

famous critic, and, as we will see, Derrida generalizes and reverses the performative beyond Austin's wildest imaginings. But an illuminating *rapprochement* remains. Derrida's inheritance of the Austinian performative ultimately allows us to view persuasion not as a traditional communicative transaction, but as a possibility given only by way of our ongoing responsibility to and for the nonpresent other. Here, the identities of the speaker and hearer are always already interrupted.

FROM UTTERANCE TO ETHICS: PERFORMATIVITY IN GENERAL

The reason "Signature Event Context" is an important location for opening a discussion about the ethics of persuasion is because this early Derridean text radically reconceives of what it means to address (and to be addressed by) someone in a speech situation, and because it explicitly takes up Austin's claim that speech is always involved in the production of effects. The central argument of this essay is by now well rehearsed: While traditional models of communication hold that thoughts and ideas are present first, and, then and only then, carried across space and/or time by the vehicles of gesture, speech, and writing, Derrida argues that "speech, consciousness, meaning, presence, truth, etc., would only be an effect" of iterability or citationality—what Derrida calls (among other terms) "general writing" (329). Above all, then, the essay is an argument about the priority of the other within any concept of the same, and while it "could appear that Austin has exploded the concept of communication as a purely semiotic, linguistic, or symbolic concept" (322), Derrida will go on to show that he nonetheless relies on the very semantic assumptions he had worked so hard to avoid. This is the reason, Derrida suggests, that it is necessary "to go beyond [. . .] the problematic of the *performative*" (321).

This critique is centered on Austin's account of the "total speech situation" (52). Despite Austin's move away from logical positivism's preoccupation with verifiability, he nonetheless tethers performative utterances to the contexts he claims can finally organize and authorize them. It is for this reason, Derrida argues, that "performative communication once more becomes the communication of an intentional meaning" (322). As I noted above, I read in Austin's open, curious approach (particularly in his willingness to cast aside the very

---

exceeds any traditional interpretation and definition" (108), and Fritsch, who has argued that "it is not always appreciated that the many ethical and political concepts that populate Derrida's later texts [. . .] are different ways of thinking the event of being and the ineluctably performative relation to it" ("The Performative" 98).

diagnostic categories he himself creates) an implicit wariness about the full presence or purity of the utterance-origin. When he ties abuses to misfires, that is, he (*nearly* and perhaps uncomfortably) acknowledges that the purity of intention is always interrupted by the repetition of convention. And yet, even after the so called "sea-change" (150), when Austin gives up any hope of distinguishing a constative from a performative utterance (turning instead to locutionary, illocutionary, and perlocutionary utterances—categories that allow him to consider with more precision the "senses in which to say something may be to do something" [91]), context serves to anchor and authorize speech acts. For example, and according to Austin's account of how illocutionary speech acts function, a judge is able to sentence a convicted criminal to jail time ("I sentence you . . .") because the state has conferred upon her the legitimate power to do so and because she has followed the appropriate legal procedures. This emphasis on protocol is precisely where Derrida takes Austin a step further. While Austin treats convention as the organizing presence that grounds and surrounds illocutionary utterances, Derrida argues that "a certain intrinsic conventionality [. . .] constitutes locution itself" ("Signature" 323). Where Austin settles for a "very historically sedimented notion of 'convention'" (323), a single moment in time that serves to authorize a single utterance, Derrida contends that each conventional event is constituted and so divided by all of the past and future instantiations of the ritual—by their constituting capacity to break from context. This iterability or breaking force, in other words, creates the structure of self on which ethics rests: It inaugurates a constitutive encounter with illimitable future others.[12] Thus, that singular moment when a judge sentences gets its seeming presence from all past and future sentencings and is divided in advance by them as well. In turn, the "I" of the "I sentence you . . ." is dispersed in the face of infinite repetition. Briefly put, the basis of Derrida's critique of Austin is that the latter's reliance on context allows institutional power to corral and contain the uncontrollable arrival of alterity.

What this critique demonstrates as well, however, is the way that Derrida also takes "help from [. . .] the problematic of the *performative*" ("Signature" 321) by initiating a certain generalization and reversal of the concept. Where Austin posits an institutionally authorized utterance-origin first and an illocutionary utterance that follows from it, Derrida insists that it is only in response to alterity's demand (which is initiated in the emergence of the mark) that the identity of a speaking subject could ever come to be in the first place. Instead

---

12. See also Nealon: "Derrida's linguistics is not primarily the force of *lack* or the demonstration of an inevitable absence, but is rather the positive or affirmative force of context breaking, the necessity of responding to emergence or the event" ("Beyond" 163).

of attributing performativity to an utterance, in other words, Derrida ascribes it to the event of being itself. It is not so much that the utterance "I sentence you . . ." is performative, but that the "I" of the "I sentence you . . ." is performative. Before any speaking subject could issue a performative speech act, that is, she will have already been addressed by the other in what Derrida has characterized as an "originary performativity that does not conform to preexisting conventions" (*Specters* 31). Taken from the perspective of traditional speech act theory, this "pre-performative force," as he also sometimes calls it, is a generalization that would seem to produce a temporally backwards understanding of where performative power comes from (*Acts of Literature* 298). Rather than beginning with an authorized speaker who intentionally utters a performative speech act, being is initiated only because it *has already been* addressed by the other. In this generalized account, the power to initiate empirical speech acts is made possible only because the "I" has gathered itself together in the activity of responding to the other, whose demand comes first. As Fritsch notes, a certain counterintuitive passivity is required before it is possible to issue an empirical speech act: "Deconstructive 'hauntology' insists that the spectres that no ontology can ever fully capture have already addressed us, the human performers" ("The Performative" 88).

Not simply there or present, neither simply true nor false, identity is incapable of being adequately described or reported upon. Instead, Derrida suggests that identity is structured like Austin's performative utterance (a speech act that does not *refer* but instead *invents*). Always and for all time gathering itself together in *response* to the other that gives it its being (while simultaneously making being-as-such impossible), identity is performative in the sense that it is an ongoing activity of answering to and for the other. As he puts this in "The University without Condition," for example, the ongoing affirmation of alterity "*resemble[s]* a performative speech act." He adds, "It neither describes nor states anything; it engages by responding" (301). Derrida will return to this Austinian idiom regularly, especially when he wishes to emphasize identity's constitutive encounter with alterity and the immediate necessity of response. Here we begin to see why Derrida so often uses terminology related to speech acts in order to discuss the ethics of deconstruction. When he uses variations of those terms I noted above related to *speaking, addressing, listening, calling, saying 'yes,'* etc., he emphasizes the structural similarity between performative speech acts and identity itself. Although he radically transforms Austin's notion of the performative utterance by positing it at the hauntological level (and thus prior to the level of the linguistic utterance), there remains, I believe, an important *rapprochement* through which Derrida brings Austin's uniquely rhetorical approach into his ethical perspective. To view Derrida's articulation of ethics in this context, furthermore, is also to understand the classical art of persuasion as just one part of a deeper and more nuanced ethical field. More than a series of carefully crafted perlocutionary utterances, persuasion—when it is understood in relation to this generalized sense of performativity—involves an unsettling *rapprochement* with the other.

PERSUASION'S ETHICAL FORCE

> But who is it that is addressing you? Since it is not an "author," a "narrator," or a "deus ex machina," it is an "I" that is both part of the spectacle and part of the audience; an "I" that, a bit like "you," attends (undergoes) its own incessant, violent reinscription within the arithmetical machinery; an "I" that [...] is not some singular and irreplaceable existence, some subject or "life," but only, moving between life and death, reality and fiction, etc., a mere function or phantom.
>
> —Jacques Derrida, *Dissemination*, 325

How is the classical tradition of persuasion transformed or reconceived when we begin with the aporetic ethical perspective tied, as I have just described, to the pre-performative address? In a certain sense, this book does nothing so much as pursue this question. But at this juncture I hope it is enough to say that because each of us bears the mark of a difference that divides conscious identity in advance, persuasion cannot be *simply* understood as a form of perlocutionary communication in which speakers utter phrases that subsequently affect audience members and innocent passersby. True, the history of rhetoric is made up in large part of theories, pedagogies, and practices oriented toward managing the distance between speech act and effect, but when viewed anew, from the theoretical perspective I've described here, these traditional notions of rhetorical communication are always interrupted by alterity. That is, even though the art of persuasion involves the calculated analysis of an audience, followed by the strategic deployment of language for the purpose of creating certain effects, the subject positions of speaker and hearer have already been unsettled in an encounter with difference. Neither is simply there; rather, each is invented in the moment of the persuasive event—in the response to nonpresent otherness.

In this way, persuasion involves two senses of force—perlocutionary force (in the Austinian sense) and force as constitutive difference (in the Derridean sense)—and persuasion's ethics emerges when the latter interrupts the former, which is always from the very first instance. If, as Derrida suggests, "one is no longer certain where to find the identity of the 'speaker' or the 'hearer' (visibly identified with the conscious ego), [or] where to find the identity of an intention [...] or of an effect" ("Limited Inc" 75), then the art of persuasion cannot simply be perlocutionary in the sense that a speaker *initiates* an utterance that in the end will have touched its receiver (or missed the mark). This is because such utterances bear within themselves the disruptive force that puts being into question. The essential components of any particular persuasive act—the speaker, the listener, and the circumstances that make each rhetorical situation unique—do not rule the scene.[13] They are disrupted by persuasion's force in the very moment they seem to ground or control it. What this means is that in addition to the calculating attempts to manage the distance between perlocutionary speech act and effect, persuasion involves the response to an other, a response in which both self and other are transformed.

What Derrida brings to the discussion of rhetoric, then, is reason to insist on the powerful ethics that circulates through each and every persuasive address. His work allows us to identify in the classical tradition exemplary instances of what Davis has characterized as "persuasion without a rhetorician" (*Inessential* 57), a phrase that speaks to the interruptive exposure to otherness that gives rise to subjectivity as well as what she calls the fundamentally rhetorical structure of this exposure. The classical rhetorical tradition, furthermore, is an ideal location to examine this concept at work because, even as its central texts make an art of mastering techniques of linguistic rule, they can be shown to demonstrate that persuasive utterances (which we could characterize with Austin as perlocutionary) are defined—essentially, constitutively—by otherness. Perhaps this is why Derrida's early work on the performative remains such an important element of his late work on ethics. What Derrida seemed to recognize was that the disjunctive rapport with the other was in fact a rhetorical relation, perhaps even a persuasive one. This idea echoes through Chapter 2, in which I consider the ethical force of what on the surface reads like an unmatched example of persuasion *with* a rhetorician—Gorgias' *Encomium of Helen*—but which, in its seeming celebration of persuasion's instrumental capacities, also provides ample evidence of a constitutive or pre-performative ethics of persuasion.

---

13. See Barbara A. Biesecker's "Rethinking the Rhetorical Situation from Within the Thematic of *Différance*" for an important account of this argument.

CHAPTER 2

Gorgias's Pre-Performative Address

> What cause then prevents the conclusion that Helen similarly, against her will, might have come under the influence of speech, just as if ravished by the force of the mighty?
>
> —GORGIAS, *ENCOMIUM OF HELEN*, 12

> I think that there is, in the opening of a context of argumentation and discussion, a reference—unknown, indeterminate, but none the less thinkable—to disarmament. I agree that such disarmament is never simply present, even in the most pacific moment of persuasion, and therefore that a certain force and violence is irreducible, but none the less this violence can only be practised and can only appear as such on the basis of a non-violence, a vulnerability, an exposition. I do not believe in non-violence as a descriptive and determinable experience, but rather as an irreducible promise and of the relation to the other as essentially non-instrumental.
>
> —JACQUES DERRIDA, "REMARKS ON DECONSTRUCTION AND PRAGMATISM," 83

If a single figure could bear the full weight of rhetoric's bad reputation—its seductive and deceptive potentialities, its self-serving nature, and its rejection of philosophical and moral certainties—it could be no other than Gorgias of Leontini (500–392 BCE).[1] Although the Older Sophist was a well-regarded and in-demand teacher of rhetoric and a celebrated performer of epideictic speeches in the late fifth and early fourth centuries, his advocacy of the disastrous Sicilian Expedition,[2] his antifoundationalist epistemology,[3] and his reputation as a purveyor of style over substance have irrevocably associ-

---

1. See Richard Leo Enos's "The Epistemology of Gorgias' Rhetoric: A Re-examination" for an account of how this biographical dating has come to be accepted (38). See also W. K. C. Guthrie's *The Sophists* (269).

2. See Diodorus Siculus, who names Gorgias "chief of the delegation" of ambassadors who appealed to Athens, "asking the democracy to come to their aid as quickly as possible" from the Syracusans (qtd. in Sprague 32), and Mario Untersteiner (93).

3. See, in particular, Scott Consigny, who explains that an antifoundationalist reading of Gorgias holds that the sophist "repudiates the notion that there is a foundational 'truth' in the

ated Gorgias with the pernicious capacities of persuasion. Praised for being "in power of speech by far the most eminent of the men of his time" (Diodorus Siculus, qtd. in Sprague 32) and for his ability to make speech "sweeter than it ha[d] been and more impressive" (Philostratus, qtd. in Sprague 30), Gorgias was also judged harshly for his belief (and his teaching) that persuasive speech was a powerful, though not necessarily virtuous, means of linguistic influence. Plato attributes to him in *Philebus*, for example, the view that "the art of persuasion was greatly superior to all others" because it "subjugated all things not by violence but by willing submission" (58a).[4] His legacy thus characterized, Gorgias became the representative figure of the dangers of persuasive speechmaking, which Plato saw as a manipulative instrument whose end is often mercenary self-interest.[5]

Plato, of course, has played a powerful role in the production and lasting influence of this partial narrative, the fullest expression of which we find in *Gorgias*. This dialogue vividly—if unfairly—attributes to the sophist an instrumental view of persuasive rhetoric as a means of bending audiences to an orator's will. When asked by Socrates to describe precisely what he claims to teach, the dramatized Gorgias argues, paradoxically, that his art "brings freedom to mankind in general and to each man dominion over others in his own country" (452d).[6] Pressed further, his baser motives are revealed: "Possessed of such power [i.e., the power to persuade people in all areas of political, legal, and public life] you will make the doctor, you will make the trainer your slave, and your businessman will prove to be making money, not for himself, but for another, for you who can speak and persuade multitudes" (452e). What becomes clear is that Gorgias's art—which does not require exact

---

world, that knowledge consists in the apprehension of this truth, and that words acquire meaning by representing an independent 'reality'" (*Gorgias* 29).

4. This section number refers to Plato's *Philebus*, in *Plato: The Collected Dialogues*, edited by Edith Hamilton and Huntington Cairns, Princeton UP, 1961, pp. 1086–150.

5. As Edward Schiappa has argued, it is not historically accurate to assume a clear distinction between sophistic and philosophical discourse and teaching during Gorgias's active period. Plato's view of rhetoric, and his use of that term, is a fourth-century phenomenon that would have been alien to Gorgias. Schiappa notes, "Fifth-century texts concerning *logos*—such as Gorgias's *Helen*—differ substantially from fourth-century texts concerning Rhetoric (*rhētorikē*)—such as Plato's *Gorgias*, Alkidamas' *On Those Writing Written Speeches*, the *Rhetoric to Alexander*, and Aristotle's *On Rhetoric*" ("Gorgias's *Helen*" 310). For this reason, Schiappa argues that it is important to understand Gorgias's *Helen* as a "predisciplinary" text, and he thus focuses on its "contributions to fifth-century discourse practices" ("Gorgias's *Helen*" 310). I want to acknowledge this point while nonetheless emphasizing the way Gorgias's views—and perhaps more importantly, his very identity—have come to stand in for suspicious views of persuasion as a deceptive instrument of control.

6. The following section numbers refer to Plato's *Gorgias*, in *Plato: The Collected Dialogues*, edited by Edith Hamilton and Huntington Cairns, Princeton UP, 1961, pp. 229–307.

knowledge of any particular subject—is first and foremost an instrument of power and control. As James Stuart Murray has characterized this decidedly Platonic portrayal, "In Gorgias' school, the main motivation for the incoming student is the prospect of power, and the main payoff for the graduate is the practice of it" (358). The dramatized Gorgias famously defends this position by arguing that rhetoric is, in fact, an ethically neutral "competitive art," much like boxing (456d). Just as it would be absurd to blame the trainer if a skilled boxer harmed an innocent friend or family member rather than an opponent in the ring (457a), so too would it be foolish to blame the rhetoric teacher if one of his students "makes a wrongful use" of persuasive speech (457b). Gorgias abdicates responsibility, in other words, for all of those instances in which his purportedly ethically neutral art is put to work by unethical practitioners for nefarious ends. But when his acolytes Polus and Callicles take up the conversation with Socrates and reveal themselves to be increasingly bent on satisfying their own passions by whatever means necessary, Gorgias's claim rings especially hollow. As James I. Porter has noted, this dramatic portrayal represents Gorgias as "unable to offer a convincing definition of rhetoric [. . .] and producing exasperation and bafflement more than any other response in his audience" (269).

There are many reasons, of course, not to take Plato's depiction of Gorgias at face value, not least the pair's incompatible beliefs about truth and its relation to language. For Plato, philosophy is, at least in part, the practice of differentiating itself from sophistry. This phenomenon may be observed not only in *Gorgias*, as noted above, but also in texts such as *Phaedrus*, *Protagoras*, and *Sophist*, each one a dialogue that depicts and discusses sophists and their beliefs primarily to articulate, by way of contrast, what counts as philosophy. Plato's interest in essences, furthermore—his primary concern with what Socrates refers to in *Phaedrus* as "being that really is what it is" (247c)— is diametrically opposed to the antifoundationalist thinking of Gorgias, who famously argued in his treatise *On the Non-Existent, or On Nature* that "nothing exists; [. . .] even if it exists it is inapprehensible to man; [and] even if it is apprehensible, still it is without a doubt incapable of being expressed or explained" (Sextus Empiricus, qtd. in Sprague 42). Challenging the Eleatic insistence on a unified, unvarying being that is capable, as W. K. C. Guthrie explains, of being "grasped by an infallible reason," Gorgias held instead that the ever-changing realm of opinion (*doxa*) ruled the scene (*The Sophists* 273). According to this thinking, appearances are incapable of being verified as true or false, and so what mattered was the capacity of language to shape the realm of experience. While Plato would tolerate rhetoric only when it was used by those in possession of true knowledge, Gorgias was content to accept that there was no truth—no "being that really is what it is"—only, as Thomas G. Rosenmeyer argues, "the supersession of the world of *logos*," which involves the "frequent discrepancy between words and things" (232). Or as Michelle Ballif reads Gorgias's famed fragment: "We never know things 'in themselves,' truth 'in itself,' being 'in itself.' All we know—if knowledge is possible—is *logos*. And this *logos* does not [. . .] correspond (really or truly or directly) to things in themselves" (*Seduction* 72).[7]

Given Plato's caricatured portrayal of Gorgias, which may be attributed to the two thinkers' irreconcilable views, it might seem that the sophist's own preserved writings on the power, purpose, and function of persuasive speech would add some dimension and nuance to the ethical picture. However, in his *Encomium of Helen*, the famed showpiece on moral responsibility and the overwhelming capacities of *logos*, Gorgias gives us reason to believe that perhaps Plato was not so far off the mark after all. In what Alexander P. D. Mourelatos calls "a panegyric on the powers of *logos*" (135), Gorgias's *Encomium* describes persuasive speech as an instrument that can, in fact, be used for the purpose of "enslaving" others. Indeed, he seems to celebrate this very possibility. This paean to speech is staged within a defense of the legendary and seemingly indefensible Helen of Troy, when Gorgias suggests that Helen herself is not responsible for running off with Paris and so inciting a catastrophic war: "For either by will of Fate and decision of the gods and vote of Necessity did she do what she did, or by force reduced or by words seduced <or by love possessed>" (6). No matter which of these led to her betrayal of Menelaus, he insists, Helen played no active role. While Gorgias claims at the outset that his speech is a praise of Helen, readers soon learn that the real object of acclaim is *logos* itself, which dominates the text both spatially and thematically. Above all, Gorgias argues that persuasive speech—because it functions just as powerfully as divine intervention, physical coercion, magical spells, and drugs—disables active judgment; it overpowers the hearer's critical capacities and leaves no room for resistance. As Charles P. Segal has argued, Gorgias figures *logos* as "almost an independent external power which forces the hearer to do its will" and "an active force impinging on the psyche from without" (121). Guthrie also highlights the especially forceful nature that Gorgias attributes to *logos*: "In the eyes of Gorgias 'the word' was a despot who could do anything" (25).

---

7. As George A. Kennedy notes, "*Logos* has many meanings through the long history of the Greek language; it is anything that is 'said,' but that can be a word, a sentence, part of a speech or of a written work, or a whole speech" (*A New History* 11). For further readings of *On Nature*, see Porter and Mourelatos.

If we are to take the *Encomium* at its word, then—an interpretive decision that, as we will see, is the matter of considerable debate—Gorgias represents his own views on the dangerous capacities of persuasion in very much the same way that Plato does. He describes, even embraces, an art of persuasion that is highly instrumental. As a result, what has taken hold in our cultural memory is the portrait of Gorgias as a decidedly unethical practitioner of persuasion. As Porter notes, "From the older handbooks to the more recent scholarly literature one finds accounts that seem to take Gorgias and Plato literally [. . .]: conjured up in all these accounts is the image of a hearer irresistibly overwhelmed [. . .] by Gorgias's apagogic and psychagogic persuasions" (269). Furthermore, because Gorgias was known for his ornate, affected style, which emphasized poetry and musicality over correct speaking (Guthrie, *The Sophists* 270), the sophist's greatest asset—his ability to make speech "sweeter" and "more impressive"—becomes another weapon in his persuasive armory. Expressly unconcerned with truth, and known instead for his use of figures of speech (including antithesis, anadiplosis, assonance, and parisosis), Gorgias has been, as Scott Consigny explains, dismissed as "not a serious philosopher at all, but rather a mere 'stylist,' an orator who deploys poetic devices to embellish his speeches" ("The Styles" 43). What remains then is the image of a speech artist and an audience pleaser whose facility with words poses a threat to those hearers unable to discern between true and false appearances. Gorgias celebrates his art for its capacity to gain power over others, and in this sense, he has come to personify all that is unethical about the instrumental force of persuasion.

In this chapter, I propose to complicate Gorgias's ethical legacy, to add a dimension that both co-responds to and interrupts the predominant understanding of the sophist as a practitioner of and an advocate for marshaling stylistic artifice to subjugate easily manipulated hearers. While I believe that Gorgias's *Encomium* thematizes and performs the instrumental and deceptive power of speech, it also, I will argue, stages a presubjective drama in which Helen's performative power is consigned in advance to the multiple others who address her (the gods, Paris, and the despot that is speech). Gorgias portrays Helen, that is, as engaged prior to the formation of her will, and so he depicts and thus calls attention to the affirmative response to alterity that is implied in every (perlocutionary) persuasive address. Because Helen's performative responsivity is painted across the backdrop of an argument for the instrumental power of speech, furthermore, the *Encomium* conveys the idea that a presubjective *rapprochement* with an ultimately unassimilable other is the condition of possibility of all persuasive speech acts. Thus, in addition to celebrating the capacity of speech to exert influence over others, Gorgias's

Encomium depicts a pre-performative scene that precedes and exceeds this very instrumental capacity. By my reading of the speech, in other words, the *Encomium* posits an ethical relation that ultimately interrupts the perlocutionary force of persuasion.

Such a reading, of course, relies on a contemporary theoretical framework to reconsider an ancient artifact as it draws on Derrida's generalized understanding of performativity, which, as I described in Chapter 1, sees the identity of a speaking subject as an effect and as the ongoing activity of response to the other's address. I am aware that this approach flouts the historicist dictate—as forwarded by G. B. Kerferd, Jacqueline de Romilly, and Edward Schiappa—that we must come to classical texts free of our own modern biases, and that it does, to borrow Schiappa's words, "anachronistically inject later developed abstractions" into ancient intellectual productions ("History" 310). Rather than seeing anachronism as a problem, however, I am persuaded by Ballif's claim that a responsible historiographical approach requires "a certain uncertainty regarding temporality and address" ("Historiography" 141), and I am influenced by Derrida's understanding of the tradition as something with an essential relation to the future. That said, I do want to make it clear that I am making no claims for a correct, final accounting of what Gorgias's multivalent *Encomium* actually *means,* or that I have any insight on the sophist's authorial intentions. On this issue I agree with John Poulakos, who argues that, "inasmuch as the sophists' purpose was to demonstrate that the world could always be recreated linguistically, restated in other words, and thus understood otherwise, the search for their essential doctrines is in vain" (*Sophistical* 25). At the very least, "the search for their essential doctrines" is not the only thing, or even the most obvious thing, that the sophists' enigmatic textual remains inspire us to do. Just as importantly, though, I hope that my reading of Gorgias's *Encomium* coaxes out some of the alterities within the text and that, rather than reduce the famed *epideoxis* to an object of knowledge, I provoke a defamiliarizing scholarly encounter with a speech that has become an emblem for persuasion itself.

RECOVERING GORGIAS AND THE *ENCOMIUM OF HELEN*

Plato, of course, has not had the final word on Gorgias, and in the years since the nineteenth-century rehabilitation of the sophists initiated by G. W. F. Hegel and George Grote, he has come to be understood as both a serious thinker on the topic of language and its relation to truth and an important artist whose creative innovations brought poetic language to the discourse of the polis. In recent years, furthermore, his work has drawn favorable comparisons to twentieth-century theory, and scholars have looked to his fragments to chart a distinctive intellectual through-line from classical to contemporary rhetoric. Victor Vitanza, for example, names Gorgias a "proto-Third Sophistic thinker" who prefigures the deconstructive impulse to disrupt those binary oppositions (such as presence/absence, man/woman) that smuggle in and authorize oppressive relations of power (244). And Sharon Crowley has argued that when he "free[s] language from any ties to objective reality," Gorgias anticipates Derrida's argument that arche-writing or writing in general is conceptually prior to both speech and thought (281). Characterizing both Gorgias and Derrida as "rhetorical men," moreover, Stanley Fish posits that the two thinkers share a flexible, antifoundationalist worldview that understands the philosophical insistence on being as such as "just another style, not the state of having escaped style" (484). No longer castigated for advancing little more than a pernicious *techne* of deception, and understood instead as a thinker who has as much to teach us about the present as he does the past, Gorgias has been, as Bruce E. Gronbeck has argued, "like his Helen, [...] 'freed ... from evil reputation'" (38).

Just as Gorgias himself has been reconsidered in terms beyond those that Plato set for him centuries ago, so too has the *Encomium of Helen*, a speech whose style, ingenuity, and complexity has invited seemingly endless interpretations of its purpose, its meaning, and what it has to teach us about rhetoric and persuasion. To read the array of scholarship on the *Encomium* is to understand how powerfully this text has struck a chord with modern readers and to marvel at the interpretive possibilities it has enabled. Particularly notable among these readings—for our purposes here at least—is the way that the *Encomium*'s ethics have been roundly refigured. Largely abandoning the idea that Gorgias uses the speech to advocate for unethical uses of persuasion, scholars have begun to suggest that he has a far more nuanced agenda in mind. Porter, for example, argues that Gorgias should not be taken at his word when he says, over the course of defending Helen, that persuasive speech has the capacity to overwhelm the hearer's free will. Instead, he suggests, Gorgias renders indistinguishable the four reasons to free Helen from blame, and so "the accent falls on the *vulnerability,* not the power of *logos*" (277). Contrary to interpretations like Segal's, Kerferd's, and up to a point mine, Porter claims that "persuasion's only claim to remarkability in *Helen* is the formal dissonance that it installs within the argument" (285). Rather than deeming this a failure, however, Porter credits Gorgias for performatively demonstrating that "we lack the words to describe what it is that *logos* 'does'" (286). The suggestion is that the *Encomium* is not a paean to the irresistible powers of persuasive speech over and above the unavoidable necessity of reality, but instead an artful performance of the precariousness of both. Poulakos also makes a claim for Gorgias's ethics on the basis of the *Encomium*'s rhetorical virtuosity. Arguing that Gorgias's aim in the speech is to cast Helen as an analogue for rhetoric, Poulakos notes that "both are attractive, both are unfaithful, and both have a bad reputation" ("Gorgias' *Encomium*" 5). What Gorgias sets out to do in the *Encomium*, then, is to rehabilitate rhetoric's reputation by arguing that just as the responsibility should be placed on those—like the gods—who use Helen for their own purposes rather on Helen herself, so too is the art of rhetoric innocent when it is misused (9–10). But more than this, Poulakos explains, Gorgias is out to insist that practitioners of rhetoric must assume responsibility for their use of linguistic force and that "rhetoric next to physical violence is helpless" (10). Vessela Valiavitcharska takes a similar tack in her reading of the *Encomium*, although she presses the point about Gorgias's insistence on upright ethical action even further. Noting that Gorgias "does not see his own art as deception, nor does he think that it necessarily rests on opinion" (149), she argues that he views persuasion with suspicion and that he deems it something that "is not a desirable outcome in a speech [. . .] [because] its influence is corruptive" (151). Drawing in part on Gorgias's claim in the *Encomium*'s introduction that "what is becoming [. . .] to a speech [is] truth" (1), Valiavitcharska argues that Gorgias believes in "an intrinsic connection between truthful speech [. . .] and correct speech" (149). This is a remarkable reading in that it claims for Gorgias an interest in determining the worth of being in itself (thus rejecting any claims to an antifoundationalist epistemology), and further still that it ascribes to him the view that *logos* involves an "obligation for ethical use" (161).

To look ahead, I will briefly note here that my own view of the *Encomium*'s ethics diverges significantly from those that ascribe to Gorgias prescriptive moral beliefs. I will suggest, by contrast, that the ethics that emerges from the speech takes the form of a presubjective *rapprochement* with alterity. I theorize this claim with Derrida's idea of the "yes/yes" or the "arche-originary *yes*," which, as he argues, "*resembles* an absolute performative" (Derrida, Ronnell, and Holmes 129). Such an approach is more conceptually aligned with recent treatments of Gorgias arguing that the sophist uses the *Encomium* to refigure the ethical realm entirely. Consigny, for example, argues that Gorgias "characterizes morality as adherence to the social conventions of particular communities" (*Gorgias* 29) and that the *Encomium* functions as a kind of invitation to the audience to enter into the discourse on Helen as part of an ongoing debate that invents and redefines ethical terms as it proceeds (189). Rather than recovering Gorgias, that is, on the basis of a softening of his claims to the ascendency of *logos* over truth, Consigny reframes what counts as ethical from the sophist's perspective. Ballif, too, articulates the way that Gorgias redefines the ethical field, arguing that, in Gorgias's hands, Helen (whom she views, like Poulakos, as an analogue for rhetoric) allows us to rethink traditional conceptions of subjectivity and so "challenges our contemporary belief that moral and ethical behavior is a function of choosing (after rational deliberation) some action in the face of being free to do otherwise" (*Seduction* 80). Like Ballif, I believe that that the *Encomium*'s most powerful ethical implications emerge when the text prompts us to think beyond the realms of self-present subjectivity and autonomous free will. Building on her insight that Gorgias's Helen functions to unravel the clear distinctions between subject/object and activity/passivity, I argue that Gorgias depicts Helen's performative power as committed in advance to the others who address her. Engaged before her free will, her responsibility is given by way of an affirmation of the other—of an inaudible 'yes' to the other's call—which serves as a reminder of the "pre-performative" force that precedes and exceeds the perlocutionary effects of persuasion.

"'YES' WITHOUT A WORD": HELEN'S ACQUIESCENCE

> Yes is the transcendental condition of all performative dimensions. A promise, an oath, an order, a commitment always implies a yes, I sign. [. . .] Any event brought about by a performative mark, any writing in the widest sense of the word, involves a yes, whether this is phenomenalized or not, that is, verbalized or adverbalized as such. [. . .] Yes indicates that there is address to the other. This address is not necessarily a dialogue or an interlocution, since it assumes neither voice nor symmetry, but the haste, in advance, of a response that is already asking. For if there is some other, if there is some yes, then the other no longer lets itself be produced by the same or by the ego.
>
> —Jacques Derrida, "Ulysses Gramophone: Hear Say Yes in Joyce," 298–99

One of the most compelling things about the *Encomium of Helen*, I believe, is that it is uniquely interested in various notions of responsibility. Ostensibly, Gorgias claims to be invested in the moral and juridical senses of responsibility, both of which imply some measure of control on the part of the actor. He insists, for example, that it is the rhetorician's duty to properly assign blame and to carefully determine with whom culpability lies: "Man and woman and speech and deed and city and object should be honored with praise if praiseworthy and incur blame if unworthy. [. . .] It is the duty of one and the same man both to speak the needful rightly and refute the unrightfully spoken" (1–2). But this proclamation is a bit odd because the *Encomium* works in the opposite direction. Helen is not responsible, Gorgias says, for betraying her husband, for abandoning her homeland, or for launching those thousand ships: "How then can one regard blame of Helen as just, since she is utterly acquitted of all charge, whether she did what she did through falling in love or persuaded by speech or ravished by force or constrained by divine constraint?" (20). He *says* he is interested in moral responsibility, in other words, but he also gives us good reason to question his sincerity on this point. After all, it matters little to Gorgias which of the causes (fate, force, speech, or love) led to Helen's betrayal, and he ultimately declines to single out one of the four possibilities. All that seems to matter is that Helen is not accountable whatever the circumstances. Thus, properly assigning responsibility, despite all of Gorgias's claims to the contrary, doesn't seem so important after all. Although he maintains that "it is right for the responsible one to be held responsible" (6), in other words, Gorgias gives us ample reason to consider that he might not be referring to the traditional conception of responsibility in which an unchanging subject is the cause of its actions. To the contrary, he casts Helen as an effect, and he seems to suggest that her very identity is given by way of its response to the others who address her.

If Helen is a subject whose being is given by way of its exposure to the other's unwilled address, then any ethical account would have to examine Helen's responsibility from a different perspective and in an entirely different register. This is the case because, in its very structure, Gorgias's argument that we must free Helen from blame rests on a series of four hypothetical imaginings that he requires us to consider in turn. In three of those four cases (fate, speech, and love), we are made to presuppose Helen's acquiescence. Her assent is inaudible (she does not speak, she does not *do* much of anything in the speech), but in order to entertain the question of her culpability so that he may dismiss it, Gorgias forces the audience to assume her consent in a serial form: "Now if through the first [i.e., the gods] [. . .] But if it was speech which persuaded her [. . .] If it was love that did all these things [. . .]" (6–15). Thus, in order to adjudicate her culpability at all, Gorgias requires us to imagine that she did acquiesce to the gods, that she did allow herself to be persuaded, and that she did choose love over duty. Of course, his point will be to argue that there is no active consent in any of these instances, but before Gorgias can begin to make such a claim, Helen must have said "yes."

Given his insistence on the affirmative quality of deconstruction, it is perhaps no surprise that the word "yes" maintains an important place in Derrida's oeuvre. In "Ulysses Gramophone," an address delivered in 1984 before an international gathering of Joyce scholars, Derrida describes the "yes" as the "pre-performative force" that is the condition of possibility for all linguistic utterances, prior to any convention or intention (298). Positioning himself, once again, in relation to speech act theory, Derrida understands the "yes" as a generalized or quasi-transcendental performative that signals a presubjective alliance with the other. This, in turn, is what gives rise to ethical and political responsibility. Not an empirical utterance—not even, he notes, a word—"yes" is both the "departure point of all discourse" (279) and a relay through the other that "interferes with the so-called monologue" (271–72). While Derrida wryly questions what value his idiosyncratic reading of *Ulysses* has to the Joycean scholarly establishment, he takes the opportunity to explain that, "for a very long time, the question of the *yes* has mobilized or traversed everything I have been trying to think, write, teach, or read" (287). A rigorous thinking of the "yes," in other words, is essential to deconstruction. And when Derrida tells Alan Montefiore in their 2001 interview that "deconstruction is *mainly* affirmation" and that this "means a "constant reference to a *yes*" ("Talking" 180), he refers to this "yes" in particular—the affirmative obligation to the other that comes prior to the formation of individual will.

Derrida is very careful to distinguish this "yes" from the Austinian performative, noting that while it is "radically non-constative" in that it designates or describes nothing, it nonetheless does not conform to the traditional account of the performative utterance (298). The difference here is that while an Austinian performative "must be a [. . .] sentence sufficiently endowed with meaning in itself, in a given conventional context, to bring about a determined event," Derrida's pre-performative or quasi-transcendental "yes" generalizes and reverses the conceptual ordering of what we might call performative power (298). Before any subject is capable of making a conscious choice (such as Helen, persuaded by Paris, agreeing to betray her husband), she has already been exposed to the other beyond any instance of choosing. The "yes" must be taken as an answer, Derrida explains, as an affirmative response that "occurs after the other, to answer a request or a question, at least implicit, of the other" (265). The significance here is that we see the necessity of alterity in every instance of identity, and before any subject is capable of actively choosing, it will have undergone a certain experience of passivity. "Being," Derrida explains, "presupposes the responsibility of the *yes*" (302), and thus it is caught up in a relation to the other that can never be untangled. In this way, each is bound to the other by way of a consent that precedes and exceeds conscious choice. There would be no subject, no "I," without this first "yes," and so we are invented by way of response to an unwilled address from the other.

While Derrida is clear about the crucial distinctions between the "yes," which, he says "is through and through and *par excellence* a performative," and Austin's performative utterance (tied, as it is, to the logic of context), his account nonetheless maintains something of the Austinian structure (298). In both instances, that is, there is a turn toward or an engagement with the other that is best described as an activity of address. Where Austin's performative accounts for empirical speech acts, however, Derrida's "yes" is a presubjective affirmation that is "co-extensive with every statement" (296). Derrida's notion of the "yes," moreover, installs repetition in the heart of Austin's utterance origin: With the first "yes" to the other, we sign on, we are given our "being" even if this "being" is not simply present and even if it is ultimately owed to the other. But this signal promise is not a once and done deal. It is not as though we say "yes" and then we get to "be," forever and all time, "ourselves." The first "yes," what Derrida calls elsewhere the "arche-originary yes," depends for its possibility on all of its infinite future instantiations ("A Number" 126). In other words, with the first "yes," we consent and make a promise to the other, but this "first" one must be confirmed by the innumerable "yeses" that follow. As Derrida explains, "The *yes* can only state *itself* by promising itself its own memory. The affirmation of the *yes* is the affirmation of memory. *Yes* must preserve itself, and thus reiterate itself, archive its voice in order to allow it once again to be heard" ("Ulysses" 276). What this means is that this arche-originary "yes"—the one that opens all questioning and through which the "I" is invented—is not simply original. Reproducibility is inscribed at its origin in such a way that the rigorous purity of the origin is fundamentally contaminated. Derrida likens this reproducibility to a "telephonic interiority" that is "at work within the voice [. . .] inscribing remoteness, distance, *différance*, and spacing" (271). Because the "I" inaugurated by the first "yes" is haunted by the infinite future deployments of the "yes," neither the "I," nor the will that would seem to issue from it is identical to itself. What the repetitions of the "yes" thus require is an ongoing negotiation with otherness that can never be settled. Because we are invented each time in our affirmative answer to the other's address, we can never count on a single, determined moral code to govern our encounters with alterity. It is in this way that Derrida's "yes" is aporetic in the sense I elaborated in Chapter 1: It hesitates before ethics *per se* and focuses instead on that which enables and gives rise to ethical and political responsibility.

It is in this sense that Derrida's pre-performative "yes" provides a way of making sense of the difficult notion of responsibility Gorgias sets out in the

Encomium. As I suggested above, Helen is noticeably inert in the *Encomium*, appearing for the most part as a prop in the sophist's drama. Porter suggests that "the Helen who emerges from Gorgias's speech is painted, as it were, in negative relief" (274), and he adds that "in sheer narrative terms Helen embodies her own self-difference" (280). She is not, to put it another way, portrayed as a fully formed subject, nor is she a literary woman invested with any personal or political agency: Poulakos deems her a "pretext" for Gorgias's real argument about the ethics of persuasive speech ("Gorgias's *Encomium*" 4), and Nancy Worman argues that "the speech uses Helen's desirable body to organize its arguments" (173). Despite these rather dismal gender politics, it would be too easy, as Porter's, Worman's, and Ballif's analyses suggest, to dismiss the speech simply on the basis of its portrayal of a passive feminine subject. Worman, for example, argues that while "Helen functions as the emotional reactant to the manipulations of persuasive speech," still other portions of the *Encomium* feature "the movement of Helen's body and those of others in a visual field" (176). In this way, she argues, "Helen's body vacillates between the subject and object position" (174). Ballif, too, posits a more complicated positioning of Helen, whose rhetorical figure, she argues, "flow[s] beyond the false dichotomy of subject/object" (*Seduction* 88). This is the case, she says, because Gorgias figures Helen as *both* a subject and an object, a woman who was willingly seduced and forcefully abducted (87). Unless we think Helen beyond the standard subject/object, active/passive binary oppositions, Ballif insists, we will continue to use her figure to maintain unjust structures of power, and in so doing "sustain[ ] relationships between Man and Man, and Man and his self" at the expense of woman (88).

What each of these readings about Helen's vacillating (non)being suggests is that her responsibility is far too complicated a matter to be explained in terms of free will or active choice. In fact, I believe that Gorgias depicts Helen not as a full and spontaneous subject capable of freely chosen action, but as a differential identity whose performative power is consigned in advance to the others who address her. In the speech, her being is inaugurated when she responds to the approach of the other, and Gorgias renders this responsivity in a serio-repetitive form that suggests that the production of the self in relation to others is work that will never be finished. The speech, as I have noted, does not ever reveal the precise reason for Helen's fall. Instead, it requires the audience to imagine that she has said "yes" to the gods, "yes" to the honey-tongued Paris, and "yes" to love. Ultimately—and disturbingly—these affirmations are rendered indistinguishable from the trauma of having been taken against her will. And yet this uneasy comparison serves to remind us that the other's address is uninvited and that the relation to the other always involves a certain cracking open from the "inside" of the safe home of one's being. This is an ethical responsibility, in other words, that involves a certain violent interruption. But as Derrida suggests in the epigraph that opens this chapter, such violence "can only appear as such on the basis of a non-violence, a vulnerability, an exposition" ("Remarks" 83).

The first way that Gorgias foregrounds Helen's pre-performative responsivity is by insisting on the priority of the other's address at the temporal level: He depicts her as responding to an appeal that has already been issued. While early in the speech Gorgias lauds Helen's "godlike beauty" (4) and the way it motivates great men to do great things, his discussion of Helen is less about that beauty than it is about her formative *relations* to those who act on her. First among those Gorgias puts in relation to Helen are the gods—who "cannot be hindered by human premeditation" (6). He shows us on the level of the sentence that Helen-as-grammatical-subject comes into being only *after* the gods' demand. It is only *after* Gorgias has argued that it is "right for the responsible one to be held responsible," that the strong are not "hindered by the weak," and that "it is the nature of things [. . .] for the weaker to be ruled and drawn by the stronger" (6) that Helen makes her appearance, at the end of the last line of the section. Helen's responsiveness to this divine command recalls Derrida's account of the "yes" as a "response to a request that has always already been made" ("Ulysses" 299) in that her emergence on the scene is made possible by gods whose approach she can neither control nor refuse.

The frame of Gorgias's speech, furthermore, has it so that Helen's first "yes"—yes to the demand of the gods—is narratively and structurally tied to her subsequent yeses to speech and love. As readers of Gorgias well know, only speech—that powerful lord whose pharmaceutical effects are tangible enough to stop fear, banish grief, nurture pity, and cause shuddering pain—is more divine and irresistible than the gods themselves. Gorgias depicts Helen as thoroughly "constrained" by speech (12), utterly open to its effects. Not only does speech summon her as if by magic and render her powerless, but it also inscribes her, marking her internally as she affirms its address. Describing Helen's relation to Paris, Gorgias argues "that persuasion, when added to speech, is wont also to impress the soul as it wishes" (13). What Worman makes of this is that Gorgias figures Helen's "immobile body [. . .] [as] so sensitive to the chime and impress of speech that it is impossible to distinguish these reactions from physical force" (176). If this is the case, Gorgias figures Helen as literally marked by speech, and she is inscribed by an address that comes from the outside but that nonetheless acts on her internally. From the very beginning, then, Helen is contaminated by the other's address.

Gorgias stages Helen's final affirmation when he closes the speech by asking us to imagine that love drew Helen to Troy. In this closing act, Gorgias frames love as a matter of sight, suggesting that affecting visions can cause people to lose "presence of mind for the present moment" (17). He hypothesizes that Helen was so pleased by Paris's beautiful image that she could not possibly "reject and refuse it" (19). Gorgias also dramatizes the "internal" fissures that result from Helen's affirmation of love's address: "Through sight the soul receives an *impression* even in its inner features" (15, emphasis added). And he adds: "In this way the sight *engraves* upon the mind images of things which have been seen. And many frightening *impressions* linger, and what lingers is exactly analogous to <what is> spoken" (17, emphasis added). In the moment of responding to love's call before or beyond the capacity of choosing to do so (this is because love, Gorgias claims, is either an affliction or a divine imperative), Helen is marked, engraved, *written* by what is radically other to her. She is constituted—yet again—by the other who addresses her, and so her being is dislocated at one and the same time. In this way, Gorgias suggests that Helen is literally composed when she acquiesces to those who address her. She is not simply a passive woman who, because of significant political, cultural, and material constraints, cannot refuse the divine, linguistic, and human agents who come for her. Rather, she is an actor in a presubjective drama. Her capacity to respond is given by the others who address her, and the only possible answer is "yes." Helen's "*yes* without a word" (this is a phrase Derrida uses to indicate that affirmation is the condition of possibility for all linguistic utterances) signals her preoriginary alliance with the other ("Ulysses" 296).

I have argued here that the *Encomium* dramatizes a series of three of Helen's inaudible affirmations—the repeated "yes" I have characterized with Derrida as a founding and ongoing alliance with and relation to the other that is prior to both utterance and free will. In order to argue that Helen is free from blame, that is, Gorgias requires us to imagine that she did indeed say "yes" to the gods, to speech, and to love. He frames each of these affirmations as occurring somehow beyond Helen's active choosing; in each case his argument emphasizes that Helen could do nothing other than say "yes." In this way, and also in the way that he writes Helen as having no personal agency (she says nothing, she does nothing in the speech other than inaudibly respond), Gorgias grants conceptual, and even at times temporal, priority to the others who address Helen. For all of these reasons, it seems that Gorgias depicts a prelusive or pre-performative scene. Helen emerges into subjectivity by way of her inaudible "yes"; her being is always a response to the other's address, and "she" never really catches up. This is an account of identity that can never be described in a constative mode. Always responding to the address of an unassimilable other, Helen is engaged prior to her will. Gorgias's *Encomium*, however, isn't simply about a passive woman with no options. Instead, the speech is an aporetic exercise: It requires us to hesitate before "everyday" moral and ethical responsibility and focus for a moment on the primordial living in relation to otherness, which is always found at its root.

INTERRUPTING "THE INFLUENCE OF SPEECH"

For rhetoric scholars, one of the most notable features of the *Encomium of Helen* is what Robert Wardy calls "the text's own partial occlusion of its central topic and true genre" (28). Even Isocrates criticized Gorgias for promising an encomium but delivering an apologia instead (*Helen* 14–15).[8] If any character in the *Encomium* is the object of Gorgias's praise, of course, it is not Helen, but speech, and what seems at first to be a paean to a troubled beauty becomes something altogether different. Gorgias's most glowing lines are devoted to *logos,* and in them he links speech's great power to its capacity for deception. "Sacred incantations sung with words are bearers of pleasure and banishers of pain," he says "for, merging with opinion in the soul, the power of the incantation is wont to beguile it and persuade it and alter it by witchcraft" (10). Gorgias thus depicts an art that can conjure the whole spectrum of human emotion and transform one's soul. He goes so far as to suggest that persuasive speech possesses a supernatural force, although as noted above, scholars disagree over how seriously we are to take this claim.

What does seem clear to me, at the very least, is that Gorgias invites us to consider the powerful instrumental force of speech. Again, whatever his true motives on this front, Gorgias's enduring reputation is that of "a supreme sophist bent on one end: the 'enslavement' of his audiences though persuasion" (Porter "Seductions" 268). Such a reputation seems to be warranted by the *Encomium*'s ostensible claims about persuasion. In the famous sections on speech (8–14), Gorgias collapses the distinction between physical force and persuasion in order to convince his audience that Helen is not to blame even if she succumbed to Paris's arguments. He then enlists a range of metaphors to get us thinking about the psychological force of persuasion: He figures speech as a "powerful lord" and argues that this "finest and most invisible body effects the divinest works: it can stop fear and banish grief and create joy and nurture pity" (8). Such powerful poetry—"speech with meter," as Gorgias

---

8. These section numbers refer to David C. Mirhady and Yun Lee Too's translation of Isocrates's *Encomium of Helen* in *Isocrates I*: U of Texas P, 2000, pp. 31–48.

defines it—can also effect "fearful shuddering and tearful pity and grievous longing" (9), and thus we see a subtle move into the physical and material realm. Speech with meter—consisting of those "signs" we tend to imagine as working on audiences with indirect force—causes the physical responses of tears and shuddering. Gorgias then asks: "What cause then prevents the conclusion that Helen similarly, against her will, might have come under the influence of speech, just as if ravished by the force of the mighty?" (12) Suggesting that Helen would have been just as helpless amid the swirl of a dazzling rhetorical display as she would have been at the hands of a stalwart attacker, Gorgias posits persuasion as a powerful form of linguistic rule and instrument of control.

But while Gorgias sees persuasion as a mechanism through which skilled orators can seize power over others, his pre-performative account of Helen's responsivity interrupts this instrumental view. Gorgias thus stages two realms of responsibility: one in which the subject is the cause of its own actions and another in which the subject is nothing but the effect of affirming the other's unwilled address. The second realm precedes and exceeds the first and calls attention to our essential reliance on and obligation to the other, to whom our performative powers are consigned in advance. What the *Encomium* shows us, then, is that the perlocutionary force of persuasion takes place against the backdrop of an always prior, pre-performative *rapprochement* with the other. The essential dependency Gorgias emphasizes in his account of Helen challenges and interrupts the controlling, self-interested account of persuasion so often associated with his legacy. This isn't so much a denial of the considerable instrumental force that can be enacted through persuasion as it is a reminder that such perlocutionary force is always coexistent with an affinity for the other to whom the orator, "you," and "I" will always be obliged.

CHAPTER 3

Lysias's Ghost

> The logographer, in the strict sense, is a ghost writer who composes speeches for use by litigants, speeches which he himself does not pronounce, which he does not attend, so to speak, in person, and which produce their effects in his absence. In writing what he does not speak, what he would never say and, in truth, would probably never even think, the author of the written speech is already entrenched in the posture of the sophist: the man of non-presence and non-truth.
> —Jacques Derrida, *Dissemination*, 68

> He was the best of all the orators at observing human nature and ascribing to each type of person the appropriate emotions, moral qualities, and actions. I also ascribe to Lysias that most pleasing quality which is generally called characterization. I am quite unable to find a single person in this orator's speeches who is devoid of character or vitality.
> —Dionysius of Halicarnassus, *The Critical Essays Vol. 1*, 7–8[1]

Of the thirty-four extant speeches written by the famed logographer Lysias, only one was composed in the voice of the author himself. And while no one knows for sure if Lysias ever stood before an Athenian jury to make his case, this single speech provides a vivid portrait of a man who once enjoyed great wealth and privilege only to lose his fortune, his family—indeed, his very identity—to the Thirty Tyrants. In *Against Eratosthenes* (Lys. 12), Lysias makes a case against the eponymous member of the Thirty for murdering his brother Polemarchus as part of a conspiracy to rid the city of democratic-leaning metics and to confiscate their riches in the process.[2] He tells us, in fact, that the politics were merely a ruse and that the metics' money

---

1. This section number refers to Stephen Usher's translation of *Dionysius of Halicarnassus, The Critical Essays Vol. 1*, Loeb Classical Library, 1974.

2. Section numbers refer to S. C. Todd's translation of *Against Eratosthenes* (Lys. 12) in *Lysias*, U of Texas P, 2000.

was always the plot's primary target. Lysias probably wrote the speech to contest Eratosthenes's appeal for amnesty following the restoration of democracy in 403/402, and it is also likely that he later circulated it as a pamphlet, either to publicly register his grievances with Eratosthenes or to advertise his skills as a logographer (Bakewell 5, Usher "Lysias" 37).[3] Whether primarily juridical, hortatory, or promotional, *Against Eratosthenes* seeks justice for the slain Polemarchus and argues that the erstwhile oligarch should pay for his crimes despite the potential for amnesty. Given its vivid depictions of kidnapping, daring escape, and a treasure chest full of shining silver and exotic coins, *Against Eratosthenes* makes for compelling—sometimes suspenseful—drama. Far more than a vivid retelling of a past injustice, this speech exerts considerable performative force in that it both announces and enacts Lysias's becoming other—his becoming ghost. In fact, I'll argue here that it *haunts* both its speaker and its hearers and that it haunts us still. Concerned with ghosts, with thresholds, and with the all too permeable boundaries of the home, the speech is an act of hospitality in which the roles of welcoming host, invited guest, and hostage are shuffled, transformed, and rendered ontologically unstable.

Speaking, for once, in his own voice, Lysias reveals himself to be a presence that no longer corresponds to itself. Standing on the threshold between one life as a wealthy, socially connected shield manufacturer and another as a dispossessed writer of speeches for a host of Athens's most colorful and derelict characters, the Lysias of *Against Eratosthenes* becomes other in the utterance of his speech. He may be speaking for "himself," but the subject position that emerges here is tenuous, characterized by a simultaneous projection into the future and the past. Neither simply present nor absent, Lysias haunts and is haunted by a series of hosts and guests. For its part, Lysias's audience is likewise ontologically disturbed. By the conclusion of *Against Eratosthenes*, hearers are brought face to face with the dead and thus exposed to what Derrida calls in *Specters of Marx* "a spectral asymmetry [that] de-synchronizes" (6). Like Lysias, who, as I will argue, has a unique capacity to cast doubt on all presence-to-self, the audience's identities are compromised as well. In the end, *Against Eratosthenes* is a rhetorical drama that makes legible a larger ontologi-

---

3. The exact historical exigency of *Against Eratosthenes* remains a point of some disagreement. Most scholars suggest that Lysias composed it for Eratosthenes's accountability hearing following the Thirty Tyrants' defeat (Todd 113; Dover 44). As part of the reconciliation agreement of 403, the restored democracy offered amnesty to members of the Thirty who submitted themselves to these public accountability hearings. K. J. Dover notes that although Lysias frames *Against Eratosthenes* as a prosecution speech for a murder charge, he may have written it for just such a hearing (44). Loening suggests, however, that Lysias's status as a metic makes such a proposition unlikely (285–86).

cal instability that affects us all—and that serves as the basis for the aporetic ethics I have described thus far.

HOSPITALITY TO FOREIGN GUESTS

Lysias inhabited something of a liminal position in the social and political atmosphere of classical Athens. As a metic, a legally registered 'resident alien' who lived in the city, he lacked several of the rights and protections that would have been afforded to Athenian citizens, although as K. J. Dover notes, Lysias belonged to a group of privileged metics "whose wealth and personal connections made them people to be reckoned with" (48). Aristophanes of Byzantium (third century CE) provides a straightforward legal definition of the Athenian metic as "anyone who comes from a foreign (city) and lives in the city, paying tax toward certain fixed needs of the city. For so many days he is called a *parepidemos* and is free from tax, but if he outstays the specified time he becomes a *metoikos* and liable to tax" (qtd. in Whitehead 7). Unlike the foreigner (*xenos*) who merely passes through Athens, and who, as David Whitehead writes, "has, from the city's point of view, no real existence" (10), metics were formally stitched into the fabric of Athenian culture in a manner more complicated than Aristophanes's practical and tax-based definition lets on.[4] This is especially true in the case of Lysias. Although he was never granted citizen status, he was not simply a foreigner either. Born in Athens to the Syracusan Cephalus, who had settled in Attica at Pericles's invitation, Lysias "grew up," Richard C. Jebb speculates, "in the society of the most distinguished Athenians" (146). Enjoying a privileged youth in what Jebb further describes as "an intellectual centre, the scene of many such gatherings as Plato imagined" (146), Lysias travelled to Thurii when he was a teenager and reportedly studied rhetoric there, perhaps with Tisias (Dover 38). But it wasn't long before he would return to his place of birth. Following the disastrous Sicilian Expedition, anti-Athenian sentiment led Lysias (along with some 300 other residents) to flee Thurii, and he returned to Athens to take over his father's successful shield manufacturing business. He lived there comfortably as a wealthy, slave-owning metic for several years before the events described in *Against Eratosthenes* upended his world. Neither citizen nor stranger, then,

---

4. Interestingly, Whitehead argues that maintaining the status of xenos may have been preferable to "achieving" the status of metic: "The metic's life was considered (in terms of penal deterrents) no more valuable than that of the xenos. And if the 'before' and 'after' stages are briefly compared, it will be seen that being a xenos [. . .] had distinct advantages" (96). It is clear," he argues furthermore, "that to become a metoikos was no unmixed blessing" (97).

Lysias lived a life on the boundary. He had an important—even enviable—social and economic presence in Athens, but he never fully belonged in the city he called home. Describing the autochthony that "sanctioned views of Athenian exceptionalism and ethnic distinctiveness," Rebecca Kennedy says that even those metics who, like Lysias, were themselves Athenian-born, were viewed as "permanent and perennial immigrant[s]" (4–5).

These "perennial immigrants" were subject to a formal legal and economic system that dictated their contributions to the state, their capacity to own land, and their legal rights and jurisdiction, among an array of other requirements and exclusions that made them distinct from Athenian citizens. Metics were indeed legally recognized individuals: They formally registered with the polemarch, the city official who kept track of metics and in whose courts their private suits (*dikai*) were adjudicated (Kamen 44, Kennedy *Immigrant* 12, Patterson 98), and their tax burden was "unique in Athens in being not merely a direct tax but a poll-tax, levied on the person rather than his (or her) property or activities" (Whitehead 75–76). This legal personage, however, came with a number of risks and vulnerabilities. As Cynthia Patterson argues, metics were dangerously isolated within an Athenian legal system built on household and family structures: "The metic is registered as 'living in' one deme or another, but he cannot own land in Attica and cannot be a part of, or have a share in, either deme or tribe" (98). Unable to own land, and likely disconnected from a large kinship structure that would signal some substantive measure of belonging, metics in court faced juries that viewed them as outsiders. Once situated within this potentially hostile milieu, furthermore, metics were subject to prosecutions unique to their status, and they could be sold into slavery if they were convicted of these offenses (failure to pay the metic tax [*metoikion*], for example, or impersonating a citizen) (Hunter 18–23, Patterson 97–98). As Virginia Hunter puts it, more ominously, "Slavery threatened any metic who appeared to step outside the bounds of his or her status" (19). Yes, metics were legally recognized individuals, but this complicated recognition served both to mark metics as *non*-citizens and to uphold the primacy of the citizens' status.

When metics themselves were victims of crimes, furthermore, their legal personage did not quite equal that of citizens. As we shall see with Lysias and his brother in *Against Eratosthenes,* metics were especially vulnerable to summary arrest (*apagoge*), and when they were murdered, their killers were not punished as severely as those convicted of murdering citizens. "Put on the same footing as the unpremeditated homicide of a citizen," the murder of a metic warranted exile, rather than death (Whitehead 93). And while metics bore the burden of protecting the Athenian state during times of war—they were required to fight in special metic regiments (Whitehead 84, Patterson

96)—they did not reap the benefits of that service in terms of political rights. Whitehead notes that unlike citizens, metics had no share in "political life in its widest sense": They had no right to hold office, no right to take part in the assembly, and no right to sit on juries (70). The collection of demands and restrictions placed on metics in classical Athens speaks, of course, to the difficulties resident aliens faced within the communal space of their adopted home. But it also speaks to the fraught relationship between Athens and its metics: Although the state (and only the state) was invested with the power to welcome outsiders, it did so by virtue of a system that marked these outsiders as potential threats to its own power. The legal limits placed on metics seem to suggest an anxiety on the part of the state and its citizenry: *The outsider within had to be contained.*

Much was required of metics, then, and much was denied them, but some metics—Lysias among them—enjoyed privileges that signaled their importance to and recognition by the Athenian state. Lysias was an *isoteles*, a privileged metic who, at the very least, was exempt from paying the basic metic tax of twelve drachmas per year (independent women were required to pay six) (Whitehead 75).[5] According to Lysias's own descriptions in *Against Erastothenes*, he was quite wealthy and furthermore honored to pay the more substantive taxes for sponsoring choral performances (*choregia*) and contributing to the costs of war (*eisphorai*) (20). In other words, being spared the cost of twelve drachmas per year was probably less important to him than being granted the *isoteleia* in and of itself.[6] According to Whitehead, the metic tax was a powerful and not altogether favorable symbol of difference—"the stamp of metic-status, and a constant reminder of the citizen/metic divide" (76). To be free of such a "stamp" would be no small benefit. Deborah Kamen argues, furthermore, that even subtle differences within categories of individual social statuses in classical Athens had important practical and ideological effects: "Given that any metic granted privileges was (ideologically, at least) being rewarded for services rendered to the city, he was implicitly more favored and more embraced by the citizens of Athens than were 'regular' metics. [. . .]

---

5. As Whitehead notes, scholars have long debated what other benefits, if any, this honor bestowed. According to Whitehead, scholars tend to minimize or to maximize the benefits *isoteleia* conferred. He argues that there is no real evidence to suggest that *isoteleia* was necessarily connected to any greater benefit such as land ownership or enhanced legal status but that it likely did come with a few smaller perks, such as exclusion from a market tax (11–12. See also Kamen 56–57).

6. According to Kamen, this would generally be the case: "This exemption was primarily symbolic, since anyone granted *isoteleia* was presumably sufficiently well off to afford the yearly twelve-drachma tax (roughly the equivalent of one or two weeks' pay for a manual laborer). The 'honor' was that *isoteleia* brought them conceptually closer to citizen status" (56).

He was not a citizen to be sure, but legally and socially he edged even closer" (61). Neither 'regular' metic nor Athenian citizen, Lysias was an officially recognized—even honored—guest of the Athenian state. Such a guest, of course, is defined by virtue of his not belonging to begin with, and the hospitality the state granted Lysias was, as *Against Eratosthenes* makes abundantly clear, extended with all the benevolence of a baseball bat to the knees. Neither insider nor outsider, Lysias hovered uncertainly on the borderline. On the basis of a host of conditions stipulated by the Athenian state, he was invited to stay, but once he took his place inside, he became a threat not only to the sanctity of the state, but also to the purity of the clean, Attic style he would later come to represent. What is particularly interesting about Lysias is the way his occupation as a ghostwriter ultimately allowed him to haunt the system that worked so hard to circumscribe him. In him we clearly see that the purity of the Athenian state was always already constituted by the foreigner and that the Athenian hospitality so famously offered to foreign guests was equal parts calculated strategy and unabated risk-taking.

Although metics were in many respects more vulnerable than their citizen counterparts, the state offered them a system, a status, and even certain protections and honors that constitute what Derrida calls "hospitality by right" (*Of Hospitality* 25). Composed of "laws (in the plural), those rights and duties that are always conditioned and conditional" (77), hospitality by right is granted by the state and bestowed upon a "foreigner 'as a family,' represented and protected by his or her family name" (23). No simple offer of generosity, hospitality by right pulls welcomed guests into an economy of reciprocity—even violence. When the state extends rights to foreigners, that is, it does so by virtue of its sovereignty and by requiring the foreigner to recognize and submit to that sovereignty. These conditional rights, furthermore, require foreigners "to have names, to be subjects in law, [. . .] to be equipped with nameable identities, and proper names" (23). In this sense, the foreigner is not *absolutely* foreign; he or she is a known quantity, neatly incorporated into a system that elides difference as such and transforms it into difference of the same kind. Thus hospitality by right enacts an essential violence on the person to whom it is offered. Foreigners remain foreign but not other, and the state requires that they offer something in return for the hospitality extended to them. They are required "to be questioned and liable, to have crimes imputed to them, to be held responsible" (23). There are strings attached, in other words, and the ongoing exchange always plays out on terms dictated by the state. While he doesn't put it in quite the same theoretical terms, Whitehead suggests that this is precisely the nature of the hospitality that Athens offered its resident aliens: "The *metoika* was intended to be the automatic destination of resident foreigners, and the progression was designed less to offer incentives of itself than to allow the whole machinery of concessions *and responsibilities* to come into play" (96).

The conditional laws of "hospitality by right," then, ensure that acts of invitation and welcome become matters of codified exchange with known, and in this case, officially registered persons. Once these conditions are in place, they function to secure the sanctity of the state's borders, as well as its mastery and authority as host. Such is the case of the Athenian metic: Whitehead suggests that the state and its citizens received far more from metics than they ever offered, and Patterson notes that despite the hospitality (or *xenia*) Athens prided itself on offering foreigners (*xenoi*), "the metic is a *xenos*, and, despite the conventions of *xenia*, relations with *xenoi* are always potentially hostile" (97). Thus one primary function of the resident alien was to shore up the boundaries of the state that welcomed him or her across the threshold in the first place.

As the complicated mix of rights and restrictions offered to (and imposed upon) Athenian metics demonstrates, hospitality by right isn't simply hospitable, at least not in the positive sense of that term, which typically refers to kindly, open, and generous actions. Because the rights offered to metics functioned primarily to strengthen and solidify the sovereignty of the state, this instantiation of hospitality undercuts the generosity and goodwill that would seem to be essential to the concept. In fact, the self-contradictory nature of Athenian hospitality is no anomaly. Derrida has long insisted on the violent contradiction that lies at the heart of hospitality, noting the troubling Latin origin of the word, "which allows itself to be parasitized by its opposite 'hostility'" ("Hostipitality" 3). This contradiction reveals itself in classic displays of hospitality insofar as the moment a host welcomes a foreign guest across the threshold "the one who receives, lodges, or *gives asylum* remains the *patron*, the master of the household" ("Hostipitality" 4). There is no generous welcome, in other words, that doesn't also assert authority and control over the guest being ushered through the door, and so welcoming always involves no small dose of *in*hospitality: *Come in, why don't you? And take a seat. But keep in mind that all of this belongs to me, and while you're here you'll submit to my rule.* Derrida deems the welcome a "performative contradiction"—an aporia that functions according to "the law of iterability at the heart of every law of hospitality" ("Hostipitality" 6–7) by virtue of the host violently imposing his or her mastery over the guest. "Hospitality gives and takes more than once in its own home," Derrida writes. "It gives, it offers, it holds out, but what it gives, offers, holds out, is the greeting which comprehends and makes or lets come into one's home, folding the foreign other into the internal law of the host" ("Hostipitality" 7). As the vexed experience of the Athenian metic demonstrates, hospitality by right is a double-edged sword that at once grants safe passage to the guest *and* violently apprehends him the moment he crosses the threshold, incorporating him into a system built to track and maintain his outsider status.

By necessity, hospitality by right operates on the basis of knowing the foreigner's name—of comprehending him, defining him, linking him to a family, and, in the case of an Athenian metic like Lysias, assigning him to a citizen patron whose function was both to protect and police his charge. As Derrida explains, hospitality by right begins with identity: "The right to hospitality commits a household, a line of descent, a family, a familial or ethnic group receiving a familial or ethnic group" (*Of Hospitality* 23). Here the host and the guest are "contracting parties" (23) who willingly enter into a system of exchange that regulates political and legal life by maintaining a distinction between inside and outside and by tightly controlling the relations between the state and its foreign guests. And yet Derrida also argues that these conditional, plural laws of hospitality function only by virtue of their bond to an unconditional, singular law of hospitality that both makes the plural laws possible and contradicts them at every turn. "Between an unconditional law or an absolute desire for hospitality on the one hand and, on the other, a law, a politics, a conditional ethics," he writes, "there is a distinction, a radical heterogeneity, but also indissociability. One calls forth, involves, or prescribes the other" (*Of Hospitality* 147). While the conditional laws of hospitality by right strive to maintain political and legal order, unconditional or absolute hospitality is "ethicity itself, the whole and principle of ethics" (*Adieu* 50). And while these politically oriented laws of hospitality require identifiable contracting parties who can be held liable for their intentions and actions, the unconditional law of hospitality interrupts identity and intention.

There would be no conditional laws of hospitality, in other words, (such as the laws that regulated the resident outsider status of metics like Lysias) without an open and giving disposition toward the other *before* any instance of recognition or identification. Why? Because, for the offering of hospitality to be truly hospitable, it cannot be an easily calculated gesture that ultimately benefits the host, nor can it neatly subsume the welcomed guest into a system of the host's design. For this reason, Derrida argues that "hospitality [. . .]—if there is any—must, would have to, open itself to an other that is not mine" (*Acts of Religion* 363), and "hospitality undoes, should undo, the grip, the seizure [. . .] the force or the violence of the taking [*prendre*] as comprehending [*comprendre*]" (362). While hospitality by right begins when the foreigner presents his papers, unconditional or absolute hospitality begins before the foreigner is identified as a foreigner. In fact, it begins even before the host is identified as host, putting the master of the house—or the state itself—in a far more vulnerable position than the conditional laws of hospitality would seem to guard against. The singular law of hospitality that makes possible the conditional and regulating laws is not a conscious, calculated choice. Nor is it a kindness granted on the basis of the host's power and authority. Instead it is "unconditional but without sovereignty" (*On Cosmopolitanism* 59), given not simply to those lucky or well-connected enough to be included on the guest list, but to anyone and everyone who might appear at the door, even—especially—if they appear unexpectedly.

If absolute hospitality is something granted to all—whenever these unidentified guests may choose to arrive—then the unpreparedness of the host and penetrability of the home's boundaries become abundantly clear. Less about invitation than *visitation*, the unconditional law of hospitality takes place before the identities of the host and guest are assured, a conceptual priority Derrida often tied to the ambiguity of the French word *hôte*, which translates as either "host" or "guest." While an invitation is a matter of the host's choice and authority, a visitation is unbidden; it has religious and supernatural connotations—such as the visit from God or from a ghost—that radically undermine the sovereignty of host. Imagine the shifting power differential amidst an otherworldly appearance of a ghost in your home. Such a visitation would clearly demonstrate the ways that the home is far less under your control than might otherwise seem the case.[7] Absolute hospitality thus welcomes a nonpresent subject, a visitor Derrida refers to as the "*hôte as ghost*" (*Acts of Religion* 359) and "the absolute *arrivant*, who is not even a guest" (*Aporias* 34). This *arrivant*, he adds, "surprises the host—who is not yet a host or an inviting power—enough to call into question, to the point of annihilating or rendering indeterminate, all the distinctive signs of a prior identity, beginning with the very border that delineated a legitimate home and assured lineage" (34). In absolute hospitality, guests are not invited across the threshold by cognizant and empowered hosts. Instead, they visit unannounced, and the host, "who is not yet a host," is perpetually interrupted—internally disturbed—by the "*hôte as ghost*" whose arrival is as imminent as it is uncertain. The imminence of the *arrivant* disperses the sovereignty of the host across the boundless unknowability of the visitor. No longer master of the house, the host is held in the thrall of an uncanny combination of expectation and surprise. "To wait without waiting, awaiting absolute surprise, the unexpected visitor,"

---

7. Paul K. Saint-Amour makes a similar argument in "'Christmas Yet to Come': Hospitality, Futurity, the *Carol*, and 'The Dead.'"

Derrida explains, "is indeed [. . .] the madness *of* hospitality" (*Acts of Religion* 362). The (not yet) host is ontologically disturbed by the visitor prior to the visitation, and this means that both the borders of the home and the borders of the subject are torn open from the inside. Thus absolute hospitality's logic of visitation "exceeds every dialogical relation between host and guest. It must from all time have exceeded them. Its traumatizing effraction must have preceded what is so easily called hospitality" (*Adieu* 63).

If the "traumatizing effraction" of absolute hospitality precedes all of the typical gestures of welcome (such as opening one's door to a friend or inviting a foreigner to make her home in the polis), then patronage involves significant risks. While only hosts and sovereign states have the authority to invite, unconditional hospitality shows just how easily the so-called master of the house becomes a hostage in "his own" home. "To be hospitable," Derrida writes, "is to let oneself be overtaken [*surprendre*], *to be ready to not be ready*, if such is possible, to let oneself be overtaken, to not even *let* oneself be overtaken, to be surprised, in a fashion almost violent, violated and raped [*violée*], stolen [*volée*]" (*Acts of Religion* 361). In one sense, the authority that enables the sovereign to grant safe passage to a foreign guest provides little protection from the outsider who has gained admittance. Think, for example, of those vaguely uncomfortable moments when a friend stays a few days too long in your home, or the far more disturbing ones in a domestic horror film like *Pacific Heights*, in which Michael Keaton's character terrorizes the bohemian couple who rented him a room in their charming San Francisco Victorian. Even a warm, stylish television commercial for Airbnb, the 'sharing' economy's hotelier clearinghouse, points to how truly creepy it can be to welcome an outsider into the home. In the spot aptly titled "Never a Stranger," an attractive, well-dressed world traveler narrates a thank-you note to her unknown hosts who, from Paris to Tokyo, have allowed her to stay in their ideally located digs. "Your home was perfect. Oh, and then I met your friends. They reminded me of my friends. It felt like I had known them for years" (Airbnb). To be sure, the ad features only the most positive aspects of the Airbnb phenomenon; there is, nonetheless, an uncanny discomfort here that speaks to the vulnerability and risk associated with hospitality.

But hosts are not simply vulnerable to their visitors in this conscious or experiential sense; in fact, their subjectivity actually comes from the others they await "without waiting" (Derrida *Acts of Religion* 362). That is, there would be no inviting subject, no *one* at home, without this openness to the unnamed, unknown other whose imminence (and immanence) is equal parts ontologically threatening and subject-forming. Derrida explains that the master's "subjectivity is hostage" to the guest (*Of Hospitality* 123), noting that there would be no authority—indeed, no subjectivity—without the visitor who at first seemed subject to the host's intentions:

> It is indeed the master, the one who invites, the inviting host, who becomes the hostage—and who really always has been. And the guest, the invited hostage, becomes the one who invites the one who invites, the master of the host. The guest becomes the host's host. The guest (*hôte*) becomes the host (*hôte*) of the host (*hôte*). These substitutions make everyone into everyone else's hostage. (*Of Hospitality* 123, 125)

Not only does the host's authority to invite come by way of the guest, but so too does his subject position, which is constituted by its openness to the other. In fact, Derrida characterizes hospitality as "an interruption of the self" (*Adieu* 51) that involves giving everything one has—"one's home and oneself" (*Of Hospitality* 77)—to the new arrival, with neither condition nor expectation. Unconditional hospitality, then, requires a welcoming prior to the sovereignty of conditional hospitality, a welcoming that is, as Derrida explains, "beyond the capacity of the I" (*Adieu* 26).

Because absolute hospitality refers to an open relation to otherness that gives rise to subjectivity, one is never in the position of choosing to be either absolutely or conditionally hospitable. Or, as Michael Naas aptly puts it, "Unconditional hospitality is not some goal or telos toward which we must strive; it is not some utopic ideal on which we must keep our eyes fixed" (*Derrida From Now* 24). Indeed, because absolute hospitality takes (and gives) place before the *hôte* is identified as either host or guest, there is no conscious calculation or decision-making involved in the phenomenon. From an ontological perspective, the open doors of absolute hospitality are the case; they characterize our radical openness to otherness such that everyone is made into "everyone else's hostage" (*Of Hospitality* 125). Or, as Diane Davis writes, "As a singularity, finite and exposed, 'I' come into being only inasmuch as 'I' respond to the other" (*Inessential* 114). Given that hospitality begins by owing everything to everyone, it makes a certain kind of sense that conditional hospitality is noticeably, even if futilely, oriented toward circumscribing the invited guest and shoring up the boundaries of the self and home. It is as though conditional hospitality attempts to retroactively enclose and protect the "self" that is constituted by its wide-open passages to the outside world. The two regimes of hospitality are thus opposed to one another—so radically different that each makes the other impossible—and yet, as Derrida has often insisted, they are nonetheless bound in "insoluble antimony, a non-dialectizable antimony" (*Of Hospitality* 77). In order for the laws of conditional hospitality to function, in other words, they must transgress the law of absolute hospitality that insists we must give all to the *arrivant*, and the reverse is just as true: unconditional hospitality requires that we transgress all of the conditional laws. "It is as though hospitality were the impossible," Derrida writes, "as though the law of hospitality defined this very impossibility, as if it were only possible to transgress it, as though *the* law of absolute, unconditional hyperbolical hospitality [. . .] commanded that we transgress all the laws (in the plural) of hospitality, namely the conditions, the norms, the rights and the duties that are imposed on hosts and hostesses [. . .] as well as the men or women who receive it" (*Of Hospitality* 75, 77).

While the two regimes of hospitality may be antinomic, each requires the other for its possibility. The conditional laws need the law and vice versa, although the relationship between the two is not simply symmetrical: "*The* law is above the laws," Derrida explains. "It is thus illegal, transgressive, outside the law, like a lawless law, *nomos anomos*" (*Of Hospitality* 79). This means that, on the one hand, conditional laws are "guided, given inspiration, given aspiration, required, even, by the law of unconditional hospitality" (79). As the complex situation of the Athenian metics demonstrates, however, there is no guarantee that absolute hospitality's open and giving disposition will be reflected in the conditional laws. In fact, the conditional laws often work to the opposite effect, as in the case of metics who entered into a series of detrimental contractual obligations that primarily benefitted the state. And yet in the best possible situations, Derrida suggests, there is a certain affinity between the two regimes of hospitality. Hospitality by right always requires that foreign guests present their papers, but it can do so "while avoiding this question becoming a 'condition,' a police inquisition, a registration of information, or a straightforward frontier control" (*Paper* 67). As Davis argues compellingly in her account of these ethical and political faces of hospitality, the preconscious law of absolute hospitality, though radically unwilled, is precisely what enables and gives rise to conscious ethical engagement. There would be no careful judgment, no generosity, she argues, without the preoriginary hostage situation that nonetheless provides the opening for all responsible advocacy (*Inessential* 131–43).

But the unconditional law isn't simply running the show; it too depends for its possibility on its seeming opposite, the conditional laws: "*The* unconditional law of hospitality needs the laws, it *requires* them. This demand is constitutive. It wouldn't be effectively unconditional, the law, if it didn't *have to become* effective, concrete, determined, if that were not its being as having-to-be. It would risk being abstract, utopian, illusory, and so turning over into its opposite" (Derrida *Of Hospitality* 79). And so while the other-before-me imperative of absolute hospitality is what gives rise to and hopefully, if we're lucky, in some sense influences the application of the conditional laws, *the* law also depends for its possibility on the laws it nonetheless makes possible. If the unconditional law did not involve itself in the impossible negotiation between the multiple singularities—the countless hosts, visitors, and hostages—who need it across various historical and political realities, it would become a static rule to be applied the same way in every case. With nothing at stake, the law of absolute hospitality would simply be an empty gesture, a meaningless copy of the same benefit given to everyone who comes to the door.

Thus the two regimes of hospitality, perpetually in the midst of an impossible negotiation, take place on the threshold, as Naas has argued of both Derrida's concept of hospitality and of deconstruction itself (*Derrida From Now* 28). While the unconditional welcome takes place, in Naas's words, "before any knowledge, recognition, or conditions, indeed, before any names or identities" (21), it must ultimately be enacted by hosts and guests whose names and identities are known. The difficulty, of course, is that the conditional laws of hospitality will inevitably corrupt the unconditional law, and so vigilance is always required. On this threshold, the welcome must be adjusted in response to the other. This adjustment, Derrida suggests, is a mode of learning that cannot be reduced to mastering statements and propositions. Instead, "at the internal border or the external border, it is a heterodidactics between life and death" (*Specters* xviii). As an Athenian-born metic on the border between citizen and stranger, Lysias is precisely the kind of interrogative figure fit for exploring the threshold ethics of hospitality. And it is the threshold, furthermore, in which everything of importance in *Against Eratosthenes* takes place.

BECOMING GHOST IN *AGAINST ERATOSTHENES*

Because all but one of the extant Lysias speeches are written in the voices of the logographer's clients, we hear most often in them an ancient cast of characters who come alive in the details and idiosyncrasies crafted by the master speechwriter. Only in *Against Eratosthenes* do we get a glimpse into the life of a man who was otherwise entirely hidden behind the rhetorical scene. The speech is a rich, if highly subjective, source of information about Lysias's biography (nearly everything we know about him comes from this text). And it provides a crucial piece of the puzzle for understanding how and why Lysias came to be a logographer to begin with. Given its status in Lysias's oeuvre, furthermore, *Against Eratosthenes* has also served as an important location for diagnosing the speechwriter's stylistic tendencies: Several scholars have analyzed *Against Eratosthenes* in order to make claims about Lysias's use of rhetorical figures (Fogelmark and Bateman), his use of affective appeals (Howland and Wooten), and his capacity to characterize the individual players in his personal legal drama (Usher "Individual" and Murphy). As we'll shortly see, not all of this analysis is favorable, as *Against Eratosthenes* is occasionally disparaged for its "overheated rhetoric" (Howland 189). But what is perhaps most striking of all—at least for our purposes here—is that the speech is also a serious meditation on hospitality. In it, Lysias stages his own transfiguration from guest to host to hostage to "*hôte* as ghost." And without fail, the narrative's most dramatic moments take place on the threshold—the threshold of Lysias's home, the threshold of the home in which he is later held hostage, and the threshold of Lysias's "being" itself, which is performatively transformed in the speech's delivery.

Of course, there is a strong persuasive element in *Against Eratosthenes*, as well, and Lysias is nothing if not forthright about the ways he hopes to influence his judging listeners. In the speech, he demonstrates a sophisticated awareness of his stratified audience amidst the tumultuous political landscape, and he deftly addresses the two primary constituencies on the jury: Athenians who supported the Thirty (members of the Three Thousand who remained in Athens during the eight-month rule of the oligarchy) *and* democratic revolutionaries who, like Lysias, were forced to wander foreign lands during the Thirty's reign (92). He implores this audience to hold Eratosthenes and his colleagues from the Thirty accountable for both Polemarchus's death and for larger crimes against Athens, crimes he consistently frames as trespasses against the ancestral home. He does so by reminding the one-time supporters of the oligarchy that the Thirty forced them "to fight a war against [their] brothers, [their] sons, and [their] fellow citizens" (92) and that they "were banished from the city that [their] fathers handed down to [them]" (95). In both cases, Lysias suggests, the Thirty violated the sanctity of the Athenian homeland, and he leverages these inhospitable offenses as reasons the jury should cast their votes against Eratosthenes.

As several commentators have pointed out, furthermore, *Against Eratosthenes* is a powerful and compelling argument, notable for its moving, vivid depictions of the Thirty's greed and malice and for its powerful persuasive acumen. Bakewell, for one, argues that Lysias's evocative depiction of the Thirty's avarice allows him to expertly redirect cultural prejudices many Athenians would have held against metics toward the (bad) citizens who became oligarchs. "In their devotion to lucre," Bakewell writes, "Eratosthenes and his friends fit popular stereotypes about metics" (13). And in one particularly persuasive example from the speech, Melobius, one of the men dispatched to arrest Lysias and Polemarchus and to help confiscate their belongings, violently rips the gold earrings right out of the ears of Polemarchus's wife (119, 12.19). Cecil W. Wooten offers an extended analysis of the ways that Lysias artfully and dramatically relates this detail, which, Wooten argues, "would have surely evoked a strong emotional reaction from the jury" (30).

The flip side of this coin is that *Against Eratosthenes* has come under fire for precisely these rhetorical flourishes. Some critics complain that Lysias's highly instrumental and personally motivated approach tends toward the inflammatory, and they suggest that the speech is a manipulative, even dangerously coercive text that reveals Lysias's ethical and logical failings. For example, Jacob Howland, who makes the otherwise highly compelling argument that Plato's *Republic* is both a response to and a criticism of *Against Eratosthenes*, insists on the fundamentally unscrupulous elements of Lysias's speech. Noting that Lysias's overall claims rest on an unargued premise, Howland contends that Lysias sacrifices the public good for a private enmity. "Lysias effectively uses this judicial proceeding as a weapon of factional strife. [. . .] [His] rhetorical strategy is to inflame the anger of the jury toward the defendants and to use this anger as a reason for treating the defendants as enemies who ought to be harmed" (195–96). Just as Howland suggests that Lysias uses words as weapons, so too does Thomas M. Murphy, who claims that Lysias casts each of his enemies as an "inflammatory oligarchic type, a rhetorical figment calculated to make traditional positive aspects of class superiority appear politically suspect" (40–41). Murphy also stresses Lysias's selfish motivations for the speech, noting that he was likely attempting to "enhance his own reputation as a democratic loyalist (probably in hope of recovering money and property confiscated from his family)" (41). And while J. J. Bateman is less derisive in his overall assessment of the ethics of *Against Eratosthenes,* he too points out some of Lysias's rhetorical sleights of hand, noting the way the speechwriter covers over his logical inconsistencies with his expert use of antithesis and hypothesis (174). These modern assessments thus echo Plato's ancient claims, so artfully staged in *Phaedrus,* that Lysias is an unscrupulous con, capable of making a convincing argument, yes, but unwilling or unable to proceed in a forthright manner with the best interests of his audience in mind.

This sentiment gathers even more steam when we consider the professional and promotional purposes of *Against Eratosthenes,* which served at least in part as an advertisement for Lysias's speechwriting services. Lysias clearly knows that his speech will reach audience members beyond the members of the jury, noting the "many people [who] have come here, both citizens and foreigners, to find out [the jury members'] attitudes towards these men" (122, 12.35). One the one hand, this statement would seem to suggest *to* the jury members that they are not the only ones with the power to render a verdict. Their own decision will be seen and judged by the large audience gathered to learn about the reception of the Thirty in the wake of the restoration. The jurors are themselves under examination, Lysias seems to suggest, and so there is an internal persuasive function at work. And yet the phrase also speaks to a secondary, but perhaps no less important, audience that would hear Lysias's claims against Eratosthenes: his future clients. In addition to using the legal proceedings as a barometer of the contemporary political climate, these bystanders also likely acquired a sense of Lysias's vivid oratorical style and overall rhetorical competence.

Against Eratosthenes also had a persuasive life beyond its immediate legal setting. It went on to assume an important promotional function in the development of Lysias's career as a logographer insofar as it advertised his unique talent and newly acquired availability as a professional logographer. Christopher Carey identifies *Against Eratosthenes* as the speech that "brought [Lysias's] name to the attention of prospective clients" (*Lysias* 3), and he notes that the events described within recount the "chance concurrence of opportunity and need" (2) that led to his illustrious career as a professional speechwriter. Stephen Usher furthermore suggests that it would have been common practice for a speechwriter to circulate a speech such as *Against Eratosthenes* to showcase his oratorical acumen. Lysias, in particular, Usher suggests, was eager to showcase his work: "It may be confidently assumed not only that readers would be anxious to obtain copies of [Lysias's] works [. . .] but that the orator, in order to increase his reputation and widen his clientèle, would actively promote a market for his speeches" ("Lysias" 37). Not only is the speech a powerful indictment of a handful of tyrants, then, but it is also a telling demonstration of Lysias's admirable rhetorical talent and an announcement of his willingness to sell that skill to others. In all of these ways, *Against Eratosthenes* skillfully exerts the perlocutionary force of persuasion in the terms described in Chapter 1. At multiple levels, the text is involved in attempting to move listeners, to bring them around to Lysias's political and legal perspectives, or, at the very least, to bring some prospective clients to his doorstep.

And yet for all of the strategic planning and instrumental force, *Against Eratosthenes* relentlessly pursues the ethical implications of hospitality, and, I believe, Lysias uses it to both seek asylum from and extend a welcome to its hearers, perhaps even to those of us who encounter it in a contemporary setting. In fact, the entire persuasive apparatus of *Against Eratosthenes* is unfurled from the threshold—from the site of a founding invitation and conditional welcome from none other than Pericles himself, that "first [Athenian] citizen" (Thucydides 2.65) who originally brought Lysias's family to Athens. The invitation itself took place a generation prior to the events detailed in the narrative of *Against Eratosthenes*, but Lysias specifically locates it as the "beginning" of the story he plans to tell them (3): "My father Cephalus was invited by Pericles to move to this land, and he lived here for thirty years. Neither he nor the rest of the family was ever involved in any litigation, either as prosecutor or as defendant. We lived our lives under the democracy in such a way as to do no wrong to others and to suffer no harm from others" (4).[8] There's no doubt a strong persuasive element at work here, and a conventional one too. The tie to Pericles allows Lysias and his family to bask in the statesman's golden reputation, and the claim that the family stayed out of the courts recalls a trope from many classical speeches—the last thing a speaker wanted to seem was a sycophant. But in *recounting* this act of conditional hospitality, Lysias reenacts it as well. He presents his papers to the jury and in so doing establishes his lineage. Although he is not directly from the Athenian soil, he is no everyday metic either. He makes clear that he has been neatly incorporated into a system that recognizes his alien status, albeit in a uniquely privileged way. He is other to the Athenian citizen, but not absolutely other. He goes on to demonstrate the ways that his family more than lived up to its contractual obligations to the state: Not only did they sponsor choral performances and contribute to the Athenian war chest, but they also "had ransomed many Athenians from the foe" (20). Lysias and his family, then, strictly adhered to the conditional laws of hospitality. They diligently assumed and, by Lysias's account at least, embraced—perhaps even exceeded—the responsibilities assigned by the state.

This otherwise conventional assertion also signals an important turn in terms of Lysias's family's status in Athens. When they ransomed Athenian citizens from the foreign enemies who had captured them, the family became at one and the same time welcomed guests and welcoming hosts. No longer simply residing in Athens at the behest of a powerful patron, the guests became hosts themselves by bringing home the very citizens who would seem to have a stronger claim on the land than they had. As this situation suggests, once the outsider is welcomed in, it's often difficult to tell the hosts from the guests. This subtle shift speaks to the impossibility of the conditional laws of hospitality: Although these laws are meant to circumscribe the foreigner and to keep him separate from and in a secondary relation to the citizen, they always tend

---

8. Lysias's mention of his father Cephalus has yet another interesting link to the concept of hospitality—this by way of Plato's *Republic*. As Peter J. Steinberger notes, Cephalus is the paternal host of that dialogue, and in it he "welcomes Socrates and offers his hospitality to those who would engage in philosophical discussion" (172). Steinberger reads Cephalus's fleeting presence in the *Republic* as a moment of donation in which "the old man is abruptly and rather awkwardly whisked from the scene, having bequeathed his definition [of justice] to a suitable heir" (172). This heir, not incidentally, is Lysias's brother Polemarchus.

towards their own internal corruption. The conditional laws are there, as Derrida writes, "to prescribe their own perversion. [...] To watch over the guests and over their own perversion" (*Of Hospitality* 85).

Despite the fact that the conditional laws are meant to police and maintain a clear distinction between citizens and metics, *Against Eratosthenes* demonstrates just how easily and often such clear boundaries dissolve. In fact, Lysias goes to great lengths to demonstrate how quickly he himself is transformed from guest to host to hostage. While he uses Pericles's founding invitation to establish himself as a welcomed guest in Athens, Lysias describes his detainment by the Thirty in a manner that makes him seem a quintessential host, even if only for a moment. On the night of his arrest, Lysias explains that members of the Thirty "found me entertaining [foreign] guests at dinner, drove them out, and handed me over to Peison" (8). In the blink of an eye we see how quickly the master of the house is stripped of his sovereign rule. Holding court for a handful of foreigners one moment, Lysias loses his masterful position in relation to them in the next. His welcomed guests driven into the night, Lysias becomes a hostage in his own home. This vivid portrait of a pleasant domestic scene violently interrupted provides a sense of the profound vulnerability that haunts being at home, and it dramatizes Davis's observation that "because my home, any home, is constituted by its openings onto an outside, by its capacity for hospitality, it is never inviolable, and my sovereignty as host is never secure" (*Inessential* 131).

Now firmly within the grips of the Thirty, Lysias finds himself in a position similar to those Athenian citizens his family once ransomed. He needs Peison to accept something in exchange for his life. Lysias shares the details of their negotiations with his audience: "I asked Peison whether he would be willing to take a bribe for rescuing me. He said yes, if it was a big one. I replied that I was prepared to give him a talent of silver, and he agreed to this. [...] He swore an oath that he would rescue me if he received the talent, and he called down destruction on himself and his children" (8–10). These negotiations, of course, turn out to be in bad faith. According to Lysias, Peison abandons his oath when he gets a glimpse of Lysias's positively overflowing treasure chest and takes the whole thing.[9] He nevertheless hands Lysias off to another member of the Thirty who takes him to the home of Damnippus, where he is then held under guard. In offering a ransom for his freedom, Lysias proposes a kind of substitution that mirrors the more profound subjective experience of

---

9. Lysias describes the ample contents of his treasure chest, noting that Peison has taken possession of far more than the agreed amount. "He now had not simply the agreed amount, gentlemen of the jury, but three talents of silver, four hundred Cyzicene staters, one hundred Persian darics, and four silver cups" (11).

being as being *for* something or someone else. His experience of singularity, in other words, is simultaneously constituted and interrupted by repetition, exchangeability, and iterability—what Derrida has called "the loss of singularity as the experience of singularity itself" (*Specters* 161). His proposition thus makes explicit something that is always the case and yet is rarely so keenly felt: The subject is not a free and autonomous individual, spontaneously presenting itself to the world, but rather it is always dependent on those others that, from the beginning, make its being possible.

Because of the way he dramatizes his negotiations with Peison, in other words, Lysias's hostage situation exemplifies this state of being *for* the other. Lysias's safety and freedom—nothing less than his unique mode of inhabiting the world—depend for their existence on their capacity to be adequately exchanged for something else. Thus what Lysias experiences as a terrifying home invasion provides us with a heightened example of what it means to be a subject. As Derrida has argued in his extended analysis of Levinas in *Adieu*, "The hostage is first of all someone whose unicity endures the possibility of a *sub*stitution. It undergoes this substitution; it is a subject subjected to it, a subject that submits at the very moment when it presents itself ("here I am") in its responsibility for others" (55). Emphasizing the subject's dependent relation to the other with which it may be exchanged, Derrida argues (again, following Levinas on this point) that subjectivity itself is a matter of being held hostage. Passive, persecuted, and contingent upon a successful exchange for something or someone else, being is thus contested. The subject comes by way of and exists for someone or something else. I would argue that Lysias personifies and, within the speech, dramatically stages this subjective vulnerability. Both his status as a metic (allowed to live in Athens as an honored guest, but only at the behest of a powerful patron) and his quickly transforming position from dinner party host into political hostage suggest that "the host [*hôte*] is a hostage insofar as he is a subject put into question, obsessed (and thus besieged), persecuted, in the very place where he takes place, where as emigrant, exile, stranger, a guest [*hôte*] from the very beginning, he finds himself elected to or taken up by a residence [. . .] before himself electing or taking one up" (*Adieu* 56).

In his account of the attempt to buy back his own life, in other words, Lysias frames his subject position as a being-in-question. Although he was, in his former life, wealthy and successful, he was also profoundly vulnerable. As a resident alien—even a privileged one, his status in Athens was never fully secure, and what wealth he had attained might have to be leveraged at any time to maintain his precarious freedom and autonomy. In this practical sense, Lysias's everyday situation required that he be, in a certain impure sense, absolutely hospitable, that he be, in Derrida's words, "prepared to be unprepared, for the unexpected arrival of *any* other" (Kearney and Dooley 70). An Athenian metic like Lysias, that is, would have had to endure an ongoing political reality of being at risk. As Patterson argues, "For the resident alien in Athens [. . .] legal rules alone could not provide status or security when he or she stood outside the protective net of Athenian kin and household relationships" (95).[10] Despite his wealth and the frequent company of his aristocratic friends, Lysias was perennially exposed, and the passage suggests to me that this exposure underscored and, in some sense, defined his being in the world. With his brief but vivid and disturbing description of being taken hostage in his own home (while hosting foreign guests no less) Lysias highlights and calls our attention to his susceptibility to the others who could have at any moment crossed his threshold. There's little question that the ongoing sense of being uniquely susceptible to a very real threat like the one Lysias describes in *Against Eratosthenes* would transform one's experience of being. Slightly less comfortable and self-assured than a citizen, perhaps, Lysias's subjective experience would resemble what in the preoriginary realm would be called absolute hospitality: a presubjective state in which "one must say *yes,* there where one does not wait, *yes,* there where one does not expect [. . .] the other [. . .], to let oneself be swept by the coming of the wholly other, the absolutely unforeseeable [. . .] stranger, the uninvited visitor, the unexpected visitation beyond welcoming apparatuses" (Derrida *Acts of Religion* 361–62).

But even as Lysias communicates the negative aspects of his profound vulnerability and his capacity to be substituted for the ample contents of a treasure chest, he returns to the theme of responsibility, and in so doing he speaks to the ethics that take priority over his persuasive aims. Just as he and his family were model metics, more than living up to the demands placed on them by the state, Lysias, in his vulnerability, defines himself as a being *for* someone or something else. He is the hostage—the guarantee for the other—answering for others before he can speak for himself. Derrida suggests that this is precisely the opening of ethical responsibility, which "begins where I am and must be the hostage of the other, delivered passively to the other before being delivered to myself" ("Hospitality" 9). And so, while this passage certainly has a persuasive function—it speaks powerfully to the greed of the Thirty and to the injustice that was brought to Lysias's door—it also reveals the high stakes

---

10. Though we are missing some pieces of the puzzle that would provide a complete picture of Lysias's family structure, Patterson notes that "while it is possible to put together a few pieces of the metic *anchisteia* [close kinship] of Lysias, the limited character of the kin connections of even this well established metic is evident" (99).

and the difficult ethics of absolute hospitality. When one passively awaits the coming of the absolute other—the unknown other who may either befriend or annihilate—being is dispersed in a fundamental way, before and beyond signification and persuasive calculation.

Having been robbed and taken hostage in his home, Lysias sees his situation continue to deteriorate. Three members of the Thirty take Lysias to the home of Damnippus to be imprisoned, while Peison continues on to Polemarchus's house to catalogue and seize its contents. Unable to contact his brother, Lysias begins to expect the worst: "It seemed to me that the situation was so dangerous that death was already staring me in the face" (13). When Lysias goes on to describe being held hostage at Damnippus's house, we learn that he is actually imprisoned in the home of a friend. Once more we get a glimpse of Lysias's borderland life as a privileged metic: He is now a hostage in a place he had once been a welcomed guest ("I was familiar with the house" Lysias explains [15]). Attempting to make the most of his social connections, Lysias pleas with Damnippus: "'You are a close friend of mine and I am in your house. I have done nothing wrong but am being killed for my wealth. Please help me in my suffering, and use your power to rescue me'" (14). Damnippus agrees to help, but says he must first consult with Theognis, a member of the Thirty who is keeping guard over other prisoners in the house. Rather than risk another bargain with the Thirty (perhaps he had learned from his previous encounter with Peison), Lysias decides to make a break for it. He embarks on a daring escape through three unlocked doors—doors that will turn out to be the passageway to an altogether different life.

Lysias's description of his escape speaks once more to the porous boundaries of the home. Just as a home's multiple passageways make it impossible to keep unwanted guests out, so too do they prevent keeping hostages inside, at least in the case of Lysias, who possesses an insider's perspective that helps him expertly navigate his environs. "As it happened, I was familiar with the house and knew it had two doors—I decided to try and save myself. [. . .] I began my escape while the others were engaged in guarding the outer door; the three doors I had to get through all happened to be open" (15–16). Focusing on just one of the thresholds, the guards leave others unwatched and vulnerable. Even within the confines of a single abode, so it would seem, policing the borders is a futile endeavor. Lysias does indeed make it out, and he takes refuge in the home of an ally in the Piraeus whom he sends to discover Polemarchus's fate. Lysias then learns that Eratosthenes had arrested his brother in the street and "dragged him off to prison" (16). Seeing no chance of saving Polemarchus, Lysias sails "the following night to Megara" (17). Later, of course, Lysias would learn that his brother had been put to death, given the customary instruction to drink hemlock (17).[11]

Now adrift (literally) and having gotten away by the skin of his teeth, Lysias becomes someone entirely other than who he once was—an altogether different person from the one he has been describing in the narrative of his speech. Having escaped through three open doors and now sailing across the Saronic Gulf, Lysias is also crossing the threshold into a new life. The Lysias en route to Megara is no longer welcome (not even conditionally welcome) in Athens, and he is no longer the recognizable resident alien he once was. The system that invited him to stay (so long as he submitted to its rule) could not, in the end, contain the outsider within. In his transition from guest to host to hostage, and in his ultimate escape from the system that by turns subjected him to recognition, circumscription, and attempted annihilation, Lysias is an ontologically unstable being. Neither an insider nor an outsider, both a host and a hostage, he is from the outset a figure on the threshold, one who undergoes a series of substitutions and so is impossible to pin down. In the delivery of his speech, furthermore—in the moment in which he relates his former hardship to the audience members present to receive his account—Lysias's subject position is temporally dispersed. Out of exile, Lysias has returned to haunt the system that once tried in vain to contain him. A *hôte* as ghost, he has taken the stage to torment his one-time tormentors.

While Eratosthenes and his colleagues from the Thirty are the primary target, Lysias doesn't let his audience members off the hook either. They too will be haunted—ontologically disturbed—by a visitation from a group of murdered metics conjured by Lysias at the conclusion of his speech. In his final appeal to the jury, he directly addresses his hearers and attempts to put them in relation, not only to the slain Polemarchus, but to all of the Thirty's victims—left nameless by Lysias but summoned nonetheless. Referring one last time to the sacred spaces the Thirty violently and thoughtlessly invaded, Lysias claims, "There is nothing lacking in my zeal—zeal for the sanctuaries that the defendants either sold or polluted by entering; zeal for the city that they weakened, for the shipyards that they destroyed, and for the dead" (99). Having reminded the jury of the Thirty's inhospitality to the Athenian homeland, Lysias then asks his audience to turn and face the victims themselves:

---

11. In the wake of Polemarchus's death, furthermore, surviving relatives were not able to use the family's homes for the burial. As Lysias explains, "His body was brought back from this prison, but they would not allow us to conduct the funeral from any of our three houses. Instead, we had to hire a shed in which to lay him out" (18). Denied hospitality even in death, in other words, Polemarchus (not to mention the family who grieved for him) was denied access to the family home.

"You may not have been able to defend them during their lifetime, but you can assist them in death. It is my belief that they can hear us and that they will *recognize* you as you cast your ballots" (99–100, emphasis added). This first part of Lysias's appeal is a common rhetorical trope with a clear persuasive function. Invoking the dead encourages the living to feel some mix of sadness, regret, and pity for those who lost their lives while, more importantly, fostering in the jury a palpable sense of responsibility for the victims—responsibility that could show itself in the form of ballots cast. Pointing out the significance of this rhetorical device in Attic oratory, Staffan Fogelmark notes that "the emotive idea of endowing the dead with the faculty of physical feeling is highly studied and deliberate; although it is in fact a variation of a similar concept according to which the gods will know how the jurors have voted" (139–40). Lysias thus seems to ask the jury members to behave as though those who are most owed justice are watching them from beyond. Furthermore, he frames the vote as an opportunity to behave responsibly with respect to the victims *in view of the victims.*

And yet the victims' nonpresent presence on the rhetorical scene effects something altogether more powerful than this perlocutionary nudge. Unnamed and hovering beyond the rational or visible realm, the dead have the capacity to bump the living present into a certain subjective uncertainty. When the "spectral *someone other looks at us,*" Derrida explains, "we feel ourselves being looked at by it, outside of any synchrony, even before and beyond any look on our part, according to an absolute anteriority [. . .] and asymmetry, according to an absolutely unmasterable disproportion" (*Specters* 7). In other words, being recognized by a cadre of unnamed murder victims wouldn't simply persuade a jury member to behave in a certain way, it would also have a profoundly unsettling effect that would supersede such rational calculation. It would interrupt his being-present by dispersing it across the boundless unknowability of the ghost—the ghost who has arrived without invitation and whose appearance constitutes an immediate demand.

Lysias's audience members are brought face to face with the dead in the instant of his address, and, at least for a moment, the firm boundary between life and death wavers. The clear divide between presence and absence is blurred when the living present are haunted by ghosts of the past. Of course these conjured victims aren't the only ghosts around here; Lysias, too, has the capacity to haunt. First a guest (invited by Pericles and welcomed into Athens's prominent social circles), then a host (ransoming kidnapped Athenians and entertaining foreigners in his home), then a hostage (forcibly taken by the Thirty), the Lysias who addresses the audience is the ultimate *hôte* as ghost. In the only extant speech written for himself—the speech from which we glean nearly everything we know about him—Lysias reveals nothing so much as the difference between "himself" and the man described in his narrative, between his own ontological instability and his being *for* the other. Having returned to address an Athenian jury, he now haunts the place that once offered him a very impure kind of welcome—a haunting he would continue in his storied career as a logographer.

LYSIAS AS GHOSTWRITER, LYSIAS AS GHOST

Carey pinpoints *Against Eratosthenes* (and the dramatic events described within) as a turning point in Lysias's life and career. Noting that the speech would have provided him with a "new notoriety" (*Lysias* 3), Carey suggests that Lysias likely turned to professional rhetoric in the period after its composition and possible delivery in 403, in large part to earn back the livelihood stolen from him by the Thirty.[12] Because Lysias could not own land, much of his former wealth would have been in cash and thus "totally irrecoverable" (*Lysias* 3). And so Lysias, who received formal rhetorical training during his time in Thurii, turned to professional speechwriting in order to make a living. Although his metic status prevented his full access to the political and legal systems so integral to Athenian life and culture, Lysias haunted those systems as the ghostwriter of political and forensic speeches delivered by the clients who sought his professional services. At one time, upward of 200 speeches were attributed to Lysias, and thirty-four of them survive in full, although some of these are generally recognized as spurious (Edwards *Attic* 21, Todd "Introduction" 9). If, as I've attempted to argue, *Against Eratosthenes* demonstrates that calculated persuasive force also includes a transformative encounter with nonpresent otherness, then Lysias's celebrated career as a logographer enacts this movement. Famous for his ability to disappear into the language and characters he created for others, Lysias maintains what Derrida characterizes in *Specters of Marx* as "the *frequency* of a certain visibility. But the visibility of the invisible" (100). Like Derrida's deconstructive figure of the specter, he eludes the order of knowledge and so calls into question our comfortable certainties about being. In his surviving speeches, in the critical narratives we have constructed about both the man and his work, and in his dramatic representation by Plato in the *Phaedrus,* the historical figure we know as "Lysias" is transformed into a series of repetitions that interrupt expression, the fantasy

---

12. Edwards and Usher concur, noting that Lysias wrote "most of his speeches between the ages of 54 and 76" (125).

of communication, and presence itself. And like Derrida's specter, which is "among other things, what one imagines, what one thinks one sees and which one projects," "Lysias" keeps us waiting and watchful for the arrival of the other (100–101).

Lauded for his vivid writing style, his compelling and persuasive narratives, and a certain lively charm that animates his speeches, Lysias is perhaps most recognized for two major contributions to Greek oratory: 1) An elegant but unadorned style that conceals its own art, and 2) ethopoeia, or the dramatic representation of character. (In discussions of Lysias, ethopoeia primarily refers to the character of the speaker as it comes across in subtle details within the speech, but it sometimes also refers to the character of an opponent described there). Known for his ability to disappear into the rhetorical scene, Lysias's authorial signature is in fact his nonpresence—his noticeable ability to go unnoticed. And so perhaps it is unsurprising that long-standing debates about the little understood relationship between the ancient logographer and his clients so often center on Lysias, who is the perfect figure for confounding questions of attribution.[13] Interestingly enough, Lysias also managed to maintain his invisibility in the only speech he wrote for himself: According to Usher, who is a leading and persuasive proponent of how vividly Lysias characterizes the speakers for whom he writes, Lysias "reveals nothing of his own character" in *Against Eratosthenes* ("Individual" 114). Lysias's rhetorical legacy, in other words, is precisely his ability to unsettle his own identity, and what I'll suggest here is that this ability puts into question identity itself.

Well known for what Michael Edwards calls his "pure and lucid Attic prose [and] everyday (but dignified) language," Lysias provides in his speeches "the supreme example of the Plain Style" (*Attic* 20–21). This elegant but everyday language, free of the highly figurative and emotive flourishes that characterized the work of Gorgias, places Lysias squarely within the Attic or Plain literary tradition (long opposed to the Asiatic or Grand style). According to the first-century BCE critic and historian Dionysius of Halicarnassus, this is precisely what makes Lysias's work so worthy of emulation: "He [. . .] has invented a uniquely melodious style that is yet free from metre, in which he makes his language beautiful and attractive without bombast or vulgarity" (3). A self-professed Atticist, Dionysius appreciated Lysias's austere stylistic virtues

---

13. The exact nature of the relationship between logographers and their clients in Athens has been and remains the subject of debate, and it is often taken up in the specific instance of Lysias. See, for example, the debate between Dover and Usher on the role of authorship in Lysias's speeches as well as M. Lavency's "The Written Plea of the Logographer." This logistical mystery was one of the key questions addressed in the International Society for the History of Rhetoric seminar, "Lysias and Logography," presented by Michael Edwards in May 2014 at the Rhetoric Society of America.

and espoused them for budding orators who, he argued, would be well served to use Lysias as a model.

Lysias's plain style, however, is important for reasons beyond stylistic ideology. The clear and understated prose seems so natural, so everyday, that all rhetorical artistry is concealed. Lysias's clients deliver speeches that seem very much like what they would say in less formal settings, and so they convey a natural-seeming, guileless ethos. As Dionysius notes of Lysias's "simple and straightforward" composing style, "The distinctive nature [. . .] seems [. . .] not to be contrived or formed by any conscious art, and it would not surprise me if every layman, and even many of those scholars who have not specialized in oratory, should receive the impression that this arrangement has not been deliberately and artistically devised, but is somehow spontaneous and fortuitous" (8). Lysias encourages this impression of spontaneity, according to Carey, by using simple sentences in the "strung-together-style," which "create[s] the impression that events are narrated without artifice as they present themselves to the speaker's mind" (*Lysias* 8). Speaking as if extemporaneously, Lysias's clients would appear, as Carey suggests, "untutored novice[s] attempting to present the unadorned truth in [their] own words" ("Rhetorical" 410). In this way the logographer is, stylistically at least, twice removed from the scene. Not only do the speeches seem such a natural fit for their speakers that they do not appear to have been written in advance by a professional, but they also mirror "ordinary speech and prose" so well that they do not seem to be prepared in advance at all—not even by the person delivering the speech (Carey *Lysias* 8).

If Lysias's elegant, understated prose has come to represent the pinnacle of the plain style, then his primary rhetorical innovation is the persuasive use of ethopoeia—the distinctive, fitting, and unique dramatization of character used, at least in part, as an argument from probability. While the speeches of Lysias do sometimes vividly characterize opponents (as in *Against Eratosthenes*, which offers a long ethical digression on Theramenes, a member of the Thirty) or other figures in the legal drama at hand (such as *On the Death of Eratosthenes* [Lys. 1], which contains several small but telling details that portray the duplicitous character of an unfaithful wife), Lysias's great rhetorical contribution is how well he manages to reveal the unique character of his speaking clients to strategic persuasive effect. While logographers before him (Antiphon, for example) appreciated the importance of establishing a favorable ethos and a style that suited their speakers' circumstances, Lysias was the only one who "fully appreciated the potential of dramatic characterization" (Carey "Rhetorical" 411). According to Carey, many of Lysias's speakers reveal a "vivid and consistent" character for the duration of their speeches, and in a strategically subtle way: "This does not amount to a detailed character portrayal. Too much detail would obtrude, and might actually impede the purpose of the speech by diverting attention from the 'facts' and the speaker's arguments. Lysias simply selects one or two distinctive characteristics and by presenting these consistently creates the illusion of depth of characterization" ("Rhetorical" 411–12).

This depth of characterization—an illusion, certainly—is a key weapon in Lysias's persuasive armory. Carey notes the several instances in which Lysias uses "characterization [. . .] to confirm the speaker's version of his case by presenting an implied argument from probability" ("Rhetorical" 413).[14] And Usher claims that Lysias's character portrayals are highly individualized to the clients and uniquely suited to the circumstances and demands of the cases at hand.[15] These skillfully crafted personae lend themselves to the speakers' believability and to their overall standing in court, even when the character is flawed. A speaker would reveal a few minor failings, Usher suggests, and he would become more relatable and believable by virtue of his venial weaknesses. Lysias would often establish for his clients some particular shortcoming or quirk that didn't necessarily endear them to their respective juries, but that somehow worked on their behalf depending on the details of their cases (Usher "Individual"). In one particularly notable example, *For the Disabled Man* (Lys. 24), the client—a speaker with a physical impairment and claims to poverty—argues for his continued pension from the state despite his admission that his property value would disqualify him. Here Usher argues that Lysias makes use of the man's sarcasm and surprising dignity to create a humorous tone that draws attention away from the weak legal merits of the case ("Individual" 111–12). Although this does not amount to the goodwill, good sense, and good moral character that Aristotle would recommend for all orators in Book 2 of the *Rhetoric*, it nonetheless creates a powerful persuasive effect. As Kennedy notes of the forensic setting in particular, "If the facts were in doubt, as they often were, the question became one of what such a person

---

14. Dionysius makes a similar claim about the way that Lysias uses characterization as a form of proof: "He also seems to me to show very notable skill in constructing proofs from character. He often makes us believe in his client's good character by referring to the circumstances of his life and his parentage, and often again by describing his past actions and the principles governing them" (19).

15. There is some debate about this claim to individualized characterization. While there's a general consensus that Lysias was talented at creating vivid and memorable characters, some argue that his characters are stock types, not uniquely dramatized individuals. For examples of this argument about character types in Lysias see William Levering Devries' *Ethopoiia: A Rhetorical Study of the Types of Character in the Orations of Lysias*, John R. Porter's "Adultery by the Book: Lysias 1," and Sophie Trenkner's *The Greek Novella in the Classical Period*.

as the defendant or the prosecutor was likely to have done. His character was the key" (*A New History* 67).

What Lysias pioneered in practice is what Aristotle would later theorize as ethos and deem "the most authoritative form of persuasion" (*Rhetoric* 1.2.4).[16] These qualities of the speaker's character, furthermore, "result from the speech, not from a previous opinion that the speaker is a certain kind of person" (*Rhetoric* 1.2.4) and so they necessarily arise from and lend themselves to a certain amount of conscious coding and decoding on behalf of both the person composing the speech and the audience receiving it. The art of character making, as it's practiced by Lysias and theorized by Aristotle, in other words, functions by way of interpretive acts that systematically foreclose otherness. Here, otherness is transformed into dramatic character—by no means an authentic representation of the speaker's attributes, but instead, a handful of subtle yet readable clues to a larger story that the audience is encouraged to piece together. Where Lysias's self-presentation in *Against Eratosthenes* works to incessantly destabilize his ontological positioning, his renowned talent for ethopoeia tends in the opposite direction. By carefully choosing and subtly revealing a handful of character traits that make the speaker seem an innocent victim in whatever legal predicament he has become unfairly ensnared, Lysias creates a character that can be spread out, examined, and pinned down like an artfully displayed butterfly. Thus the overall experience of reading Lysias's collected speeches is something like encountering a shadow box full of vibrant species of Lepidoptera: There's Euphiletus (Lys. 1), a naive farmer prone to violence when he becomes aware—quite late in the game—of his wife's extramarital dalliances. There's the young, overconfident Mantitheus (Lys. 16), who, though too boastful and not deferential enough to the jury, appears incapable of deceit. There's the unnamed speaker of *Against Simon* (Lys. 3), whose meek disposition makes him an unlikely perpetrator of assault. And these are just a few of Lysias's most fully analyzed and most often discussed rhetorical characters.[17]

These are characters that can be read, fully understood in the context of their unique legal situations, and—thanks to Lysias's self-concealing art-

---

16. In "Persuasive *Ethopoeia* in Dionysius's *Lysias*," Kristine Bruss argues that Dionysius stresses the persuasive function of Lysias's ethopoeia as opposed to its propriety-oriented function, which is often assumed. She also offers a lucid account of the different possible meanings of ethopoeia and provides important insight on the way that Dionysius's account of ethopoeia enriches and enhances Aristotle's account of persuasive ethos in Book 2 of the *Rhetoric*.

17. For a thorough analysis of individual characterization in the speeches of Lysias, including a close reading of Lysias's rhetorical figures and persuasive tactics, see Usher's "Individual Characterisation in Lysias." My brief accounts here are indebted to his close readings and to Carey's, which can be found in "Rhetorical Means of Persuasion."

istry—vividly imagined. Even though we've never met them—even when we hold no illusions about determining what these little-known, often unnamed clients must have been like, Lysias manages to make them sound somehow *like themselves*. Usher hints towards just how compelling and evocative these characters remain for modern readers when he notes somewhat speculatively that "the special care with which certain clients are portrayed may be partly explained by reference to the individual needs of their cases; but the present writer finds it impossible to escape the impression that these clients stimulated Lysias's imagination more than others" ("Individual" 119). It's hard not to imagine, in other words, the very real and fascinating person behind the ventriloquized speech. Lysias's elegant but everyday language produces the illusion that his clients are speaking spontaneously, and their characteristics are unique enough to make one speaker discernable from the next. The clients are thus made present, reduced to meaning, and in a manner of speaking, ossified—both for ancient jury members, who were asked to reconcile the content of their character traits with the details of their cases, and for contemporary readers, who have the luxury of seeing the perhaps not full but nonetheless admirable collection on display.

And yet a certain nonpresent force escapes this expert thematization. The very notion of making someone appear *like themselves*, as Clare Connors argues, "suggests something bogus about identity" (13). "To have even a minimal sameness," she adds, noting Derrida's claims about iterability, "[identity] must always repeat itself, en-act itself though time" (13–14). And so, while Lysias's subtle but vivid portraits of his clients might seem to represent something unique, authentic, or essential about them, in fact they call attention to identity's internal division and alteration. The logographer's lifelike characterizations, especially when perceived alongside Lysias's renown for ethopoiea, put into question the rigor and purity of the very thing that was supposed to have been present to begin with. As Derrida once asked about Richard M. Nixon, "In what sense did Nixon pretend to be Nixon, President of the United States up to a certain date? Who will ever know this, in all rigor? He himself?" ("Limited Inc." 106). Thus the prevailing conceptual question that arises from Lysias's ethopoetic talent, is not, as Usher is tempted to wonder, "Did Lysias accurately represent the most interesting of his clients?" Instead, it is something more along the lines of, "In what sense were the clients' identities already dispersed by an internal, differential repetition?" If Lysias's lifelike portrayals encourage us to entertain the first question, in any case, they also demand an answer to the second.

Just as Lysias's ability to vividly characterize his speaking clients shows us that these clients' identities are precisely *not* self-identical, so too does it suggest as much for the identity of Lysias 'himself.' This begins as a practical and professional consideration: For the ancient logographer, ethopoeia was a job requirement. The vividly drawn character of a client provided good cover for the person behind the scenes who had strategic reasons for wanting to go unseen. Even though it was normal practice to hire a logographer, the Athenian speaker could not reveal that he had employed such assistance without harming his relationship with the audience, which, by and large, demanded authenticity. This speaker not only had to win over the audience with the particular qualities of his character, but, as William Devries explains, he had to do so in part by convincing his audience that he had composed the speech himself. Hence the central role of ethopoeia: "It was the necessity of concealing the hand of the logographer by giving each speech individual traits," Devries writes, "as the professional speechwriter was not in good odor in Athens in those days, and to make use of his art was hardly credible, although customary" (13). Known for his ability to, as Dionysius says, invest "every person with life and character" (*Lysias* 13), Lysias was the preeminent ethopoet. He brought his speakers to life, and in so doing, vanished into his ability to characterize them so vividly. In this way, Lysias is a paradoxical figure: His appearance is simultaneous with a certain disappearance. He survives in our critical imagination as the innovator of ethopoeia and its most talented practitioner, and there is reason to believe that he enjoyed this renown in his own time: Carey notes that even though logographers worked in secret while their cases were active, it was common for the most accomplished logographers to publicize and circulate their speeches after their clients' cases had been resolved (Carey *Lysias* 6).[18] Thus Lysias hovers uncertainly alongside the speeches he authored for his many paying clients, at once present and absent in their delivery and always able to reappear on the scene.

In this way, Lysias is no longer simply a logographer but a *ghost*writer, who like the haunting figure this term conjures, maintains a spectral nonpresence on the rhetorical stage. Though it is a modern term that would have been unfamiliar to ancients, I believe 'ghostwriting' is an appropriate anachronism in this case because it highlights Lysias's subjective instability and the ways his simultaneous appearing/disappearing act challenges our established categories

---

18. With this phenomenon in mind, Carey points to the great paradox of Athenian oratory: "There is evidence that public opinion disapproved of the writing of speeches for pay, as it disapproved of any suggestion of professionalism in connection with the lawcourts. But Athenians also loved good oratory, and there was certainly a reading public for logographers' speeches, as is shown by the large number of speeches circulated in written form. Thus although before and during the trial the logographer worked in secret, once the issue had been decided his work was appreciated by a wider audience which could judge it for its craftsmanship" (*Lysias* 6).

of being. Lysias haunts us, just as he haunts the rhetorical tradition. He disturbs the boundaries of established categories of presence and absence, being and nonbeing, and he interrupts the fantasy of the communicative act itself. Perhaps more strongly than any other figure in the tradition, that is, Lysias encourages us to ask, 'Who speaks?'; 'In what time?'; and, 'To whom?' He encourages us to ask furthermore, 'On what basis could we possibly answer these questions?' This is because Lysias inhabits a space of pure virtuality. In his role as a gifted ethopoet and famed Athenian logographer, Lysias, like the specter, is "a paradoxical incorporation" who refuses to "present [himself] in the form of full presence" (Derrida *Specters* 6, 65). The point here isn't simply that Lysias wrote speeches in the voices of others, but that his ghostly structure interrupts being as ontology or the presumption of being itself. This spectral figure is, as Derrida explains, always still to come. This means, he adds, that the specter is "distinguished [. . .] from every living present understood as a plentitude of a presence-to-itself, as a totality of presence effectively identical to itself" (99). Never fully present and always still to come, the specter's unpredictable arrival ensures that presence is infiltrated in advance by the imminent visitation of an anachronous other.

Because the specter disturbs the boundary between presence and absence, furthermore, it radically resists being known or understood, and so Derrida insists, time and again, that it "remains [. . .] beyond the phenomenon or beyond being" (100). Far more than being something that's difficult to get a handle on (although it is that, too), the specter does not belong to the realm of knowledge: "One does not know what it *is,* what it is presently. *It is* something that one does know, precisely, and one does not know if precisely if it *is* [. . .]. One does not know: not out of ignorance, but because this nonobject [. . .] no longer belongs to knowledge" (6). Crossing every threshold, the specter is utterly incomprehensible, and so it "comes to defy semantics as much as ontology" (6). This is precisely Lysias's role in the rhetorical tradition. Famous for his unmatched talent in character making and for his uniquely self-concealing artistry, Lysias is made visible by his invisibility. He is thus a figure on the threshold—neither present nor absent—and so beyond all of our traditional ontological categories. The overall effect of his writing is likewise paradoxical. Although Lysias encourages us to invest his rhetorical characters with presence—they seem so real, so *like* themselves—he also demonstrates that being and presence are not self-identical.

Any attempts to theorize Lysias, then, must grapple with his "absolutely unmasterable disproportion," his radical inability to be contained within our established intellectual frameworks (7). Like all encounters with ghosts, this one is likely to leave us feeling a little anxious and uncertain. As Derrida has famously argued, the ghost is precisely that consternating figure with which scholars cannot deal. Typically concerned with "the sharp distinction between the real and the unreal, the actual and the inactual, the living and the nonliving, being and non-being" (11), traditional scholars trade in accepted categories of knowledge rather than in the "virtual space of spectrality" (11). In his visible invisibility, Lysias intrudes incomprehensibly and thus inaugurates what Michelle Ballif has called "that restless moment, [in which] we experience the event, the ethical moment of radical otherness, which—we will have experienced—is within/in us" ("Historiography" 145). This challenge to our available intellectual traditions may, as Colin Davis has argued, "open us up to the experience of secrecy as such: an essential unknowing which underlies and may undermine what we think we know" (377). All of this attests to the unbounded ethical potential of Lysias's rhetorical visitations. In his virtual becoming, the famed persuasive gun for hire enacts "the coming of the event, the excessive or exceeded relation to the other" (*Specters* 23). Though such a visitation might make us feel slightly ill at ease, Derrida insists that we must "correspond and have it out with [. . .] obsessive haunting, in the absence of any certainty or symmetry" (109). Maintaining this correspondence is what provides the opening for ethics itself. There would be no justice, in other words, "without the principle of some *responsibility,* beyond all living present, within that which disjoins the living present, before the ghosts of those who are not yet born or who are already dead" (xix).

If there was ever any certainty about the ill nature of Lysias's character, it would seem to have come from Plato who, in *Phaedrus,* offered up an unflattering and enduring portrait of the ghostwriter as a pernicious con artist from whose thrall eager young students must be rescued. Brilliantly mimicking Lysias's own trade, Plato attributes a speech to Lysias that demonstrates the latter's promiscuous leanings: Not unlike the nonlover for whom Plato's fictionalized Lysias advocates, professional logographers write speeches for any and all comers, regardless of the character of the client or the content of the case.[19] Within the frame of the dialogue, furthermore, Socrates is nothing if not confident in his sharp criticisms of Lysias's talent and judgment. Yet there is a surprising way in which Plato "has it out" with Lysias's obsessive haunting.

---

19. We cannot be sure if the *Eroticus,* the speech Phaedrus recites in the dialogue, was written by Lysias as Phaedrus claims or by Plato himself. Alexander Nehamas and Paul Woodruff argue that the most plausible hypothesis is that Plato wrote the speech as a work of fiction suited to his needs. What Stephen Usher finds most important about the speech's inclusion in the text is that Plato was familiar enough with Lysias that he was able to discern a "Lysianic style." He writes: "Plato, then, recognized Lysias's versatility, perhaps even as a talent kindred to his own. But he must have thought that he could distinguish a Lysianic style, in order either to imitate it, if the *Eroticus* is by Plato, or to select an authentic work of the orator, if the *Eroticus* is by Lysias" ("Lysias" 33).

Despite the largely negative portrayal, that is, Plato emphasizes the ghostwriter's spectral qualities. He dramatizes Lysias's unsettling (non)presence in a way that maintains his radical otherness and exposes us to his ghostly visitations.

While Lysias never appears as a speaking character in the *Phaedrus,* he is the engineering force of a text that seems intent on emphasizing his spectral qualities. The dialogue commences when Socrates accosts Phaedrus on a walk outside the city walls, and the budding orator explains that he has just spent the day with Lysias. Phaedrus is using the stroll, he says, to contemplate this earlier exchange, but Socrates is too clever to fall for that. He knows that Phaedrus is seeking out a place where he can memorize Lysias's speech in order to deliver it later as if it were his own. Instead of initially calling Phaedrus on his bluff, however, Socrates innocently asks: "So Lysias, I take it, is in the city?" (227b).[20] While this question serves to demonstrate Socrates's playful yet knowing demeanor, it also emphasizes something important about Lysias's position: He is at once there and not there, in town but no longer with the speech he has authored, not an active character in Plato's dialogue, but in it nonetheless. He may be in the city and at the heart of the debate between Socrates and Phaedrus, but Plato never permits him to enter the dialogue in the same way as the two speaking characters. Still, his simultaneous presence and absence enables the dialogue, for it is the written text of Lysias's speech, hidden beneath the young Phaedrus's cloak, that leads the boy and his teacher to the heated riverbanks of the Ilissus. And not unlike the speech itself, now cut loose from its author, the pair wanders away from the city to debate, among other things, the dangers of professional speechwriting. When Socrates finally persuades Phaedrus to share Lysias's speech, he demands that Phaedrus read the text rather than recite it from memory, explaining: "You can be sure that, though I love you dearly, I'll never, as long as Lysias himself is present, allow you to practice your own speechmaking on me" (228e). Socrates, once again, insists on Lysias's "presence" in the written text of his speech, while Plato withholds the logographer from the audience. We have a copy of his speech, but Lysias himself does not read it to us. Between Socrates's insistence on his presence in the speech and Plato's insistence on his absence from the dramatic action, Lysias hovers uncertainly between appearance and disappearance. The effect of this ghostly depiction of Lysias is that we clearly notice the indeterminacy of his position. Indeed, it seems as though Plato calls our attention to it.

For Socrates, what is at stake in the play of the ghostwriter's appearance and disappearance is the integrity of Phaedrus's character. The boy's intention,

---

20. The following section numbers refer to Alexander Nehamas and Paul Woodruff's translation of Plato's *Phaedrus,* Hackett Publishing Company, 1995.

as he wanders away from the city with Lysias's speech hidden away, is to memorize the defense of the nonlover so he can later deliver the clever argument as if it were his own. Socrates takes several measures to prevent this youthful and potentially soul-corrupting error, beginning with the insistence that Phaedrus read the written text aloud rather than recite what he has already begun to memorize. Forcing Phaedrus to behave as something of a ventriloquist's dummy, Socrates makes sure that "Lysias himself is present" enough to take responsibility for what is spoken. Writing, as Socrates will later insist, is a copy of speech and so external to its presumed point of origin. It would follow, then, that if Phaedrus relies on the page, he does not use his "living" speech to convey the objectionable message and therefore does not risk his soul in the process. It is the wiser and more rigorously trained Socrates who will assume this risk for the sake of Phaedrus, and he goes on to improvise a superior example of a speech on behalf of the nonlover (at least, that is, until he breaks off partway through, refusing to take the blasphemous exercise any further).

What emerges, then, is a fascinating tension between the philosopher and his ostensible mouthpiece—a tension that speaks to the impossible ethics of both spectrality and hospitality. While Socrates takes pains to protect Phaedrus from being contaminated by Lysias, Plato isn't so careful with his reading audience. By allowing Lysias to haunt the edges of the dialogue, he calls our attention to the possibility of a ghostly visitation despite Socrates's vigilant attempts at border control. It may be an anxious conjuration, but Plato's spectral representation of Lysias shows us that the ghost's always imminent arrival interrupts presence itself. He shows us the ways that the specter, to borrow Derrida's words, "intensifies and condenses itself within the very inside of life" (*Specters* 109). Despite all of Socrates's well-intentioned meddling, Phaedrus's vulnerable borders will have always been breached by the return of the ghost.

Does Plato's *Phaedrus* offer up what Derrida calls in *Specters of Marx* a "gesture of positive conjuration," or is it an invitation of another kind—one meant to safely corral Lysias's disturbing (non)being (108)? The history of the *Phaedrus*'s critical reception suggests the latter, of course. And given the way that Socrates attempts to assert control over Lysias's comings and goings, Plato's dramatization recalls the conditional hospitality offered to metics by the Athenian state. What remains, however—in addition to an enduring portrait of Lysias as an indiscriminate practitioner of an already indiscriminate profession—is a quiet insistence on the ghostwriter as "an alterity that cannot be anticipated" (65). Derrida has argued that "hospitality without reserve, which is nevertheless the condition of the event [. . .] is the impossible itself" (65). And yet, he adds, "without this experience of the impossible, one might as well give up on both justice and the event" (65). In conjuring Lysias's ghost, therefore, even if such a conjuration begins as an attempt to master that frustrating other who exceeds all categories of knowledge, Plato awaits "the absolute surprise of the *arrivant*" (65). He has it out with the ghost; he learns "from the other at the edge of life" (xviii). How could an encounter with Lysias be otherwise? As the rhetorical figure most famous for his capacity to disappear, Lysias contaminates the purity of self-presence. A disrupted identity that disrupts identity in general, "Lysias"—who undergoes a series of iterations as a privileged and persecuted Athenian metic, a critically reviled and revered writer of persuasive speeches, and an elusive Platonic invention—inaugurates that uneasy instant in which we experience the event.

CONCLUSION

> Except in the impeachment of Eratosthenes, [Lysias] appears to have had no personal contact with the affairs of the city. Yet, as in literary style he is the representative of Atticism, so in his fortunes he is closely associated with the Athenian democracy. [. . .] In his speeches for the law-courts, he became perhaps the best, because the soberest, exponent of [the democracy's] spirit—the most graceful and most versatile interpreter of ordinary Athenian life.
> —Sir Richard C. Jebb, *The Attic Orators from Lysias to Isaeos*, 142

While the Athenian state by turns conditionally welcomed Lysias and exiled him, in the end it found itself haunted by the guest/ghost it was never fully able to master. Although he was denied full participation in the law courts and assemblies so characteristic of Athenian democracy, Lysias haunted these realms as an in-demand logographer whose profession explicitly thwarted the state's every attempt to contain the outsider within. And like any ghost worthy of the name, Lysias's haunting knows no limits. Today he is the face of pure Atticism—the representative figure of the state that would have seen him sold into slavery for impersonating one of its citizens. As the outsider settled firmly yet disruptively inside the borderlines, Lysias shows us that hospitality is always a matter of welcoming an other who, as Derrida has argued, "overwhelms the self of the 'visited' and the *chezsoi* of the *hôte*" (*Acts of Religion* 372). He shows us, furthermore, that hospitality is not a phenomenon that operates according to the terms of the host, but a matter of responsibility without autonomy—a learning from the other in which the host is transformed.

CHAPTER 4

Isocrates's Promise

> Those who promise great things should not waste their time
> on trivial matters, nor say things that will not improve the life
> of those who are persuaded by them, but they should speak
> so that when their recommendations are accomplished, they
> will free themselves from their present difficulties and be
> thought by others to be responsible for the greatest benefits.
>
> —ISOCRATES, *PANEGYRICUS*, 189[1]

> Pervertibility has to be at the heart of that which is good, of the good promise, for the promise to be what it is. It must have the capability of not being a promise, of being broken, for it to be possible, to have the chance of being possible. This threat is not a bad thing; it's its chance.
>
> —JACQUES DERRIDA, "A CERTAIN IMPOSSIBLE
> POSSIBILITY OF SAYING THE EVENT," 459

In the previous chapter I emphasized Lysias's threshold position in the social and political atmosphere of classical Athens, noting the way that his status as a metic rendered him a perpetual immigrant in a culture that valued little above citizenship and the benefits such citizenship conferred. I also argued that Lysias's profession as a ghostwriter allowed him to haunt the legal and political systems to which he was denied full access: As the enduring face of the pure, understated Attic oratorical style, Lysias is a disruptive figure who demonstrates that Athenian rhetoric—the authorized language of the state's governing and legislative bodies—is haunted by the outsider. In this chapter, I shift my focus to a representative figure of the inside, Isocrates, whose influential vision of rhetoric and rhetorical education was indelibly tied to the integrity of the Athenian state. As much as Lysias posed a threat to Athenian autochthony, Isocrates celebrated it, going so far as to posit Athe-

---

1. Section numbers for *Panegyricus* refer to the translation by Terry L. Papillon, *Isocrates II*, U of Texas P, 2004, pp. 23–73.

nian exceptionalism as the ideal model for all of Hellas.[2] Where Lysias was a resident alien whose backstage rhetorical practice disrupted the purity of what it meant to be Athenian, Isocrates was a proud citizen who defined rhetoric as a practice of virtuous citizenship and who developed a rhetorical educational program designed to serve the polis and elevate the quality of civic life. With respect to the status of the Athenian city-state, then, we have two divergent rhetorical legacies. What I will show in this chapter, however, is that there is nonetheless a corresponding motif of haunting—of "being" as haunted—in the work of both thinkers. In each case, that is, rhetorical ethics emerges in the expropriating experience of encountering otherness. For Isocrates, importantly, this experience is framed as a transformative educational process in which learning involves something more than appropriating content from an outside source (the teacher, fellow students, or the substance of the curriculum) and creating objects of knowledge through the process of conceptualization. I will argue that in Isocrates's formulations of rhetorical pedagogy, learning is a matter of repeatedly encountering alterity—a discomforting experience in which the identity of the subject is put into question in the moment of responding to that which exceeds all knowledge and presence.

ISOCRATES'S DELIBERATIVE EDUCATIONAL PROMISE

When Isocrates opened the first school of rhetoric in Athens (around 390 BCE, following his early career as a logographer), he transformed the nature of rhetorical education, dramatically refiguring what had been offered a generation before him by Older Sophists like Gorgias.[3] While sophistic pedagogy was a product of those teachers' itinerant movements—"short-term," John Poulakos suggests, and "discontinuous"—Isocrates's school provided an institutional base "where the art of discourse could be studied at length and without inter-

---

2. Central to his advocacy of panhellenism was Isocrates's belief that only Athens could assume moral and intellectual leadership of a unified Greece, even if political necessity required a more practical partnership between Athens and Sparta. In *Panegyricus*, Isocrates makes this case for Athens's distinctiveness and superiority: "Our city revealed philosophy (*philosophia*), which has discovered and provided us with everything. [. . .] Our city has so far surpassed other men in thought and speech that students of Athens have become the teachers of others, and the city has made the name 'Greek' seem to be not that of a people but a way of thinking; and people are called Greeks because they share in our education (*paideusis*) rather than in our birth" (47, 50).

3. This sophistic tradition, of course, is the very educational environment in which a young Isocrates would have received his own rhetorical training. As Werner Jaeger explains, "Biographical tradition represents [Isocrates] as the pupil of Protagoras, of Prodicus, and especially of Gorgias" (48).

ruption" (*Sophistical* 132). Isocrates attests that students spent three or four years at his school (*Antidosis* 87)[4] and that this duration enabled a far more expansive educational undertaking than would have been available under a sophist's tutelage: Over time, students could study an array of subjects that served to develop their intellectual, moral, and civic sensibilities (*Antidosis* 260–66). In this way, as Werner Jaeger argues, Isocrates created "a more profound conception of the purpose of rhetorical education than had ever existed before," a purpose that far exceeded "a purely formal technique of hypnotizing the ignorant masses with persuasive talk" (90). Takis Poulakos points to a further shift in the scope and purpose of rhetorical education in Isocrates's hands. Where rhetoric had been traditionally focused on and deployed for private gain (primarily in the spheres of the courts and the assembly), now it was put to work for the welfare of the polis. "Political oratory," Poulakos argues, "rested for Isocrates on the capacity to undertake an ethico-political inquiry, a deliberation by means of which ethical choices illuminated decisions about action and choices regarding political action illuminated decisions about ethical commitments" (*Speaking* 68). By shifting rhetoric's emphasis from personal gain to public welfare, Isocrates infused oratorical practice with new moral and civic imperatives. Thus, in treatises like *Against the Sophists* and *Antidosis*, Isocrates claims to provide a training in eloquence that would develop in his students a capacity for sound political judgment. Far more than the study of persuasive speechmaking, which could too easily facilitate self-interested legal suits and miscarriages of justice, Isocrates's rhetorical pedagogy trained students to make intelligent contributions to civic life. As H. I. Marrou puts it, "His eloquence was not amoral—it had, in particular, a distinct civic and patriotic purpose" (85). Rather than its power to exert influence in the manner of a powerful lord, as Gorgias would have it, the primary benefit of *logos*, in Isocrates's view, was that it could guide people to upright action.

Just as these political and civic imperatives distinguished Isocrates's educational aims from those of the sophists, so too did they set them apart from those of his contemporary Plato, whose Academy opened roughly four years after Isocrates founded his school. The adversarial nature of the relationship between Isocrates and Plato is well-charted territory: Not only did the two vie for students in an era of newly formalized higher learning, but they also offered competing accounts of what this kind of education should entail, what its purposes were, and what larger benefits might follow from it. One important point of disagreement was the place of political and civic deliberation

---

4. Section numbers for *Antidosis* refer to the translation by David C. Mirhady and Yun Lee Too, *Isocrates I*, U of Texas P, 2000, pp. 201–64.

within the larger educational paradigm. Where Isocrates promised to help his students achieve a flexible kind of political wisdom, Plato encouraged his pupils to seek out purer forms of theoretical knowledge, exemplified in Socrates's entreaty to Phaedrus to pursue "Justice as it is" and "Knowledge [. . .] of what really is" (*Phaedrus* 247d–e).[5] Josiah Ober emphasizes the civic and political points of contention between Plato and Isocrates when he reads *Antidosis* as a deliberate misappropriation of Socrates's apology. In this text, Ober argues, Isocrates both evokes and counters the martyr figure of Socrates while making the case for "a political program [. . .] that will fulfill the needs and guarantee the just desserts of all decent persons, in the *polis* of Athens and in the broader realm of Hellas" (26).

Important distinctions between Isocrates's and Plato's educational visions are further borne out in their divergent accounts of *philosophia*.[6] In contrast to Plato's view of the concept as the dialectical striving toward transcendental essences, Isocrates's understanding was more rhetorical, practical, and pedagogically expansive. As David M. Timmerman and Edward Schiappa suggest, Isocrates vigorously advocated for a vision of *philosophia* that was grounded in his civically minded approach to rhetorical education: "Isocratean *philosophia* should be understood as the *cultivation of practical wisdom through the production of ethical civic discourse*. As an educational practice, *philosophia* for Isocrates involves ethical and intellectual training—the means and ends of which are the thoughtful creation of deliberative prose" (44). What Isocrates offered students, then, was a comprehensive educational undertaking that could be described as the study, practice, and development of virtue. Focused on building individual capacities and cultivating practical wisdom, Isocrates trained students to speak *well* in two senses of that term, persuasively and virtuously. Under Isocrates's guidance students didn't so much learn to write high-minded, technically excellent speeches as they undertook a training regimen that transformed the nature of their being. The production of civically beneficial deliberative speeches was one important by-product of this broader personal transformation, but it was not the baseline concern. The primary undertaking, from Isocrates's point of view, was the development of good character. As Marrou notes, Isocrates posits a powerful connection between studying honorable texts and behaving honorably in everyday life. "[Isocrates] is convinced that mental application to any subject worthy to be treated is a sure way of contributing to the development of character and the moral sense,

---

5. These section numbers refer to Alexander Nehamas and Paul Woodruff's translation of Plato's *Phaedrus*, Hackett Publishing Company, 1995.

6. For further discussion, see DePew "The Inscription" 160, Jaeger 49, Marrou 89, Mirhady and Too "Introduction" 3–4, Poulakos *Sophistical* 128–31, and Poulakos *Speaking* 69.

to nobility of soul" (89). He adds that Isocrates's pedagogical rational was premised on a "gradual, imperceptible shift from literature to life" grounded in the belief that the "habits of morality developed in the one must necessarily pass into the other" (89). Cultivating this kind of "nobility of the soul," the rhetorical education Isocrates offered served a larger purpose for the polis as a whole. His rhetorical educational innovations led to the production of a moral and civically minded populace whose participation in political affairs would ultimately make life better for all members of the community. When students studied worthy subjects over time, they received the benefits of moral and civic development, which in turn paid dividends to the polis at large. Structured like an investment, Isocrates's rhetorical *paideia* was a powerful form of character education whose rationale continues to inform contemporary institutions of higher learning. Any college or university promising to foster socially and culturally engaged critical thinkers owes a debt to Isocrates, who, as Marrou has suggested, "appears as the original fountainhead of the whole great current of humanist scholarship" (89).

Isocrates thus communicates his educational philosophy in the form of a two-part promise: First, he insists that his brand of rhetorical pedagogy has the capacity to develop civic virtue in those who undertake it, and second, he argues that these students will go on to have a beneficial impact on the polis at large. Claiming that he "exhorts all citizens to better and more just leadership," Isocrates explains that he tries "to persuade the whole city to undertake activities which will lead to their own happiness and will free the rest of the Greeks from their present evils" (*Antidosis* 86, 85). In order for his educational program to have such a broad impact, however, Isocrates begins locally—by focusing on developing the character and capacities of those enrolled in his course of study. Jeffrey Walker says of this forward-looking logic that "the development of good character precedes (and is a foundation for) the development of real eloquence" (*Genuine* 68). Isocrates spells out his goals for these students in *Panathenaicus*: "I call educated [. . .] those who manage well the daily affairs of their lives [. . .], those who behave appropriately and fairly toward people who are always with them [. . .], those who are always in control of their pleasures and [. . .] those who are not corrupted by their good fortune" (30–32).[7] Notice the emphasis Isocrates places here on the orderly, integral self. Efficient, self-disciplined, and virtuous, the educated man Isocrates describes is in possession of a moral compass that guides him

---

7. Section numbers for *Panathenaicus* refer to the translation by Terry L. Papillon, *Isocrates II*, U of Texas P, 2004, pp. 167–227.

toward fair and just action.⁸ In this way, the development of individual character is Isocrates's first educational concern. Once good character was fully formed—and only then—could his students begin to make contributions to the community at large. As David Fleming characterizes this developmental model, "For Isocrates, the worth of rhetorical education could only be measured by judging the character of the students who had gone through it" (180).

The importance of this first part of Isocrates's educational promise is that it subsequently elevates the quality of public life writ large. Students who undertake his unique, sustained version of rhetorical training, in other words, will develop the disposition and capacity to speak on those matters that benefit the polis—to deliver the speeches Isocrates describes in *Panegyricus* "that treat the greatest subjects, best demonstrate the speaker's talent, and most help those who hear them" (4). Thus, Isocrates relies on a deliberative, future-oriented structure to describe and market his educational program: Broadly speaking, he claims that when students undertake his course of study *today*, the polis will benefit from their contributions *tomorrow*—at some distance off in the future. The power of this deliberative structure, in other words, is that it articulates the benefits of the broad-based, not-immediately-practical course of study to a wider citizenry.

In using the term "deliberative" to describe the structure of Isocrates's educational promise, I intend to emphasize, first of all, the temporal structure of the genre of deliberative rhetoric articulated by Aristotle when he categorized and described the types of speeches that dominated the fourth-century oratorical landscape. In this well-known conceptual triad, which defines and distinguishes among forensic, epideictic, and deliberative rhetoric, Aristotle notes that "each of these [species] has its own 'time'" (*Rhetoric* 1.3.4).⁹ While forensic speakers prosecute or defend with an eye toward past actions and epideictic speakers praise or blame in light of the values that most powerfully define the present moment, deliberative speakers, Aristotle says, exhort and dissuade "about future events" (1.3.4). In urging hearers, typically in a political or civic context, about what they should (or should not) do in the future, deliberative speakers engage them in the process of conscious decision-making based, at least in part, on reasoned discourse about what would be beneficial and/or harmful for them (1.3.4). And yet while the *telos* of deliberative oratory is to

---

8. The notion of justice itself, furthermore, would have been central to Isocrates's rhetorical educational program. As Arthur E. Walzer has argued of this pedagogical approach, "Isocrates' students would be led to conclude that, regardless of the circumstances, justice should have a priority in political deliberation" (116).

9. Book, chapter, and section numbers of Aristotle's *Rhetoric* refer to the translation by George A. Kennedy, *On Rhetoric: A Theory of Civic Discourse*, 2nd edition, Oxford UP, 2007.

persuade the audience to take specific courses of action in the *future*, deliberative speakers must often draw on past evidence in order to make a compelling argument about what may yet happen. Aristotle notes, for example, that a speaker who wishes to persuade on the topic of "war and peace" will have had to "have observed not only the wars of one's own city but also those of others, in terms of their results; for like results naturally follow from like causes" (1.4.9). Thus we see a certain standard chronological pacing essential to the structure of deliberative oratory: In an attempt to make a case about what hearers should do in the future, it is often necessary to refer back to what has happened in the past. To do so is to posit a certain probabilistic continuity between the past and the future and to assert that, although past events may not repeat themselves exactly, one can nonetheless rely on them to provide a reasonable indicator about what might happen in the future.

What Isocrates promises to teach his students is just this ability to contend with the uncertain future, and so his educational promise not only has a deliberative structure but also a strong thematic emphasis on deliberative rhetoric itself: He prepares his students to be ethical and intelligent practitioners of deliberative rhetoric, able to guide the polis toward appropriate civic action. As Takis Poulakos has argued, Isocrates was a unique and innovative thinker of the deliberative genre in that he introduced a more protracted, temporally spacious understanding of the deliberative process. Concerned less with individual political speeches meant to be delivered in the assembly, Isocrates was interested in the power of *logos* to guide public deliberation writ large and to promote long-term civic action that had been carefully considered in light of ethical and moral values. In so doing, he says, Isocrates "gave to the art [of rhetoric] the gift of time" (*Speaking* 70). This contribution is demonstrated particularly well in *Panegyricus,* which Poulakos reads "as an instance of wise deliberation [. . .] as Isocrates might have understood it and taught it to his students" (89). Although this deliberative process is focused on a long-term future, the orator's knowledge and understanding of the past plays an important role because, although the past cannot simply be followed as a model, it can serve as a guide for present and future action. In this context, Poulakos argues that Isocrates relies on a flexible but nonetheless continuous conceptual thread between past, present, and future. "Once the dialectic between past and present is fixed," he says, "the orator displays phronesis by channeling all segments of society to the same end and by paying heed to link the action proposed with values revered and commitments cherished by all members of the polis" (92). As does Aristotle, then, Isocrates envisions a concept of deliberative rhetoric that is oriented towards a future characterized primarily by its unbroken link to the present and past.

The same temporal structure applies to Isocrates's claims for his unique brand of rhetorical education, which is at its heart, I want to suggest, a promise. He claims to offer his students training in eloquence that will ultimately enable them to become skilled deliberative orators in the expansive sense I have just described. As we shall see, this course of study was not limited to the examination and analysis of deliberative speeches but was instead a broad-based, nonvocational form of learning that required students to engage with time-honored texts—texts that often thematized the aforementioned "values revered" and "commitments cherished." This was a novel educational system that Walker suggests was highly successful and widely influential. With it, he says, "Isocrates launched the basic rhetorical *paideia* that worked so well and was so remarkably stable for so long" (6). Thus, in the context of newly formalized higher education in the fourth century, when he had to carve out a space for his pedagogical insights, Isocrates offered up a powerful educational promise. It turns out to have been an appeal that has lasted for more than two millennia, particularly for educators in the humanities and liberal arts, who are increasingly called upon to justify their existence in the context of shrinking budgets and the demand for educational "deliverables." From this perspective, and perhaps more than any other classical thinker, Isocrates provides a site of resistance to encroaching neoliberal (and increasingly monetizing) approaches to higher education organization and administration.

Now more than ever, Isocrates's case for the future value of an educational program focusing on literacy and the arts seems particularly important, and a number of scholars have found his discussions of *philosophia* productive for inquiries into the purposes of higher education today. One important example of scholarship devoted to reconsidering this educational legacy is Takis Poulakos and David Depew's 2004 collection, *Isocrates and Civic Education*. Here the editors argue that Isocrates offers the best insight into moral and civic educational practice, rather than Plato and Aristotle, the classical thinkers most often associated with a virtues-centered educational model. Interestingly, Poulakos and Depew make a point to note that during William J. Bennett's tenure as the chairman of the National Endowment for the Humanities, the cultural conservative and *Book of Virtues* author held Aristotle up as the epitome of "public-spirited, virtue-centered civic education" (1). One of the primary contributions of their collection, Poulakos and Depew suggest, is to counter this idea, to demonstrate that it is Isocrates—not Aristotle—who serves as a better "whetstone for our own reflections on contemporary humanistic education and its relation to the theme of civic virtue" (2).

It is certainly true that Bennett often turns to Plato and Aristotle in *The Book of Virtues*, his self-described "'how to' book for moral literacy" (11) (one or the other or both are excerpted in six of Bennett's ten chapters), and yet I find it a bit troublesome that Poulakos and Depew position their exploration of Isocrates's civic educational project within this framework. Forging such a link highlights the fundamentally conservative aspects of Isocrates's educational model (including his commitment to the elite Athenian class). While I wholeheartedly agree with Poulakos and Depew's suggestion that Isocrates's pedagogical design has a great deal to offer contemporary educators, I would suggest that this approach doesn't make the best case for Isocrates's current and future relevance precisely because it is tied too tightly to historically and culturally determined values. Furthermore, this link to Bennett puts rhetoric and rhetorical education in a secondary relation to the virtue each is said to develop. That is, if the benefit of rhetorical pedagogy is that it reinstalls already agreed upon values in the future, then the pedagogy is first and foremost in service to those already settled beliefs. It plays no productive part in the invention and transformation of those values.

To be clear, part of the case for Isocrates, according to Poulakos and Depew, is that he refuses to privilege Platonic Truth and its descendant Aristotelian idea of rhetoric as *techne*. In other words, while Plato and Aristotle place rhetoric outside the realm of ethics, Isocrates conceives of it as central to the political decisions that constitute everyday life—indeed, it is vital because of this centrality. Isocrates understands, furthermore, that the discourse we use to persuade others and make important decisions about civic life is the same discourse we use to make up our own minds (*Antidosis* 254). This is a crucial difference, and it is central to Poulakos and Depew (and to many of the authors featured in their collection) in their efforts to reclaim Isocrates as a relevant figure for thinking about the place of character development in contemporary education. And yet, despite this essential distinction, the reclamation of Isocrates based on his status as an ideal model for modern-day moral and civic education never leaves the confines of Plato's backyard: If what Isocrates does for us today is provide a less foundational and more culturally or linguistically determined way to discuss the relation between education and civic virtue, literacy and morality, then he does so entirely within the structure set up by Plato. Here, Isocrates's *logon paideia* is put in the service of predetermined ideas about virtue and what might constitute virtuous qualities, and rhetoric (once again) becomes mere ornament, a handmaiden to the state of affairs that exists apart from and before the language that describes it.[10]

---

10. In his classic essay "The Q Question" in *The Electronic Word: Democracy, Technology, and the Arts,* Richard Lanham makes a similar point about Isocrates himself. Lanham argues that any claim to produce virtuous citizens is an entirely Platonic endeavor because it takes as foundational some idea of the Good and puts rhetoric in the service of this foundation. As I

My point in this chapter is to articulate a different legacy for Isocrates, one that refigures the deliberative structure of his rhetorical pedagogy altogether. To do this I suggest that what is most exciting and productive in Isocrates's work is not his attention to virtue and its subsequent effects, per se, but the ethics of radical otherness that creep through his discourse on these concepts. In other words, while I acknowledge that Isocrates is thoroughly interested in producing a conservative and eloquent moral subject who acts with the best interests of the community in mind, the way he talks about accomplishing this actually undermines his normative claims about virtue and the Good. What I show is that Isocrates's discussion of virtue gets disrupted by his discussion of ethics—those aporetic ethics in which being is interrupted in the encounter with difference. I claim that this is the case because in Isocrates's work, presence is internally structured by the anticipation of a radically unknowable future that comes in the guise of *kairos*. The significance of this claim is that it reimagines Isocrates's ethical terrain and expands his notion of justice beyond the deliberative realm. By making this case for Isocrates's ethics, I do not claim that his interpreters have somehow misread him; there is no doubt that Isocrates was a politically conservative thinker with an expressed interest in a training in virtue that directly contributed to the improvement of the city. Despite this conservative moralism, however, I argue that a radical otherness haunts his work, and that this haunting is central to Isocrates's educational promise, both in the classical setting and for his continued relevance to contemporary education in the humanities.

MORAL LITERACY: REPRODUCING THE PAST

Despite my objections to the link proposed by Poulakos and Depew, there certainly is a way in which Isocrates would seem to be William J. Bennett's dream-come-true. The better part of the *Antidosis*, a late career treatise that defends Isocrates's life and work as a teacher in the Athenian polis, is based on the master pedagogue's capacity to develop those good, moderate men who become guardians of the city's reputation. Indeed, Isocrates argues in *Anti-*

---

will argue in the pages that follow, I think there is a good deal more going on in Isocrates than Lanham's critique suggests. For our purposes here, however, what is useful in Lanham's treatment of Isocrates is his claim about rhetoric's relation to the Good. For rhetoric to be understood as powerful and transformative in its own right, it cannot simply be put in service of some preexisting truth. This is the essence, I want to suggest, of claiming that Isocrates offers us a better version of civic education than Plato or Aristotle. Even though the thinkers who make this claim take Isocrates's version of civic education to be more culturally responsive than Plato's or Aristotle's, they nonetheless put rhetoric in service of an ideal model of civic virtue.

dosis that his students live temperate, moderate lives—a benefit that comes in part from their study of well-respected texts: "They live their daily lives in the simplest and most orderly manner," he writes. "They do not study speeches concerning private contract disputes or those that attack others, but only those that men everywhere respect" (228). Isocrates's suggestion here—that reading honorable texts leads to similarly honorable behavior—is very much the rationale behind Bennett's *Book of Virtues*. For Bennett, the thinking is that when young students read stories featuring the themes of self-discipline, courage, work, honesty, faith, and the like, they will internalize these values and take their good traits with them everywhere they go. This is precisely the kind of moral development that should take place at school, Bennett argues, especially in the English and history courses whose purview includes a wealth of rich texts treating moral themes ("Moral Literacy" 29–31).[11] In a similar vein, Isocrates suggests that his students read only the finest, most eloquent deliberative and epideictic speeches (not courtroom speeches, which might encourage them to undertake unnecessary litigation for personal gain) and that because of their work with these texts they will contribute to the polis in an appropriately honorable fashion.[12] And not unlike Bennett, who claims that reading texts with explicitly moral themes will help students preserve the principles they encounter there (*Book of Virtues* 12), Isocrates argues that working with time-honored texts "improves those who study [them]" (*Antidosis* 175). In other words, both educators are interested in the way that the study of appropriate and admirable works leads to the development of appropriate and admirable citizen subjects.[13]

In addition to stating these traditional, "Great Books" ideals to frame his goals for civic education, Isocrates goes out of his way to suggest that only the culture's elite can realize the height of eloquence, honor, and wisdom. In other words, while everyone can be made better through rhetorical education, not everyone can become a preeminent example such as Pericles. Why? Because,

---

11. For these purposes, Bennett himself is partial to Homer, Plato, Shakespeare, and the framers of the US Constitution ("Moral Literacy" 30–31).

12. In *Panathenaicus*, Isocrates clearly separates himself and his students from those who would use public speaking for personal gain rather than public good: "Everyone knows that most public speakers [. . .] have the daring to give people not advice that will benefit the city but what they expect will be profitable for themselves; I and the people around me, however, not only keep away from public funds more than others but we spend our own funds beyond our means for the needs of the city" (12).

13. Like Isocrates, Bennett stresses the temporal significance of a pedagogy aimed at developing good character: "A person who is morally literate will be immeasurably better equipped than a morally illiterate person to reach a reasoned and ethically defensible position on these tough issues. But the formation of character and the teaching of moral literacy comes first, the tough issues second" ("Moral Literacy" 33).

according to Isocrates, "abilities in speaking and all the other faculties of public life are innate in the well-born" (*Against* 14)[14] and because "in education in speaking, [. . .] nature [. . .] is paramount and stands far ahead of everything else" (*Antidosis* 189).[15]

To this main ingredient of "natural ability" (188), Isocrates adds a relatively stable moral code meant to maintain order in both the public and private spheres. He does this in part by encouraging those in his charge to make themselves living arguments by virtue of their good moral character. In *To Demonicus*, for example, a treatise in which he passes along maxims and advice to the son of a Cyprian friend, Isocrates advises his ward to respect authority by honoring his parents, obeying the laws of kings, and offering up sacraments to the gods. In addition to privileging existing (and empowered) social structures in this way, he also encourages the love of physical toil and mental strain; such actions not only condition the person who undertakes the physical and mental challenges, but they also promote a strong agricultural and intellectual community. Isocrates's advice also lends itself to maintaining the economic status quo: He advises Demonicus to work hard to achieve the wealth he deserves but at the same time to "appreciate not the excessive acquisition of material goods but their measured enjoyment" (*To Demonicus* 27).[16] Joy Connolly has argued that this conservative strand of Isocrates's thinking

> rewrites the aristocratic aesthetic of balance and self-control as the model of a moderate, rational, civil politics. This pose reinforces traditional class limits on participation and [. . .] amplifies, broadcasts, and makes utterly familiar the very propositions that may need the intensity of intellectual reflection that only a more critical politics might provide. (133)

When it's put altogether, Isocrates's advice demonstrates his interest in keeping the social, agrarian, and economic fabric intact. He provides Demonicus with a moral formula that adds up to little more than the way things are now.[17]

---

14. Section numbers for *Against the Sophists* refer to the translation by David Mirhady and Yun Lee Too, *Isocrates I*, U of Texas P, 2000, pp. 61–66.

15. See also *Against the Sophists:* "Education (*paideusis*) can make such [naturally talented] people more skillful and better equipped at discovery. [. . .] But it cannot fashion either good debaters or good speechwriters from those who lack natural ability, although it may improve them and make them more intelligent in many respects" (15).

16. Section numbers for To Demonicus refer to the translation by David Mirhady and Yun Lee Too, *Isocrates I*, U of Texas P, 2000, pp. 19–30.

17. See also Vitanza, who emphasizes the violent, appropriating logic of Isocrates's imperialism (*Negation* 125–35).

Isocrates's civic ethos, then, is fundamentally conservative, and when we couple his belief that natural ability is innate in the well born with his moral prescriptions to promote cultural stasis, it seems easy, perhaps even preferable, to dismiss the overly traditional, conformist thinking as well as the pervasive cultural elitism it symbolizes. Assuming a continuous through-line that links the past, the present, and the future together in a progression, Isocrates uses these conservative ideals to guarantee the quality of his educational program and its results. I believe, however, that he must insist so strongly on these traditionalist commitments because they are put at risk by a pedagogical design that radically transforms students. In what follows, I will suggest that Isocrates's pedagogical model promises a form of character transformation so thorough that the teacher's preferred conservative values are ultimately undermined by his commitment to a future so radically unknowable that it defies temporal logic. Isocrates's seeming desire to reproduce a past, in other words, is challenged (structurally, internally) by his promise to contend with unforeseeable events to come.

THE PROMISE OF CHARACTER: RHETORICAL CAPACITY

> A promise is always excessive. Without this essential excess, it would return to a description or knowledge of the future. Its act would have a constative structure and not a performative one. But this "too much" of the promise does not belong to a (promised) content of a promise which I would be incapable of keeping. It is within the very structure of the act of promising that this excess comes to inscribe a kind of irremediable disturbance or perversion.
>
> —JACQUES DERRIDA, *MEMOIRES FOR PAUL DE MAN*, 93–94

Derrida has characterized the promise as a performative contradiction—a disruptive utterance that requires, on the one hand, intention, consciousness, and seriousness, and on the other, a structural openness to the future that renders each of these impossible. One of the key concepts he inherits from J. L. Austin, the promise figures prominently in Derrida's work, both rhetorically and conceptually, often in order to demonstrate the way that iterability and citationality require, as Mario Ortiz-Robles puts it, "an engagement with or response to the call of the other as the horizon of performative force" (2).[18]

---

18. Derrida addresses the concept of the promise as promise most directly in "Avances," *Memiores for Paul de Man*, and the essays in *Without Alibi*, although important references to and demonstrations of the idea proliferate, notably in *Specters of Marx*.

Frequently making promises to his own readers, Derrida transforms Austin's "*explicit* [. . .] unambiguous" performative utterances (*How to Do Things* 32) into profoundly vulnerable encounters with otherness that both produce and challenge the identity of the one who swears an oath. Where Austin's understanding of the promise ("I promise . . ." as an explicit, exemplary speech act) assumes and requires an "utterance-origin" (60)—a speaking subject whose sincerity secures the success of the spoken vow—Derrida's transformation of this concept offers no such guarantees. Because it "inscribes us with its trace in language," he explains, "the promise [seizes] the *I* that promises to speak to the other" ("How to Avoid Speaking" 153). The one who swears an oath, in other words, is not the origin of the utterance, but already its effect. In the case of the promise, then, Derrida takes up an idea central to Austin's speech act theory and transforms it into an aporetic ethical concept that prioritizes the other by showing the other to be in "me," before "me." Thus unseating the speaker as an initiating source of the performative, Derrida shows that the promise is not simply a speech act in the Austinian sense, but rather an *arche*-promise inscribed in the basic structure of locution.[19] The promise is "engaged even before any explicit formulation," Derrida says, "and even in the case where I would declare, [. . .] that I did not commit myself" ("Le Parjure" 172).

Not any particular empirical promise, but instead a promise that is "inevitable as soon as we open our mouths" (*Memoires* 98), Derrida's promise is a pre-performative concept that speaks to a situation prior to the moment when an individual subject would swear an oath.[20] As he puts it, "The discursive event presupposes the open space of the promise," and so, the "promise is older than *I* am" ("How to Avoid Speaking" 151, 153). Putting into question the identity of the subject who would give one's word, this promise requires a certain performative impotency, meaning, as Diane Davis explains, that it

---

19. Derrida has often separated his conception of the promise from Austin's, although, as J. Hillis Miller has argued, Derrida's transformation of the concept nonetheless requires the speech act theory it critiques and transforms (Miller "Performativity as Performance" 231). In "How to Avoid Speaking: Denials," for example, Derrida argues that although the promise interrupts identity, Austin believes it must be grounded by intentional authority: "Here is something that appears impossible, the theoreticians of speech acts would say: like every authentic performative, a promise must be made in the present, in the first person (singular or plural) by one who is capable of saying *I* or *we*, here and now [. . .] and where I can therefore be held responsible for this speech act" (153).

20. Matthias Fritsch offers a cogent explanation of the way the promise functions for Derrida as a hauntological or quasi-transcendental concept. He writes, "The different senses of identity (the subject, content, and meaning of the promise) presupposed in empirical promising are looked at from the perspective of what makes them possible, a perspective that takes us beyond present identity and the homogenous chain of presents on which empirical promising seems to depend" ("Derrida's Democracy to Come" 576).

"remains at a certain level without power, without mastery, without authority, without sovereignty" ("Performative" 71). I will return to this idea shortly (specifically in terms of how it enables us to rethink the deliberative structure of Isocrates's educational promise), but for the moment I want to highlight the way that empirical promises—those performative utterances Austin knowingly called "awe-inspiring" (*How to Do Things* 9)—echo their hauntological counterpart. Empirical promises, in other words, are rhetorical formulations that do some of the unsettling work described above, even if in a different register. Indeed, Derrida's rhetorical practice of weaving promises into his philosophical writing itself enacts and dramatizes this contaminating exposure to alterity that both enables identity and puts it at risk. In "'Le Parjure,' *Perhaps*: Storytelling and Lying," an essay that contends with the porous boundary between literature and life in the case of Paul de Man's bigamous second marriage, Derrida elegantly illustrates the risk that underwrites all empirical promises:

> The essential destination, the structural signification of the oath or the given word, is to commit oneself not to be affected by time, to remain the same at moment B, whatever may happen, as the one who swears previously, at moment A. This sublating negation of time is the very essence of fidelity, of the oath, and of sworn faith. [...] But the perjurer [...] can always seek to be excused, if not forgiven, by alleging, on the contrary, the unsublatable thickness of time and of what it transforms, the multiplicity of times, instants, their essential discontinuity, the merciless interruption that time inscribes in "me" as it does everywhere [...]: "I sincerely promised in the past, but time has passed, precisely, passed or surpassed, and the one who promised, long ago or in the past, can remain faithful to his promise, but it is no longer me, I am no longer the same me, I am another, *I* is another [...]. I am unable to account for that, myself, ask the other who decides this for me within me." (173–74)

One of the most awe-inspiring things about promises, as Derrida seems to suggest here, is their powerfully aspirational tone. They signal a hope—often a sincere desire—to stake a claim on the future and to project oneself into that future, constancy guaranteed. But promises betray precisely this ambition. Instead, they insist on and remind us of the priority of the other, especially in those moments when we would most like to assert our constancy and control. This is the case because promises not only require us to turn toward the other to whom we make a pledge, but also to confront in advance that unforeseeable future expanse we must eventually pass through in order to (perhaps) fulfill the vow. This can be a disquieting moment, one that highlights the profound vulnerability that lies at the heart of every assurance.

And just such a vulnerability lies at the heart of Isocrates's educational promise. Deliberative in structure, his program begins with natural talent and virtue and then works to develop wisdom, good moral character, and persuasive talent so that students who have completed their training can respond ably to the civic and rhetorical demands they encounter in the future. Assuming a certain "sublating negation of time," Isocrates promises to produce eloquent subjects who will live up to and so honor the largely aristocratic values that ground his pedagogical design. But because the system's *raison d'être* is marked by the future from the very start, its deliberative promise also involves putting those traditional values at risk. We can see Isocrates's willingness to imperil such a promise—to pass through a disruptive encounter with an unknown future—even in a backward-looking speech like *Antidosis*, which takes account of his long and accomplished career. Here, Isocrates confidently guarantees the future worth of his students, accepting blame for any wrongs they might commit, all the while relinquishing praise to them should they earn it. He elaborates this idea in the lengthy defense of his former student Timotheus, a general who was—unfairly Isocrates says—charged with treason after an otherwise successful military career. Isocrates argues in *Antidosis*:

> I make the same proposal about him as about the others: if Timotheus was a bad man and committed many wrongs against you, I ask to be party to this, to be punished, and to suffer just like the guilty. But if he is shown to be a good citizen and a general unlike any other we know of, then [. . .] you should praise him and thank him. (106)

The ostensible logic of Isocrates's proposal goes something like this: If Timotheus ultimately benefitted the polis, then this is a credit to his noble character. If he caused harm, however, then Isocrates never should have taken him on in the first place, and the teacher should shoulder the blame. This is why a student's natural disposition is so important to Isocrates, whose educational promise secures right action in the future to a nobility of character. The argument about Timotheus demonstrates the larger deliberative structure I have described in that it stakes a claim for the future by taking support from a presumably unbroken link to the past.

And yet something complex happens in the interval between a student's arrival at Isocrates's school and his later intervention in public life—something that renders the causal link between past and future a little less certain. While Isocrates's promise to produce the so-called "good man speaking well" might begin with natural ability, in other words, it certainly doesn't end there. This is because Isocrates also argues that his educational model is comprehensive, powerful, and personally transformative. To make them better, more civically minded, and capable of benefitting their fellow citizens, Isocrates puts his students through an expansive educational experience that develops not simply their bases of knowledge but also their individual capacities. As Debra Hawhee argues, the primary emphasis of Isocrates's educational strategy "does not lie in material learned, but rather inheres in a learned *manner*, a kind of habit-production based on movement" ("Bodily Pedagogies" 145). Although Isocrates valued the honorable virtues featured in the fine literary works and deliberative and epideictic speeches that served as models for his students, his foremost concern was facilitating what Marrou called the "gradual, imperceptible *shift* from literature to life" (89, emphasis added). Isocrates attempted to produce in each of his students a certain condition or constitution that would enable them to think, speak, and behave in ways that reflected those ideals, a project more complicated than a simple transfer or replication of ideas. This form of character development was in some important ways linked to the conservative values Isocrates preferred, but it was more complicated than the values themselves and of an entirely other order.

Isocrates's curriculum required students to undertake a series of rhetorical practices such as memorizing and imitating model orations, developing a deep familiarity with noble themes, and practicing, under the teacher's supervision, the critical examination of prose and poetic texts. As Isocrates explains, this is a thoroughgoing process that requires the involvement of both the students and the teacher. "In particular," he says, "the pupils' responsibility is to bring the requisite natural ability, and the teachers' to be able to educate these kinds of students, but common to both is practical experience [. . .]. Teachers must meticulously oversee their students; students must resolutely follow what they have been taught" (*Antidosis* 188). Emphasizing practice, intensity, and experience, Isocrates's focus here is on what students and teachers do, over and above the content of what is learned/taught. In his detailed account of the specific practices that characterized the pedagogical work of Isocrates, Walker argues that students were put through an increasingly complex, two-stage learning process that would later come to be formalized as the progymnasmata and the declamations (*Genuine* 74–75). In the first stage of this developmental process, as Walker explains, Isocrates teaches his students various forms of discourse and helps them become acutely familiar with them "by encountering, examining, and discussing examples of them" (73). Having thus internalized these fundamental elements of rhetoric, or, as Isocrates says in *Against the Sophists*, having been successfully "molded by him" (18), students practice responding to the unique demands of specific discursive occasions by choosing from among the available rhetorical forms, now part of a newly developed repertoire (*Genuine* 74). "Such a second-stage exercise," Walker concludes, "is meant to cultivate, through practical and guided experience, that creative, kairotic sensitivity that cannot be directly taught but is the essence of skillful, even eloquent *rhêtoreia*" (74). As we can see, the overriding pedagogical approach is directed toward developing new capacities in students who, because of the indirect effects of their training, emerge from the educational process with the inner resources that enable them to respond well to contingency.

Isocrates makes special note of the indirect nature of the relationship between the content of the curriculum and the benefits borne of actively encountering it. He stresses, in other words, that the content and quality of the material to which the students devote their time *does* matter, but it matters less than the quality of their attention to and the nature of their interaction with this material. For example, although he distinguishes himself from "leaders in eristic and those who teach astrology, geometry, and other branches of learning [that] do not harm but rather benefit their students" (*Antidosis* 261), Isocrates nonetheless argues that it is a good thing to spend time learning subjects like these, even though they have no immediate utility. Though some would "regard such studies as babbling and hairsplitting" (262), he says, and though they have no obvious application in civic life, Isocrates argues that these subjects ultimately benefit those who work through them. It is this active work, he suggests, *more than the content of the subjects themselves* that readies students to undertake the more advanced components of Isocratean *philosophia*:

> When we spend time in the detail and precision of astrology and geometry, we are forced to put our minds to matters that are hard to learn. [. . .] When we are exercised and sharpened in these matters, we are able to receive and learn more important and significant material more quickly and easily. [. . .] I call such activity a "mental gymnastics" and a "preparation for philosophy." (*Antidosis* 265–66)

The point, then, of taking up and working through seemingly impractical subjects was to develop a kind of disposition or capacity of thought. As long as the subjects are difficult enough to require persistence, focus, and precise thinking from the students who learn them, they are worthwhile undertakings.[21]

---

21. Isocrates elaborates this point again in *Panathenaicus* 26–29.

Isocrates's most advanced students were also engaged in a pedagogical process whose objective was to develop their capacities to encounter the future. As Takis Poulakos argues, Isocrates focused on developing eloquent and wise citizen subjects who possessed the ability to "meet contingent occasions with good judgments and to resolve indeterminate situations through successful conjectures" ("Isocrates' Civic Education" 45). The purpose of rhetorical pedagogy, then, was to help students cultivate the capacity to assess complex political and rhetorical situations and to come to reasoned decisions about how to proceed, even when—especially when—the associated outcomes were unclear. Those who develop such capacities through *philosophia*, Isocrates argues in *Panathenaicus*, "can form an accurate judgment (*doxa*) about a situation (*kairos*) and in most cases figure out (*stochazesthai*) what is the best course of action (*to sympheron*)" (30). Poulakos refers to these faculties as "equipment for civic life" (45), an apt phrase that, with its Burkean intonations, emphasizes Isocrates's desire to parlay students' work with admirable texts into the adaptable and open-ended ability to respond well to whatever may come.

Because of this expansive view of the scope and value of rhetorical pedagogy, Isocrates is quick to criticize those rival rhetoric teachers whose conception of the discipline is so narrow as to reduce rhetoric to a set of rules and repeatable forms. Railing against their "boasts with too little caution" and their "easy promises" (*Against* 1, 16), he chastises those lesser sophists for teaching their students generalized forms and rote methods for writing speeches. Although "they promise to make their students such good orators that they will miss none of the possibilities in their cases," he says, "they say that the science of speeches is like teaching the alphabet" (9–10). In this way, Isocrates insists, they instill in their students a profound inflexibility because just as "the function of letters is unchanging and remains the same" (12), rhetorical rules and methods are merely wielded unchanging in all circumstances. As Isocrates puts it, "[These teachers] fail to notice that they are using an ordered art [. . .] as a model for a creative activity" (12). What teachers such as these are unable to communicate to their students is that "what is said by one person is not useful in a similar way for the next speaker" (12) and that a truer objective of rhetorical training is to be able to "discover things to say that are entirely different from what others have said" (12). Thus, Isocrates educates his students broadly, giving them experience in subjects he admits are not strictly useful, and putting them through difficult paces that transform the shape of their being. A good orator is made, he says, "if a person surrenders himself not to those who make easy promises" (16), but to the one whose promise maintains an open relation with the future. While his rival teachers are content to focus primarily on templates that could be applied in every circumstance, Isocrates's rhetorical pedagogy is aimed at helping students become capable of rhetorical virtuosity.

This educational philosophy begins to show us that, although Isocrates was interested in familiarizing his students with noble themes and honorable texts, he was also interested in the transformative effects of working through them. In fact, it seems as though the content itself—including the moral ideals found in the texts Isocrates preferred—takes a back seat to this active endeavor of working through. This is why Isocrates often and across multiple treatises compares his *logon paideia* with athletic training, which, as Hawhee has argued, featured methods and approaches borrowed and adapted by teachers of rhetoric, not least of all Isocrates, who posits, she says, "deep connections between the two kinds of training practices" ("Bodily Pedagogies" 145). Grounding his approach in what Hawhee calls the "three Rs of sophistic pedagogy—rhythm, repetition, and response" (145), Isocrates required his students to learn, repeatedly practice, and thus acquire rhetorical strategies they could then "use in response to particular situations" (152). Isocrates required his students to exercise their minds in the same way that gymnastics required them to exercise their bodies, and thus the term "mental gymnastics" takes on a positive, enabling connotation.

The most important thing that Isocrates offered his students was not a curriculum replete with praiseworthy and principled texts; rather, it was a series of practices (including, yes, the study of these moral texts) that ultimately changed who his students were. What's interesting here is that for Isocrates—who seems to be (along with Bill Bennett, perhaps) the ultimate conservative moralist—the single most important educational goal was to help his students become different, more capable people than they were when they entered his program. The single most important educational goal, that is, was to help them become *other*.

Who are these others? Who emerges on the other side of Isocrates's rhetorical training? On the one hand, Isocrates knows exactly who they are, or at least he says so. He claims that they are rhetorically, ethically, and politically astute citizens; they are a credit to Athenian democracy and their actions a benefit to its people. But on the other hand, Isocrates does not know them at all, and he cannot even imagine who they might be. He can never know for sure the precise choices and actions that ultimately amount to this rhetorical acumen. This is because, long after his students have left Isocrates's concerned and attentive tutelage, they alone must make their rhetorical, ethical, and political decisions. The best Isocrates can hope for is that he has helped develop in them the *capacity* to respond to the infinite rhetorical and political demands that come their way. It may be impossible to teach students everything they'll ever need to know, but what we can do—and what Isocrates claims to do—is train students to be able to respond capably to those situations we cannot foresee.

In this we can see a certain (although not yet complete) loosening of the deliberative, future-oriented structure so important to Isocrates's claims for the significance of his pedagogy. Even as he promises to reinstall today's culturally entrenched values tomorrow, Isocrates remains, in the end, open to what Derrida calls in the passage from "'Le Parjure,' Perhaps," "the unsublatable thickness of time and of what it transforms" (173). Despite their natural-born virtue, that is, the students whom Isocrates promises to fashion precisely *do not* remain the same in moment B as they were when they began, in moment A. And if Derrida's perjurer seeks to excuse himself by having been "surpassed" by time, Isocrates's well-trained students will have developed the capacity to capably respond to time's "multiplicity" and "discontinuity" (173). But such a capacity can only come by way of an absolute rupture of the integral, orderly, and virtuous self that Isocrates posits as essential to the success of his developmental program. Far from being a flaw in Isocrates's venerated discipline of discourse, as I will suggest in what follows, this rupture is precisely what makes ethical responsibility possible.

RESPONDING TO THE FUTURE-TO-COME

> When they [intelligent people] deliberate about something, they should not assume that they know (*eidenai*) what will happen, but they should think about such matters aware that they are relying on their best judgment (*doxa*) and that the future depends on chance (*tychē*).
>
> —ISOCRATES, ON THE PEACE, 8[22]

For someone who stakes his entire pedagogical and intellectual legacy on his ability to prepare students to ethically and effectively lead the polis in the future, Isocrates has quite a bit to say about the impossibility of knowing what is to come. As he suggests in the above selection from *On the Peace*, the future cannot be anticipated and even sound judgment can be undone by chance. Against such a backdrop, the task of deliberative oratory is to address contingency with as much reason and discernment as possible. And yet, because

---

22. Section numbers for *On the Peace* refer to the translation by Terry L. Papillon, *Isocrates II*, U of Texas P, 2004, pp. 134–66.

human deliberation meets its limit on the threshold of chance, even the most well-reasoned arguments and carefully considered decisions involve no small amount of risk. In this respect, Isocrates reveals himself to be something of a gambler: The same teacher who guarantees that his students will be a benefit to the polis in the future insists time and again that we cannot possibly know what lies ahead. This impossibility, furthermore, bears importantly on the present moment in that it initiates profoundly disruptive effects within Isocrates's educational paradigm. In unsettling the unity of identity (and thus the possibility of something like innate virtue) as well as the belief that conservative moral prescriptions will have relevance in the future, this disruption requires an expropriating response to otherness. And this response not only goes beyond the application of a rule or a moral code; it also exceeds Isocrates's most significant pedagogical promise, the internalized capacity to respond well to contingency.

On more than one occasion, Isocrates makes the argument that the future cannot be known. He accentuates this point in part to object to some of his rivals' teaching methods and to separate them from his own. As I outlined in the previous section, because these rivals rely on a rules-based pedagogy that ultimately instills in students a profound inflexibility, they remove rhetoric from its responsive milieu and posit it as a universal set of principles residing above specific events and situations. Unlike Isocrates, who encourages students to attend to the particulars and complexities of a given situation, these teachers merely provide rhetorical forms and rules, which they assume can be effectively deployed as though there were no circumstances capable of escaping the preexisting conventions. And so when Isocrates takes his rivals to task for "*pretend*[*ing*] *to know the future* [. . . and persuading] the young that if they study with them they will know what they need to do and through this knowledge they will become happy" (*Against* 7, 3, emphasis added), he reiterates his belief that no body of knowledge, no set of rules, no handbook of rhetorical forms could possibly account for contingency.

Yet the future Isocrates describes exceeds even these pedagogical and conceptual distinctions. We see an instance of this in *Against the Sophists*, in which Isocrates argues:

> I think it clear to all that it is not in our nature to know in advance what is going to happen. We fall so far short of this intelligence that Homer, who enjoys the highest reputation for wisdom, has written that the gods sometimes debate about the future—not because he knows their thoughts but because he wants to show us that this one thing (i.e., knowledge of the future) is impossible for human beings. (2)

There is, on the one hand, a simple practicality to these claims. In the most traditional understanding of chronological time—where past, present, and future are ordered points on a straight line—we cannot know the nature or outcome of events that lie before us. This is precisely why Isocrates values rhetorical responsiveness and capacity over forms and rules, and it is in keeping with his larger disagreement with Plato about the value and availability of exact knowledge. But here Isocrates articulates a future so boundlessly unfathomable that even his own deliberative educational and civic goals would seem to be at risk. Even as he insists that his vision for rhetorical education better prepares students to respond to what is to come, that is, he nonetheless suggests that the future is beyond the human capacities of knowledge and expectation. Further, while he points to this necessary ignorance about what is to come, he also hints at a *beyond* of this epistemological limit, gesturing toward an event that is not simply unknown (as in, yet to be known), but that is in excess of knowledge itself. The passage above from *Against the Sophists* suggests that knowledge of the future is doubly elusive, giving the slip to both humans and the gods. Escaping human comprehension and divine control, the future Isocrates describes is uniquely unmasterable—off the chronological axis altogether and beyond the horizon of knowledge itself.

From this perspective, Isocrates's educational promise seems quite lofty, indeed. How does one prepare students to respond ably to something that can neither be understood nor foreseen? How does one develop in another the capacity to respond ably to a future defined by its radical unaccountability? For Isocrates, the answer is to offer students a training in *kairos*, which, as Phillip Sipiora has argued, is *the* principle on which Isocrates's discipline of discourse is structured (7). Positing that "Isocrates' most important historical contribution [...] is his articulation of the critical importance of *kairos* in rhetorical theory and practice" (7), Sipiora explains that *kairos* permeates nearly every aspect of Isocrates's thinking, from the public to the private realms (10–14). It is a central element, furthermore, of Isocrates's educational promise, which provides students with a training in how to flexibly respond to the unique moment at hand. A touchstone concept in the history of rhetoric—particularly the work of the sophists—*kairos* refers to an oration's timeliness, appropriateness, and contextual responsivity. Effective orators understand the inventive power of *kairos*, which requires them to align content, style, and delivery with the external contingencies that comprise the "opportune moment."[23] Throughout *Against the Sophists*, Isocrates argues that what sep-

---

23. My discussion of *kairos* zeroes in on the concept's chronologically disruptive aspects as well as its resistance to knowledge, but a wealth of scholarly research addresses the historical development and rich conceptual nuances of the term. See, for example, Chapter 2 of Janet

arates truly good speeches from those that his rivals taught their students to compose is that the good ones suitably respond to the circumstances in which they emerge. His educational model is designed, he says, in order that students' "views (*doxai*) may be better adapted to the right moments (*kairoi*)" (*Antidosis* 184). And yet these "right moments," Isocrates understands, are ultimately impossible to grasp. Even though he insists that with time and guided practice, students will become better able to appropriately respond to these kairotic moments, he nevertheless concedes that, "It is not possible to learn this [*kairos*] through study, since in all activities, these opportune moments elude exact knowledge (*episteme*)" (184).

As a qualitative rather than quantitative measure of time, *kairos* cannot be assumed to "take place" in the typical sense. Not subject to any identifiable logic or numeric principle (such as the logic that helps us organize and understand *chronos*) *kairos* can only be understood as a singular event—bound by no calendar and proceeding according to no predictable schedule. Emphasizing this unpredictability, Eric Charles White argues that *kairos* requires "a conception of temporality according to which the flow of time is understood as a succession of *discontinuous* occasions rather than as duration or historical continuity" (4, emphasis added). "Instead of viewing the present occasion as continuous with a causally related sequence of events," he adds, "*kairos* regards the present as unprecedented, as a moment of decision, a moment of crisis" (4). Characterized by its discontinuity, *kairos* interrupts the deliberative structure of Isocrates's educational paradigm. His promise to produce eloquent and upright citizen subjects, that is, has a somewhat predictable schedule: After the typical three to four years under Isocrates's tutelage, students emerge better able to virtuously intervene in public life. In this way, the educational promise relies on a conceptual space that is, chronologically speaking, somewhere ahead in the distance. In the interest of keeping this schedule, however, Isocrates must develop in his students the capacity to respond to *kairos*, which carries with it a disruptive charge. Off the calendar and incapable of being reduced to knowledge, *kairos* demands a response to an unprecedented event. The significance here is that, while Isocrates seems to be primarily committed to a deliberative future—a future with a content yet unknown but with an identifiable location on the chronological horizon—in fact, his more profound concern is with this kairotic future, which has the potential to unhinge deliberative movement altogether.

Atwill's *Rhetoric Reclaimed*, Chapter 3 of Hawhee's *Bodily Arts*, Chapter 2 of John Poulakos's *Sophistical Rhetoric in Classical Greece*, Dale Sullivan's "Kairos and the Rhetoric of Belief," Eric Charles White's *Kaironomia: On the Will-to-Invent*, and Phillip Sipiora and James S. Baumlin's edited collection *Rhetoric and Kairos: Essays in History, Theory and Praxis*.

Given the unprecedented nature of the kairotic moment, as well as the simultaneous discontinuity and demand *kairos* introduces into the persuasive scene, we get a sense of the difficulty and delicacy involved in responding ably to the opportune moment. Isocrates's own insistence on the ineffability of *kairos* suggests that the complementary activities of teaching and learning this complex skill are high-wire acts in which the slightest hesitation or misstep results in disastrous rhetorical effects. We can never know when the right moment will arrive, and its possibility is given by its discordance with the chronological moment in which we happen to find it. The best we can hope for is to be able to grasp after it (for it can never be finally grasped)—and to respond to it appropriately—in the impossible instant of its appearance. Noting that *kairos* cannot be "limited to a seat of reason or conscious adherence to a set of precepts," Hawhee suggests that the response to the kairotic moment exceeds the bounds of subjective mastery (*Bodily Arts* 70). Responding to *kairos*, she elaborates, does not "require the 'rhetor'—a discreet, rational being—to decode a 'rhetorical situation' from outside (step one), and then consciously select or create 'appropriate' arguments (step two)" (78). Instead, she argues, "*kairos* provides a point of departure from reasoned, linear steps—even from consciousness" (78). Thus, responding to *kairos* requires not a calculating, masterful rhetorical agent, but instead, a subject who surrenders to the coming of an unprecedented and unpredictable moment. Because of its unpredictability, its discordance with the chronological moment in which it arrives, and its unknowability, *kairos* interrupts the deliberative subject. It requires an encounter with an event cut away from any conscious moral code, however powerfully instilled it may be.

Given Isocrates's adamant claims about the future's ambiguity along with his insistence that *kairos* is beyond comprehension, it may seem counterintuitive for him to so confidently guarantee the future benefit of his pedagogical design. It is precisely the future's radical unaccountability, however, that requires Isocrates's educational promise and gives rise to it in the first place. If it were a given that his pedagogical philosophy engendered civic virtue and rhetorical virtuosity and so elevated the quality of life for all citizens, then Isocrates would not have to so thoroughly make the case that he makes. He would not have to claim so explicitly that his methods yield exclusively beneficial results. With a certain elegant simplicity, this is what Derrida has suggested in general about promises, which he says are always "haunted or threatened by the possibility of being broken or of being bad" ("A Certain Impossible" 459). For a promise to be what it is, Derrida notes, it must from the outset be exposed to all that could go wrong. If the promise is not capable of being broken or going utterly awry, in other words, it is not a promise—

not a performative speech act through which a subject commits herself—but a descriptive statement in which the person offering up the description is not implicated in any substantive way.

As we have seen, Isocrates takes responsibility for any and all instances of his students' failure to live up to his lofty ideals, and so his promise makes him vulnerable; it involves him in an ultimately uncontrollable confrontation with chance. Beyond these considerations of reputation and personal standing, Isocrates's promise risks something even more valuable: the rigorously trained student capable of putting his innate virtue, well-honed moral literacy, and carefully developed rhetorical acuity to work for the good of the polis. In other words, the very thing Isocrates has been promising his hearers all along. This is because, in affirming the future's radical unaccountability, Isocrates installs a temporal heterogeneity at the heart of his otherwise linear developmental model. All claims for a progressive educational process come unhinged when they are interrupted from the start by a future that can neither be anticipated nor mastered. Thus, we begin to see a more radical account of the future inhabit Isocrates's discourse on teaching and learning. It is this emphasis on *kairos*, I want to suggest, that makes Isocrates a more progressive figure than even the most generous readings of his pedagogical and political interventions indicate. And it is here, I believe, that we begin to see Isocrates's discussion of ethics interrupt his better-known commentary on virtue.

To get a sense of the effect that this kairotic future has on Isocrates's rhetorical pedagogy (and what this ultimately tells us about the students who undertake it), it is helpful to consider Derrida's distinction between the traditional teleological notion of the future and *l'avenir*—the future-to-come. While the former is predictable, scheduled, and programmed, the future-to-come refers to an arrival that, though imminent, is totally unexpected and unpredictable. I may not know what will happen tomorrow, but I have a clear understanding of when tomorrow will arrive as well as a sense of myself as a subject in relation to it. The future-to-come, by contrast, is pure event; it is beyond comprehension and has nothing whatsoever to do with knowledge. Not just some measurable distance off, it is an untimely interruption, indeed, a future anterior that, Derrida says, "is in me before me" (Derrida and Ferraris 84). The future-to-come overflows all ontological determination, and this means that, to borrow Derrida's phrase, "I am not proprietor of my 'I'" (85). Instead I am interrupted in advance by the future I cannot know, and originarily marked by something that is nevertheless not present.

What Derrida is especially helpful for here is demonstrating that the future-to-come, because it is beyond the axis of knowledge, fractures self-presence. It breaks it open from the inside, simultaneously constituting it and making it impossible. If Isocrates is serious when he says that *kairos* is not subject to study because it eludes exact knowledge, then we have to consider its interruptive capacity as well. Indeed, we have to consider the way that it unhinges the deliberative structure of his educational promise, compromising, too, the unity of the well-born subject who possesses Isocrates's coveted natural ability. Derived from the Greek verb *keirein*, which means to cut or shear, *kairos* rives self-presence. It cuts through our experience of ordered, chronological time, and what it announces is that the incalculable future (indeed, the arrival of the other) is not only imminent (as in "impending") but immanent (as in "inherent"). What it means to be "me" is to be perpetually disturbed by the other. My existence is structured by the inevitable arrival of what I cannot know, and thus "to come" is not simply some distance off. It is here, now, always interrupting what I take to be my present.

As I suggested earlier in this chapter, Isocrates is a nuanced and complicated thinker of deliberative rhetoric, committed to deliberation on multiple levels, on both the large and small scale. He claims that the students he sends into the public arena will lead the city with their sound deliberative rhetoric. Because of their upright characters and their sustained encounters with moral texts (often well-respected deliberative speeches), they will not participate in self-interested forensic or courtroom speaking, which was Athenian democracy's dark underbelly and the shame of rhetorical study. Furthermore, as I have stressed throughout, Isocrates's description of his educational program is deliberative in structure: He claims that his unique approach to training students yields a larger, civic benefit in the future. This description in turn takes the form of a promise that must maintain an open relation to the future, which Isocrates understands well cannot be predicted. But when Isocrates adds *kairos* to his already complicated thinking of deliberation, he threatens the forward moving link between past and future.

Traditionally understood, deliberation implies consciousness. When we deliberate, we weigh things in our minds, in full view of the present, so that we might make the best decisions. We proceed as though our present thoughts authorize our future actions, and we assume they maintain a link, however speculative, across time and space. This is what Isocrates seems to have in mind when he carefully grounds his pedagogical model in natural ability and conservative moral values, and when he argues that this model is a benefit to the city. But as I have argued, Isocrates is preoccupied by the way the radically unknowable future interrupts being in the present. And if this being is interrupted, then there can be no consistent causal relationship between rhetorical planning and rhetorical effect. The future disrupts the present, and in this movement, deliberation in its traditional sense (the sense that views deliberation as an *effect* of consciousness) comes undone. There is no way in which present consciousness is carried forward into future action because present consciousness has always been disturbed by the future's radical unknowability. And because being is perpetually disrupted in this way, deliberations can no longer be thought to belong to any particular person or subject, no matter how carefully this person has prepared for what might come.

This is a difficult responsibility to and for the unknowable future, and it constitutes a simultaneous self-interruption and necessity of action that Derrida has discussed in terms of the decision. Just as Isocrates figures *kairos* as the elusive untimely moment that disrupts being and consciousness, Derrida shows us that the decision always belongs to the other, even if this other is located in the heart of subjectivity itself. "Decision and responsibility," Derrida argues, "always come back or come down to the other, from the other, even if it is the other in me" (*Adieu* 23). What this means is that even though our decisions seem to be ours alone, the very uncertainty that requires a decision in the first place will have interrupted being from the start. Not simply prior to and unaffected by the decision, our being is constituted by the future's interruption (and thus the future is no longer simply what's ahead; the future is the constitutive otherness that haunts being itself). What it means to be responsible, then, is to be utterly compromised in the face of the other, and 'to decide' is to suffer what Derrida calls a "tearing rupture" that pierces our seemingly coherent subjectivity (24).

We can claim no sovereign ownership, then, of our decisions and deliberations, and we find that we are utterly compromised in their making. But none of this means that we are excused from responsibility, none of this means that it doesn't matter what we do. We must act, and we must act to the best of our abilities, with the singular demands of the situation in mind. Even though we cannot know the future, Isocrates insists that his students should "spend time acquiring intelligence as quickly as possible" (*Antidosis* 271)—indeed, they should spend time attending carefully to their individual situations. Similarly, Derrida argues that prior to the decision, one must accumulate as much knowledge and intelligence as possible. Because there is no single method that can help one decide in the face of this unknowability, the individual circumstances of each event must always be closely considered.

And yet what is crucial about the decision for Derrida is precisely Isocrates's point that *kairos,* by definition, eludes exact knowledge. For a decision to "take place" (and once again, we cannot assume that it actually "takes place"), there must be a radical break from the intelligence gathering that seems to lead up to it. All of the information and consideration leading up to the decision must be of an entirely different order from the decision itself. This means that all of the research, all of the weighing of available options, and all of the soul-searching that comes prior to making important life choices are not causally linked to the decision itself. It means that there is a radical separation between the decision and the interpretive operations that occur prior to it. Thus the decision—even though it requires careful consideration and reasoning—always involves an irrecoverable risk: "One has to calculate as far as possible," Derrida argues, "but the incalculable happens [*arrive*]: it is the other, and singularity, and chance" (Derrida and Ferraris 61). What we do in the moment of decision, then, is make the ultimate wager. We give ourselves over to the infinite. The self dissolves, and reason and calculation fall away. What we find in the moment of decision is that "the space of rationality can be totally invaded by or surrendered to what we call the incalculable, chance, the other, the event" (61).

The nonprogrammable response to *kairos*, then, always involves a two-fold risk. Not only is it impossible to know what is to come, but in the face of the radical otherness of *kairos*, the self is utterly compromised. For all of the danger we are exposed to here, it would seem that we were due some resolution on the other side. Given what we must endure on the front end of rhetorical responsibility, that is, it would be nice to know after the fact if our responses have been just. But we are never afforded this sense of relief. Justice is incalculable, impossible, and unbounded; it always keeps us waiting. Its condition of possibility, as Derrida says in *Specters of Marx*, is the "*non-contemporaneity with itself of the living present*" (xix), and so the interruptive temporality of *kairos* is what leaves open the possibility of justice and gives it its chance. This is the case because, if there is to be any justice (and this is never a guarantee), it must arise from an active responsibility to alterity and *not* from an existing moral code or rhetorical method that would claim to guarantee it in advance. Such codes and methods eliminate the need for the decision. They do not require a vigilant responsibility to the unknowable "to come," and their application allows the self to remain unchanged in the encounter with what is beyond knowledge.

Justice, then, is always a risk. It can neither be guaranteed in advance of a decision nor confirmed after the fact. It requires that in the moment of response, the one who seems to be making conscious decisions undergoes a radical separation from reason. If we were able to apply a method or rely on a moral code—both principles that would tell us how to act in any given case—we would not be relating or attending to the particulars of the situation. We would simply be implementing a predetermined and repeatable set of instructions that could not account for the unique qualities of each individual event. In this sense, the application of a method or code is unresponsive, irresponsible.

Because these kairotic moments, as both Isocrates and Derrida argue, elude exact knowledge, they interrupt chronology and unhinge our traditional notions and experiences of time. By virtue of this radical cutting through and across time, *kairos* disrupts being as full presence. It subjects it to its always imminent arrival and renders it impossible. Even when human nature is understood in the most traditional guise of Isocrates, who famously suggests that one's character is prior to "mere words," it is always in response. No one insists on this responsibility more strenuously than Isocrates himself, who develops an entire pedagogical philosophy around training students in the capacity to respond to the unforeseeable future. This emphasis on responsibility is a rejection of rhetorical method. Indeed, Isocrates deems rhetorical rules inattentive to the situations that are always to come. They are a closing off of the future and precisely the way to avoid an encounter with the unknowable other.

Because Isocrates figures *kairos* as an interruption of conscious knowledge and of being itself, he suggests that no set of moral principles could finally authorize or deem any particular deliberative action as just. Decisions are not owned by subjects; they are not grounded in methods or moral codes. Because *kairos* necessitates decision in those instances of utter undecidability, it undercuts the intelligible or causal relation between moral education and subsequent virtuous civic action. What Isocrates shows us, then, is that justice requires an openness to the unknowable future and that *this openness requires training*—it is not simply the case. We must actively work to transform our dispositions and our abilities to be receptive; we must do all of the work that undecidability would seem to render unnecessary. This is our responsibility to responsibility. Isocrates's own future, then—his speculative value to a field now reappraising him at a time when his insights are most needed—should not simply be based on his interest in the capacity of rhetorical pedagogy to develop civic virtue. Rather, it should lie in his insistence that ethics interrupts virtue, that it cannot be reduced to it, and that it is always involved in a risky movement toward alterity.

CONCLUSION: ISOCRATES'S GAMBLE

Because Isocrates is so attuned to the immeasurable gamble of ethics and justice, there may yet be a way to tie him to his modern analogue, William J. Bennett. Initially I challenged the link (posited by Poulakos and Depew), arguing that such a reclamation strategy ultimately tied Isocrates too tightly to a past and put rhetoric in service to the values situated there. But in Isocrates's obsession with unknowable futurity, alongside his attempts to transform his students' (ultimately compromised) being over their doing, I see a heightened attempt to account for unaccountable contingency. Isocrates helps me see, that is, that any kind of moral educational program has an uncontainable element of risk built in. It is structured by this risk and also disturbed in the face of it. This, too, is the case for Bennett, even if he doesn't realize it, because there is no possibility of guaranteeing virtue in the face of radical alterity.

Moral education, then, conservative as it may seem, is one of the riskiest propositions going. On the surface, such an educational model would seem to attempt to reproduce a past: Both Bennett and Isocrates claim to instill important virtues *today* so they may be taken up and reinstalled *tomorrow* (and these virtues are often uncontested and oriented toward maintaining the status quo for the empowered). But this deliberative, future-oriented structure is always already disrupted; it is simultaneously designed for and disturbed by radical unknowability. Decisions are never finally owned by the people who could be said to make them because presence and consciousness are perpetually interrupted by a future that is, in Derrida's words, "absolutely non-reappropriable" (Derrida and Ferraris 21). Perhaps, then, it shouldn't have been as surprising as it was when reports of Bennett's multimillion-dollar gambling habit shocked (and, let's face it, *delighted*) the masses who knew him best for his lectures on virtue, his loud condemnations of personal weaknesses, and his insistence that American culture was too permissive about indulging its own appetites. But when the *Washington Monthly*'s Joshua Green and *Newsweek*'s Jonathan Alter reported that Bennett had lost an estimated $8 million on the slots and video poker machines in Las Vegas and Atlantic City from 1993 to 2003, columnists and talking heads around the country responded with a spate of gleeful commentaries that might best be summed up in a single word: "Gotcha." Green cleverly titled his *Washington Monthly* entry "The Bookie of Virtue," while *Slate*'s Michael Kinsley noted that "sinners have long cherished the fantasy that William Bennett, the virtue magnate, might be among our number."

Beyond the obvious schadenfreude, however, I think we have something to gain from the revelation of Bennett's high rolling. If we think about Isocrates's interest in futurity and chance alongside Bennett's predilection for wagering millions on spinning reels and five-card draw, we might discover an unexpected affinity between the two conservative moralists. And what's more, this affinity might tell us something about moral education and deliberative action itself. The so-called morality czar was, in the end, a compulsive gambler, and what's most interesting about this is that those two identities are not necessarily at odds. On the clock, he devised moral educational policy, he spoke to eager audiences about the virtues he believed would strengthen American culture, and he fervently espoused a conservative political agenda grounded in these same ideals. Off the clock, he played $500-a-pull slots in the exclusive high-limit rooms of Bellagio Las Vegas and Caesars Boardwalk Regency (Alter and Green). Despite the surprise elicited by the news of Bennett's habit, there's a remarkable consistency across these seemingly divergent activities: Both involve a movement toward radical otherness and a dispersal of the self in this movement. Perhaps, then, it's not an accident or an instance of hypocrisy that the virtue maven is also a gambler. Moral education is always a dice throw. Though it seems to be grounded in virtue and invested in the reproduction of the same, it must give its students—and virtue itself—over to sheer unpredictability, and its deliberative movement is disturbed when presence is retroactively pierced by the unknowable future.

When he was contacted by Alter and Green for comment on their story, Bennett did not deny the claims—supported by casino documents and other sources—that he was a "preferred customer." Instead he defended his practices as harmful to no one and not beyond his considerable resources (virtue, after all, had been quite lucrative for Bennett). "I don't play the 'milk money,'" he said. "I don't put my family at risk" (Alter and Green). More interesting than his main defense, though, was the way Bennett characterized his play and his identity as a gambler. Alter and Green quote Bennett as saying: "I've been a machine person. When I go to the tables, people talk—and they want to talk about politics. I don't want that. I do this for three hours to relax." It would seem, then, that Bennett preferred to keep his games of chance separate: Deliberative politics and conservative moralizing during the day, and video poker and high-limit slots at night. One may be more relaxing than the other (with slots, it would seem, you get all of the chance with none of the decision), but it's risky business all around.

I don't know if Isocrates wagered his tuition earnings in some ancient backroom game of dice, but I know he was a gambler. With his rhetorical pedagogical design, he wagered time and again what seemed to be most important to him: the conservative moral values he attempted to instill in his students. Although he clearly articulated these values in *Antidosis*, *To Demonicus*, and *Against the Sophists*, he argued in those very pieces that the content of these value claims must take a back seat to his students' active working through texts that feature them. Furthermore, Isocrates risked the security—the very ground—of these conservative values by acknowledging that, in and of themselves, they might not be enough to take students into the unknowable future.

No particular content, he argued, could ever prepare students for the unknowable to come. And even when he had successfully transformed his students' *being* over their *doing* (the transformation that I've argued was his ultimate educational goal), he suggested that this being was haunted by the radical unknowability of *kairos*. Isocrates, in other words, played only the highest stakes. He wagered the thing he seemed to hold most dear—virtue—for the chance of ethics, for an openness to otherness that puts both subjectivity and moral ground at risk. We can see this openness to contingency in Isocrates's edict, "Let no one think that I mean that a sense of justice is teachable; I contend that there is no sort of art that can convert those who by nature lack virtue to soundness of mind and a sense of justice" (*Against* 21). Here, Isocrates seems to acknowledge that his entire educational undertaking—the thing on which he built his career and his reputation—comes with no guarantee. He seems to acknowledge that justice is always a risk. No *thing* in and of itself, justice is at best a "sense" beyond reason. It cannot be reduced to a set of constative morals or guaranteed by a set of rhetorical methods. No matter how much Isocrates might like to contain it, then, it is this uncontainable risk that is the best chance for justice.

CHAPTER 5

Plato's Friendship

> I don't even know in what way one person becomes a friend of another.
> —Socrates, to Lysis and Menexenus, in Plato, *Lysis*, 212A[1]

> Let us dream of a friendship which goes beyond this proximity of the congeneric double, beyond parenthood, the most as well as the least natural of parenthoods, when it leaves its signature, from the outset, on the name as on a double mirror of such a couple. Let us ask ourselves what would then be the politics of such a "beyond the principle of fraternity."
> —Jacques Derrida, *Politics of Friendship*, VIII

I argued in the previous chapter that Isocrates understands learning as the quintessential risk-taking activity: Learning occurs only as an expropriating encounter with alterity in which the self is transformed, and the purpose of his pedagogical design (precarious though it may be) is to provide a training in and a preparation for this ultimately incalculable experience. What I will contend here is that Plato's dialogue *Lysis* communicates a similar, if somewhat surprising view about persuasion and its relation to learning. Ostensibly about friendship, the *Lysis* also suggests (by way of a Socratic demonstration) that the calculated art of persuasion initiates a certain experience of the impossible in which mastery and self-identification are disturbed. What emerges from the dialogue, in other words, is an account of friendship that is essentially tied to an iterable address—an address that installs difference in the heart of every other who would be called a friend.

One of the founding texts on the concept of friendship in the Western philosophical tradition, Plato's *Lysis* was long read, at best, as "one of those earlier dialogues where Plato's thought still moves within the ambit of his Socratic heritage" (Vlastos 6)—or, in other words, as an immature version of the *Phaedrus* or the *Symposium*. At worst, it was a "failure [of] method and

---

1. Section numbers for *Lysis* refer to the translation by Terry Penner and Christopher Rowe, Cambridge UP, 2009.

presentation" (Guthrie 143) because it introduces and considers notions of friendship and love without developing a precise or incisive theory of either. By this reasoning, it "appears to make no positive contribution to the Greek tradition on friendship" (Glidden 39), and even efforts to cast the dialogue as a success often did so by extrapolating beyond the *Lysis* and connecting it to the more carefully developed Theory of Forms.[2] Fittingly, from these perspectives, the dialogue ends in failure, with Socrates deeming himself and his fellow conversationalists "ridiculous" for not having been able to discover the meaning of friendship (223b).

Scholarship over the past three decades, however, rejects this narrative of failure by reading the dialogue more generously and opening it up to a variety of critical and analytical approaches.[3] Among other recent texts that engage the *Lysis* in this manner, the most comprehensive is, perhaps, Terry Penner and Christopher Rowe's book-length translation and analysis, *Plato's* Lysis. Their project, which goes to great lengths to treat the literary and dramatic elements of the dialogue as carefully as the philosophical ones, concludes that the *Lysis* "pursues a single line of argument from beginning to end" and offers up a theory not just of friendship, love, and desire, but of "what drives our actions in general" (xii). Seeing this single line of argument is vital, Penner and Rowe say, to grasping the nuanced whole of the *Lysis,* rather than its often-confounding parts, and to understanding why the readings of so many "modern interpreters [. . .] tend to run into the sand, taking the dialogue along with them" (xiii). Mary P. Nichols and Catherine H. Zuckert likewise see the *Lysis* as a rich resource for theorizing not just friendship and love but philosophy itself. Nichols, in *Socrates on Friendship and Community,* seeks to "recover the place of friendship and community in Socratic philosophizing as an antidote to the alienating aspects of modern thought" (2). She argues that the "twofold character of friendship"—a relationship that blurs distinctions between self and other—is analogous to the experience of philosophy: The other simultaneously reveals our need for wisdom (when we experience our own as other) and makes gaining that wisdom seem possible (when we experience an other as our own) (1). For Nichols, the *Lysis* shows us how the dynamics of friendship (the drive to attain friends, the reciprocity[4] needed to

---

2. See Glidden's account of K. Glaser's 1935 study on the *Lysis* in the German publication *Wiener Studien.*

3. See, for example, T. Brian Mooney's "Plato's Theory of Love in the 'Lysis': A Defence" for details of what he calls the reinstatement of the dialogue as an important Platonic work (134).

4. Nichols acknowledges that the relationship between the philosopher and truth is not, per se, reciprocal. Her point is that "philosophy must understand itself as a friend of wisdom" to avoid falling into a possibly alienating love for wisdom (155).

maintain community) relate to the pursuit of wisdom. "If the truth were in no way our own," she writes, "philosophy would not be possible. If the truth were in no way other, [. . .] philosophy would not be necessary" (154). Like Nichols, Zuckert incorporates her reading of *Lysis*, in *Plato's Philosophers*, into a larger argument about how studying the dialogues in their dramatic order can offer a more comprehensive understanding of Plato's ideas as they developed. Because "serious questions have been raised about the evidence" for the traditional chronology of composition of the dialogues (3), Zuckert reads the texts in an order based on what she calls their "dramatic dates," which she derives by using the "philological, philosophical, and archaeological work of many scholars" (9). This, she argues, allows us to more fully see what Plato is showing us: "And Plato only shows; he does not state or say anything in his own name" (7). Zuckert places the *Lysis* in the last decade of the fifth century BCE, rejecting the idea that it was an early (and thus immature) dialogue. What Plato shows us, she writes, when we read the dialogue in its dramatic context, is the "character of the philosophical friendship [Socrates] tried to form with younger men" as he tried to help them "acquire the kind of self-knowledge he himself was seeking" (530). Zuckert's analysis of the aporetic ending of the *Lysis*, like Nichols's, rejects the notion that the failed quest to define the friend means the dialogue itself is a failure. Rather, Zuckert writes, the conclusion "images the character of philosophy as a never-ending, essentially uncertain search" (512). Echoing Isocrates's notion of education as a series of encounters with the event, the *Lysis*, too, suggests that pedagogy is more a matter of disruptive defamiliarization than a process of acquiring knowledge.

Paul W. Ludwig, too, in "Without Foundations: Plato's 'Lysis' and Postmodern Friendship," sees the dialogue as a rich and vital source—in this case, for political theory—because it offers a platform for analyzing the "problem of foundations"[5] (the need for our rejection of stable, continuous conceptual edifices upon which to build) and because it "illuminat[es] an intimate aspect of the philosophic experience" as a whole (136). In his article, Ludwig addresses the tensions among ancient conceptions of civic friendship, modern liberals' determination that friendship falls in the private realm, and postmodern theories that erase the boundaries between these two camps. The *Lysis*, he argues, can help us understand how the "problem of foundations is intriguingly bound up with the problem of friendship" (134). Echoing Nichols's explanation of the "twofold character of friendship," Ludwig uses Derrida, Foucault, and others to map the public/private (foundational/anti-

---

5. Ludwig defines 'foundations' as a modern substitute for metaphysics, dating back to Descartes, and writes that "epistemology and ontology became the successor disciplines to metaphysics" (134).

foundational) tensions with which any theory of friendship must contend. To navigate these tensions, Ludwig focuses on the "ontological flexibility" (149) that Plato ascribes to Socrates in the *Lysis,* building an argument that is as much about philosophical method as it is about the dialogue itself. "Socrates appears to choose his foundational accounts opportunistically, letting the subject matter determine his ontology" and showing an instructive ability and willingness to adapt his approach (135). For Ludwig, Socrates seems positively postmodern in his "ontological and epistemological skepticism" of foundational questions surrounding friendship, but his willingness to adapt his approach to fit his needs "stands in contrast to the blanket application of foundational skepticism [. . .] in much postmodern theory" (135).[6] In the end, Ludwig presents this flexibility as a model for modern political theorists who wish, as he puts it, to moderate liberal individualism with civic friendship: "Swapping and alternating ontologies, although seemingly insouciant, would fulfill a dual purpose of keeping ontological dimensions in mind, while preventing ontology from prescribing political results" (148). For Ludwig, as for other recent scholars, the *Lysis* proves to be an especially valuable guide to gaining a fuller understanding of Plato's thinking on friendship and how those ideas can be applied in a variety of ethical, educational, and political settings.

Productive readings like these recall Derrida's claim, even if implicitly, that the only way to approach what we might call ethics is to first undertake a passage through *aporia,* an experience of the impossible that "surprise[s] both the freedom and the will of every subject" (*Politics of Friendship* 68). As the authors above have begun to suggest, we get a glimpse of such surprise, I believe, in Plato's aporetic dialogues, which depict Socrates putting his interlocuters through an elenctic questioning that ultimately reveals their shared understanding of the central topic to be unsatisfactory. The purpose of this subversion of will is ultimately a pedagogical one: Socrates hopes to instill in his conversational partners a desire for further philosophical investigation. And so, when in the *Lysis* Socrates declares to Lysis and Menexenus at the end of their conversation that "we've made ourselves ridiculous" (223b), when he compares their endeavor to "something soft and smooth and slippery" (216c5), and when, seemingly exasperated, he asks them, "What use, then, could we still make of our argument?" (222e1), we are witness to their encounter with an impasse that has disturbed whatever comfortable feelings of mastery they may have entertained prior to the encounter.

---

6. Including, he argues, in the work of Derrida specifically (144).

Like Penner and Rowe, Nichols, Zuckert, Ludwig, and others, I believe these aporetic pronouncements make the *Lysis* a valuable resource. What I hope to add to this conversation is that this often-perplexing dialogue has as much to offer rhetoric as it does philosophy. The *Lysis* has, in fact, already sparked some interest in this regard. Eugene Garver examines the rhetorical significance of the dialogue in his essay "The Rhetoric of Friendship in Plato's *Lysis*," arguing that it "dramatizes the rhetorical nature of commitment" (127) by exploring the often-strained relationship between being a friend and being able to articulate what it means to be a friend. This "rhetorical problem of friendship" (128) is characterized, Garver says, by Hippothales (in love but unable to talk about it) and Socrates (outside of love but able to recognize, understand, and speak about it). "The paradox of the inarticulate lover and the articulate theoretician of love sets the *Lysis* apart from other dialogues," Garver writes (129). So, too, I argue does the dialogue's underlying claim about the limits of instrumental persuasion. Quite unlike *Gorgias*, that is, which casts rhetoric as a potentially dangerous instrument of power, and even unlike *Phaedrus*, which makes allowances for the use of rhetoric, but only in the service of dialectic, the *Lysis* frames persuasion as an interruptive encounter with difference in which both the speaker and the audience members are fundamentally disturbed.

Like *Phaedrus* in that it stages a scene of seduction that eventually directs the titular character towards philosophical rather than sexual pursuits, the *Lysis* makes a more complicated suggestion about persuasion's ethical force: Calculated persuasive tactics, Socrates shows us, always meet their limit at the radical unknowability of the intended audience. What the dialogue offers to the study of rhetoric—what it can tell us about the ethics of the most calculated and instrumental persuasive acts—is rooted in Plato's dramatization of Socrates's explicitly persuasive interactions with his young interlocutors. I do not mean by this that Socrates simply proves himself to be a talented rhetorician; this is a fact, of course, that we have always known. Rather, Plato depicts Socrates as putting on several persuasive demonstrations in which he shows off how effectively he can appeal to specific audience members for specific purposes. The dialogue is composed, that is, of a series of encounters in which Socrates attempts to persuade one audience for the benefit of another. In each case, furthermore, Socrates's demonstration is meant to serve as a model— it is meant to be repeated later by the interested party who watches from a distance. Significantly, these scenes recall the structural *raison d'être* of *Phaedrus*, in which the eponymous student is positively burning to recite Lysias's argument for the nonlover to Socrates when he encounters him just beyond the city walls. The important difference here is that it is Socrates who plays the role of would-be ventriloquist; in the *Lysis*, he becomes the figure whose speech acts are meant to be reenacted later for seductive or antagonistic effect. These encounters allow Socrates to clearly demonstrate his capacity to adapt his persuasive tactics depending on the disposition of the one with whom he speaks. But this movement of persuasive force is ultimately dispersed by the dialogue's topic, friendship, because Socrates finds that he cannot finally define what a friend is. Socrates tells his young interlocutors that he would "wish for a good friend more than [. . .] the gold of Darius" (211e), but in the end he suggests that friendship is not a matter of possession. Further still, Socrates suggests that friendship cannot be explained on the basis of similarity or difference, and so the dialogue concludes by figuring the friend—frustratingly for the interlocutors—as something of an elusive stranger. What the text ultimately suggests with this display, I believe, is that the instrumental force of persuasion is frustrated in advance by the impossibility of finally knowing the audience.

DERRIDA'S FRIENDSHIP WITHOUT FRIENDS

There is no way to separate Derrida's contribution to the philosophical concept of friendship from what I described in Chapter 1 as his transformative inheritance of Austin's performative utterance. I would add, as well, that there is no way to separate it from his own rhetorical performance in *Politics of Friendship*, a book Michael Naas characterizes as both a deconstruction of the "philosophical treatment of friendship" and a "*call* or *invocation*" to think about this tradition differently (*Taking* 139). I emphasize the importance of performance and performativity because Derrida's interrogation of the always fraternal links between theories of friendship and theories of politics is initiated, sustained, and ultimately bound together by an often-repeated citation of a citation: "O my friends, there is no friend." Attributed to Aristotle by Diogenes Laertes (and quoted by many of the thinkers Derrida treats in his book), this direct address—with its paradoxical performative and constative modes—reverberates throughout *Politics of Friendship* and dramatizes the originary performativity that Derrida insists is prior to all linguistic utterances.

> We do not know to whom Aristotle is said to have said this or that, but it is not only the reader or auditor who is 'entailed' by the structure of the utterance. A minimum of friendship or consent must be supposed of them; there must be an appeal to such a minimal consensus if anything at all is to be said. Whether this appeal corresponds, *in fact*, to a comprehension or an

agreement, if only on the meaning of what is said, appears to us secondary with regard to the appeal itself. [. . .] It rings in the performative space of a call, prior to its very first word. (214)

Before one friend can call out to another to simultaneously confirm and deny a friendship, in other words, there is a prior "consent" that precedes and exceeds both subjectivity and conscious choice. And before there can be anything like a subjective experience of friendship, there is an "appeal [. . .] prior to its very first word" (214). What Derrida describes here is not friendship in itself, but something prior to friendship—"a friendship beyond friendship, [. . .] a promise of friendship," and indeed, a presubjective entanglement that would give rise to and sustain "the *dream* of an unusable friendship" (217–18, emphasis added).

The lived experience of such an "unusable friendship," however, is impossible to achieve and maintain. Derrida bears witness to this impossibility in his review of the philosophical tradition's dominant Graeco-Roman model of friendship, which begins, he says, in Plato's *Lysis*. This model privileges presence and mutual recognition, thus making friendship into "a sort of narcissistic circuit of self-reflection" (Naas *Taking* 141). In the *Lysis*, Derrida notes, Socrates emphasizes that friendship is born of proximity and familiarity. "The value of *oikeiotes* [suitability] dominates the end of the dialogue," Derrida explains, "it frequently qualifies the bond of friendship itself, an always natural bond" (154). The Greek term *oikeiotes* is thematically important, Derrida continues, because of its

> indissociable network of significations [. . .] assembled, precisely, around the hearth (*oikos*), the home, habitat, domicile—and grave: kinship—literal or metaphorical—domesticity, familiarity, property, therefore appropriability, proximity: everything an *economy* can reconcile, adjust or harmonize, I will go so far as to say *present*, in the *familiarity* of the *near* and the *neighbor*. (154)

Friendship, in this model, is a matter of finding those in whom we see ourselves. And once we recognize these commonalities, we possess the friend in such a way that reduces his otherness to our horizon of knowledge. The essence of friendship, in other words, is that the friend is like me—and, further still, belongs to me.

Unable to account for the friend's essential difference, and organizing itself instead on an appropriative comparison of shared traits and desires, this is precisely the model Derrida hopes to interrupt. Characterizing his project as an attempt to divert the *Lysis* tradition and "to move what is said to us in the dialogue elsewhere" (*Politics* 6), Derrida prefers instead a model of friendship epitomized in Maurice Blanchot's memorial text for Michel Foucault. Blanchot's is an account of friendship defined by distance and reserve; it does not assume that friends share anything in common, and by this view, the relation between friends is one of unbridgeable distance. Thus, any friendship worthy of the name would be characterized by a relation of distance, unfamiliarity, dissymmetry, and heterogeneity. The difficulty here, of course, is that it is impossible to legislate appropriating narcissism out of friendship altogether. In the case of "Blanchot's declaration of friendship" for Foucault, as Paul Allen Miller has argued, what is clear is that such a declaration "can come only after Foucault has died and only in the form of a declaration addressed to friends that declares the impossibility of that friendship, the necessary absence, ambivalence, and aggression that lies at the heart of the most genuine affections" (*Postmodern Spiritual* 173–74). What would be required, in other words, is an address to an infinitely other, ultimately unreachable addressee, and so friendship as such remains an impossibility—a promise that can never be fulfilled.

For the most part, Derrida reads the *Lysis* as adhering to the dominant strain of narcissistic friendship, although he does indicate a willingness to believe that the dialogue's aporetic ending might hold such a friendship in suspension (*Politics* 155). Picking up this loose thread, I argue that when Socrates and his cohort turn away in frustration from their ostensible task, we see the limits of persuasion: Socrates's targeted manipulations have been in vain because his audience—his friends—are beyond his comprehension and calculation.

SOCRATES'S FRIENDLY ADVICE

Because of its extensive propositional exploration of the definition and inner workings of friendship, the *Lysis* isn't typically thought to hold a place alongside Plato's rhetorically themed dialogues. While texts such as *Sophist*, *Protagoras*, *Gorgias*, and *Phaedrus* explicitly thematize rhetorical thinkers or concepts, the bulk of the *Lysis*'s conversation is devoted to questions concerning what precisely friends have in common, what attracts one friend to the other, how best to acquire friends, and whether friendship is reciprocal. Furthermore, it gives readers a glimpse of two distinct sets of friends interacting with each other as Socrates liaises (or interferes) with each. Set first outside and then inside a newly constructed wrestling school, the *Lysis* places the slightly combative friendship of (older boys) Hippothales and Ctesippus in relation to the more amiable though still competitive one between (younger boys) Lysis and Menexenus. Madly in love with Lysis, but unable to articulate his feelings to the boy, Hippothales agrees to let Socrates show him how to woo a beloved, and so the famed teacher has reason to visit with both sets of friends, granting us access to them as well.

Thematically and dramatically, then, friends and friendship are at the heart of the matter. But, as Garver has pointed out, the *Lysis* possesses a unique design that places persuasion front and center, as well. Indeed, persuasion and friendship interact significantly, perhaps even inseparably, in the dialogue. This is in part because—more than *Sophist, Protagoras, Gorgias*, and *Phaedrus*—the *Lysis* reads like a stage play in the sense that Socrates flits from one set of interlocutors to the next, and with each move he's aware (and we're aware) that his interaction with the new audience is being scrutinized by the previous one. Of course, it is not unusual for setting to figure importantly in Plato's work. Socrates and Phaedrus, for example, have their chat away from the city, near where Boreas abducted Orithyia, and so the scenery is suggestive of the erotic danger that plays out between the two. But here the setting contains characters who watch Socrates work his persuasive wiles on targets of their choosing, and so the dialogue features a voyeuristic, watching-from-the-edge-of-the-stage component that transforms the effects of the centerstage action. Socrates's acts of appealing to various audiences are placed *en abyme*, and this strategy infinitely reflects (and so disperses) one of the dialogue's central demonstrations: that the act of persuasion involves targeting an audience. It involves judging an audience in advance and formulating linguistic techniques meant to attend to and make the most of that audience's particularities. For Socrates, in this case, this includes playing on the weaknesses and insecurities of his interlocutors and handling them roughly along the way. What is most interesting about this serial-persuasive form, however, is that, when coupled with the thematic impossibility friendship poses for Socrates and his friends, it also highlights the impossibility of such careful targeting. Friends, speakers, and audiences are all put into question here. Despite their proximity, none is ever allowed to appropriate the other in the form of a constative identity.

The *Lysis* opens with Socrates, the dialogue's narrator, en route from the Academy to the Lyceum. As Socrates approaches a group of boys and young men that includes Hippothales and Ctesippus, the former calls out, hoping that the eloquent teacher will join him and his group of friends as they head into their palaestra. "Come straight here to us," Hippothales exclaims, "Won't you come over? [. . .] We spend most of our time in discussions (*logoi*), and would gladly make you a part of them" (203b–4a). His interest piqued—as it always seems to be by the potential of a new audience—Socrates wants to know more and asks about the "us" that Hippothales has offered up. One word in the response by the (we soon learn) lovesick lad sets the dialogue in motion: Hippothales describes the participants as "those of us here now and others as well—quite a lot of them, and *beauties*, too" (203b, emphasis added). Socrates picks up on this cue and presses Hippothales to tell him "who the beauty is" (204b).[7] Hippothales deeply blushes at the question, and his response tells Socrates much of what he wants to know: The young man is far less interested in any "discussions" than in the object of his desire (204a). Socrates, in turn, shows his hand: "I know that you're not only in love," he says to Hippothales, "but already pretty far along in your love" (204b). All that is left for him to discern is the identity of Hippothales's beloved. With the ever-reddening Hippothales tongue-tied, his friend Ctesippus reveals the name: Lysis.

Here, in these opening lines of the dialogue, Plato builds into the backstory one persuasive effort important primarily for its ongoing failure and sets the stage for another that will prove remarkably successful. We learn of the first—Hippothales's hapless wooing of the young, desirable Lysis—through Socrates's incisive questions, Ctesippus's responses in the face of his friend's embarrassed silence, and, finally, Hippothales's own halting and naïve declarations. The second unfolds as Socrates delivers a bravura lesson in the art of persuasion once he turns his attention to Lysis and Menexenus (it is these conversations with the younger boys that will make up the bulk of the dialogue). Thus, Socrates's dressing down of Hippothales for his rhetorical inability—his failure to seduce a beautiful boy—is what leads to the stated topic of the dialogue, the nature of friendship. Knowing that he will be able to succeed where Hippothales has failed, Socrates steps in, effectively becoming, as Ludwig notes, Cyrano to Hippothales's Christian. Speaking strictly in terms of the dialogue's form, then, we get Socrates's discussion of the impossibility of friendship—one that plays out thematically in his discussions with Lysis and Menexenus—only by way of a calculated perlocutionary scene.

That Hippothales is smitten with Lysis is beyond doubt, even if we lack Socrates's "capacity to recognize quickly a lover and an object of love" (204c). Just as obvious—despite the fact that it is part of the narrative that has taken place offstage—is Hippothales's rhetorical clumsiness: This becomes painfully clear thanks to Ctesippus's recollections, infused with the commentary of an exasperated wingman, and to Socrates's keen observations. Garver, for one,

---

7. J. Wright, in Edith Hamilton and Huntington Cairns's *Plato: The Collected Dialogues*, translates this line as "who is your prime beauty" (204b).

casts Hippothales's as a problem of articulation: He is in love but can't talk about it, and thus can't hope to persuade his beloved—this "individual audience"—to reciprocate (128). Not that he isn't trying. This we learn from the increasingly impatient Ctesippus, who, set off by one too many of Hippothales's deep blushes at Socrates's questions, lets loose about how much his friend talks about the object of his desire—and about how little he has to say. The problem according to Ctesippus is that Hippothales knows neither *what* to say to Lysis nor *how* to say it. At first, he can do little more around his friends than say the name that he is reluctant to reveal to Socrates: "He's deafened *our* ears by stuffing them with 'Lysis'" (204c–d). When Hippothales does manage to push beyond this appellative obsession, nothing really improves. "The things he says are ridiculous," Ctesippus tells Socrates (205b). And even though he is besotted with Lysis, Hippothales "doesn't have anything of his own to say that even—a *boy* couldn't say" (205c).[8] Instead, he blathers on about Lysis's family history and accomplishments and "stuff that's even older news than that" (205b–c), Ctesippus says, reminding Socrates once again of his, and his companions', unwanted expertise in the matter: "These are the things that this person talks and sings about, forcing us as well to be his audience" (205d). And as annoying as these things are, Ctesippus implies—and, later, Socrates declares—that they are only part of Hippothales's rhetorical failure. The lovelorn young man is equally clueless about *how* to say the things he wants to say to Lysis. The words that spill out "in ordinary conversation" are "hardly terrible at all compared with the poems that he tries to pour over our heads, and the bits of prose," Ctesippus tells Socrates (204d). Worse still are the songs, sung in "an extraordinary voice that *we* have to put up with listening to" (204d). Yes, Ctesippus feels put upon. His pointed description of Hippothales's behavior and his emphasis on being an unwilling audience member make this clear. But these scenes do more than simply showcase one friend's complaints about another, however entertaining they might be: They also demonstrate the ways that the dialogue explicitly thematizes the rhetorical considerations of audience, invention, style, and delivery.

For his part, Socrates is quick to offer the hapless lover a bit of advice, and what his position as coach, mentor, and, ultimately, model ensures is that we view Socrates's subsequent conversations with Lysis and Menexenus as examples of effective persuasion, examples that take into account the very things Ctesippus shows us that Hippothales has entirely forgotten or never knew to

---

8. Or, as Wright translates it, Hippothales can think of nothing of a "personal interest" to break the ice.

begin with. When Socrates hears Ctesippus's account of his friend's failed rhetorical attempts, he offers the following critique:

> The person who's an expert in erotics, my friend, doesn't praise the one he loves until he catches him [. . .]. And at the same time whenever anyone praises them and builds them up, the beautiful ones get full of proud and arrogant thoughts; or don't you think so? [. . .] So what sort of hunter would it be, in your view, that started up his prey and made it more difficult to catch? (206a)

Putting aside for the moment any disturbing similarities to a good bit of contemporary dating advice, the passage is significant because, in it, Socrates places himself in the position of ersatz rhetoric coach. Suggesting that praise is getting Hippothales nowhere, he advises him to view his persuasive endeavors as something more like a hunt: The object of the hunt is to catch the prey, just as the object of wooing is to persuade a beloved. Socrates casts this as a lesson in seduction, of course, telling Hippothales initially that he wants to "establish the way you're applying yourself to your beloved" (205b) and, later, that he will "demonstrate" the things that Hippothales *should* say to win Lysis over (206c). But all of this is staged so that we recognize luring a beloved as a rhetorical problem and, more specifically, as a problem of knowing the audience and how to make that audience pliable.

We come to see this in part because, from the beginning, Socrates showcases his ability in reading audience members. Almost from the moment he sees him outside the palaestra, for example, Socrates begins to read Hippothales: his eagerness to invite and entice Socrates to join him and his companions ("It really will be worth your while" [203b]); his naïve vagueness ("One of us thinks it's one person [. . .] another another [204b]); his uncontrollable blushing (204b–c). From these cues, Socrates deduces that Hippothales is desperately—and desperately inept—in love and that the young man not only will accept help but can be moved to practically beg for it. To get there, to the point where Hippothales beseeches him for advice, Socrates alternately teases, flatters, chides, and corrects the young man. The teacher recognizes the student's bashful evasions and presses one button ("Who do *you* think" the prime beauty is? [204b]). He hears the name of the student's beloved and presses another ("Well now [. . .] Hippothales, how noble and dashing a love this is that you've discovered" [204e]). He takes in Ctesippus's version of Hippothales's efforts and presses a third ("Ridiculous Hippothales [. . .]" [205d]). The result: Hippothales readily acknowledges everything that he has done wrong in pursuit of Lysis, assures Socrates that he has opened up to him completely, and asks desperately for the direction that Socrates has been ready to provide from the beginning. "If you've something else up your sleeve," Hippothales says, "give your advice about the line a person should take in conversation, or what he should do, to become an object of love for a beloved" (206c).[9]

Having snared Hippothales, Socrates maneuvers to begin the main event, his own seductive encounter with Lysis. With little more than a nudge, Socrates learns from Hippothales how best to lure Lysis, while making it seem that none of this is his idea at all: "If you were prepared to get him [Lysis] to come and exchange words with me," Socrates says to Hippothales, "perhaps I'd be able to demonstrate to you what one should say in conversation with him" (206c). In his response, Hippothales suggests a course of action and, more importantly, reveals to Socrates a couple of golden nuggets about Lysis himself: "If you go in with Ctesippus here and sit down and have a conversation, my thinking is that he'll actually come over to you himself, because, you see [. . .] he's got this outstanding love of listening" (206c–d). And, a few lines later: "In fact it's Menexenus he goes around with more than anybody else" (206d). Like a cardsharp lying in wait at a low-limit table, Socrates now has another bit of information that will help him read the players about to join the game. Not that Plato wants us to see Socrates's various interlocutors as victims. As Garver notes, the "people in the *Lysis* know that they are living in a rhetorical world"; like Socrates, they show an awareness of the disconnect between being a friend and being able to talk about being a friend (131–32). Thus, Hippothales, Lysis, and Menexenus willingly engage with Socrates, they want to know what he knows and is willing to share with them, even if they aren't fully aware of the persuasive strategies being deployed against them. As readers, however, we are meant to be aware of the persuasive force that makes the *Lysis* so much more than an aporetic inquiry into the nature of friendship.

Clearly, Hippothales's lack of rhetorical skill—made glaringly apparent in comparison to the persuasive performances of others—figures importantly in the dialogue. And because we begin by focusing on this ineptitude, we view the subsequent interactions between Socrates and his audiences as better models of seduction. As Gary Scott argues, "Plato's audience is placed in the role of judge and is challenged to assess which of the two erotic approaches—Hippothales' or Socrates'—is most appropriate" (59). One significant reason for this is that we have no choice but to view Socrates's conversations on friendship (conversations he'll have with Lysis alone and with Lysis and Menexenus together) as a persuasive demonstration put on for the benefit of Hippothales.

---

9. Wright's translation places more emphasis on Hippothales's state of mind: "I put myself in your hands, and beg you to give me any advice you may have."

When Socrates shifts his attention from the first group of friends to the second, he does so precisely with Hippothales in mind. As if on cue, the lovesick lad "took his opportunity, since he could see several people placing themselves close, to use them as a cover and take a close position himself in such a way that he thought Lysis wouldn't catch sight of him" (207b). Close enough to see and hear but removed from the view of the participants, Hippothales "set[s] to listening" (207b). Thus, we see Hippothales assume a position that is similar to our own, and like him, we await Socrates's demonstration.

PERSUASION, REPETITION, INTERRUPTION

With Socrates in position and Hippothales looking on, we finally meet Lysis and Menexenus, who mirror some of the competitive behaviors of the older Hippothales and Ctesippus. Socrates, ever the keen observer, notices and immediately exploits this similarity when Menexenus responds to a question about who is older with: "We have different views about that" (207c). Fully engaging now, Socrates artfully pursues the conversation with a series of follow-ups that draw Lysis in. "Then you'll also dispute about which of you is the better born?" he asks Menexenus, whose hearty affirmative Socrates clearly expects (207c), using it to get to the questions to which the heretofore silent Lysis will be compelled to respond:

> "And about which of you is the more *beautiful,* too, in the same way."
> They both laughed at that.
> "I shan't ask you, though," I said, "which of you is the richer; after all, the two of you are friends, aren't you?"
> "Yes, absolutely," they said together. (207c)

Here, then, after but a handful of incisive queries and comments, Socrates has enticed Lysis to join the conversation without really asking and has positioned himself to show Hippothales "how one *should* converse with one's beloved" (210e). This also means, of course, that Socrates is free to seduce the young beauty himself (into philosophical rather than romantic pursuits) while masking his efforts as a lesson in persuasion delivered for the benefit of someone else. That Menexenus is then called away only intensifies this effect. Socrates is able to focus his persuasive salvos on precisely the target he and Hippothales have discussed, and because Menexenus exits and then later reenters the scene, we notice the different tactics Socrates reserves for distinct audience members.

With Lysis as his sole interlocutor—at least for a time—Socrates again shows his persuasive dexterity, shifting from the series of questions meant to lead Menexenus and Lysis to examine the nature of their friendship to his interrogation of Lysis about his parents' love for their son. The purpose of what Penner and Rowe call this "rather badly misread" passage (because Socrates treats Lysis so roughly here and because he defines love according to utility) quickly becomes clear, given Socrates's admonition to Hippothales in 205e-6b not to "start [. . .] up his prey and [make] it more difficult to catch" (206a): This will be a demonstration of how to tame that prey and ready it for capture.[10] At the heart of Socrates's performance is the teacher's infamous humbling of Lysis, which serves not only as a lesson to Hippothales in how to cut one's beloved down to size (210e) but also as a first step in Socrates's pedagogical seduction of the boy. Socrates begins, after the departure of Menexenus, with a simple question: "I suppose, Lysis, [. . .] that your father, and your mother, love you very much?" (207d). Lysis, secure in his world and in his parents' love, responds as Socrates knows he will: "Yes, certainly" (207d). The teacher then proceeds to chip away at what his student thinks he knows about his parents' affections. Do they want him to be happy? Lysis is sure they do. But Socrates walks him through various scenarios that would seem to prove otherwise and that raise doubts about the boy's assumptions. Piercing the cocoon Lysis has grown to know and love, comparing the boy's lot unfavorably to that of even a slave, Socrates points to a simple conclusion: "*You* control nothing, Lysis, and you don't do a single one of the things you desire" (209a).

Although Lysis musters what seems to be a reasonable response—"That's because I'm not yet grown up" (209a)—Socrates presses on. Having defamiliarized the familial bonds with which Lysis has been so comfortable, making the boy feel a bit less at home in his own life, Socrates shifts the conversation, both to show the student a way to reset his foundations and to punctuate the dressing down. He leads Lysis, in 209a-10d, through a series of questions and comments that point to knowledge and the utility that comes with it as the source of authority, power, and love ("If you become wise, everyone will be friends to you and everyone will belong to you" [210d]). Just as he inflames the boy's intellectual passions, however, just as he dangles the promise of knowledge as the key to all that Lysis really wants, Socrates adds a twist. Reaffirming for Hippothales, who has been watching nervously from the crowd, that there must be no "puffing [. . .] up" of the prey (210e), Socrates casually leads Lysis to the conclusions that "if *you're* in need of a teacher, *you* aren't

---

10. The nature of this misreading, according to Penner and Rowe, involves a misunderstanding of Socrates's argumentative strategy and of various conceptions of love and happiness as presented in the passage (231-36).

yet thinking" and that there can't be "anything big about your thoughts, if in fact you're still thoughtless" (210d). If knowledge is the key, in other words, the door remains locked tight for Lysis until, as Penner and Rowe put it, he ventures out to "strive for knowledge wherever he can find it, even in a lover" (236). Scott offers a similar analysis of Socrates's pedagogical strategy here: It begins with a "psychic purgative" that decenters Lysis and leaves him ripe for the "Socratic arousal" that follows; lest the student get too excited, the teacher then quickly shows him just how poorly equipped he is to get what he wants and "which steps the boy must take next to further his goals" (63). Once again, Plato frames all of this as a persuasive show put on for the sake of Hippothales, still hidden on the scene. After his humbling discussion with Lysis, Socrates "glanced at Hippothales, and almost slipped up" (210e). Explaining his near mistake, Socrates says, "What came into my head was to say 'That, Hippothales, is how one *should* converse with one's beloved, humbling him and cutting him down to size'" (210e).

Having showcased these persuasive approaches—defamiliarization, humbling, intellectual arousal, and the promise of more—Socrates simultaneously demonstrates how to seduce and actually seduces: He performs the persuasive act *for* Hippothales and *on* Lysis. And the effect of Socrates's words on Lysis is similar to that which we saw on Hippothales a few lines earlier in at least one important way: In both cases, Socrates manages to move his interlocutors to practically beg for his rhetorical assistance—when Hippothales asks for advice to woo Lysis and when Lysis seeks a Socratic comeuppance for his friend Menexenus. While nudging the dialogue toward a more explicit discussion of friendship, each of these requests also sets up a scene in the developing mini-drama that Plato scripts to exhibit the impressive force of Socrates's persuasive skills. When Lysis, now made fully aware of his "thoughtless" state of being (210d), asks Socrates to run Menexenus through the same wringer from which he has just emerged, we get for a third time in the first half of the dialogue an example of the teacher's rhetorical acuity and uncanny sense of audience. We see that, once again, Socrates is willing to present himself as a rhetorical model, someone whose abilities in individualized persuasion can be imparted through demonstration.

When Lysis good-naturedly beseeches Socrates to give Menexenus this lesson, the teacher suggests that since he has just had it himself, he should do it on his own: "Try, then, [. . .] to recall it as far as you can, so that you can report everything clearly to him" (211a–b). But even though Lysis was "paying complete attention" (211a), it seems as though both he and Socrates know that he isn't quite ready for prime time. Sensing that the one-time encounter was not sufficient, Socrates offers Lysis some future tutoring: "If you forget anything, ask me again when you come across me next" (211b). Lysis gratefully accepts—"I'll do that, [...] you can be sure of it" (211b)—but Socrates has so inflamed his passions that the boy seeks immediate relief and asks the teacher to "say something else to [Menexenus] so that I too can hear it" (211b). Like Hippothales before him, Lysis entreats Socrates to put on a rhetorical demonstration. He seeks a model, one he can take in and apply to his own future interactions with Menexenus. (Beyond his hopes of developing his own rhetorical acumen, Lysis seems to view this as a source of entertainment as well. He notes that he wants to see Menexenus get "some punishment" at the hands of Socrates [211c].) Plato's readers, then, are left with something of a comical scene (but one that is significant nonetheless): Hippothales watches while Socrates seduces Lysis, and Lysis, in turn, sets Socrates to enacting a similar kind of maneuver on Menexenus. The persuasive frame is thus doubled back on itself (and all this after we've already seen Socrates masterfully manipulate Hippothales at the outset of the dialogue). All that we pick up about friendship along the way, in other words, comes to us by way of Socrates's carefully modulated addresses—addresses that Plato's readers have been clearly instructed to view as rhetorical models put on for the sake of first Hippothales and then Lysis.

When Menexenus returns to the scene, Socrates prepares to display his persuasive skills one final time—at the behest of Lysis, of course. Widely known to be "a great one for disputing" (211b), Menexenus is a different kind of audience member from Lysis. Not nearly as shy and far happier to jump in and argue with the more experienced visitor, he provides us with the opportunity to see one more shift in Socrates's persuasive capabilities. As Scott points out, Socrates's maneuvering is driven in part by Lysis's and Menexenus's "propensities for trusting different things"—the former puts his faith in "his natural gifts and in traditional authorities," while the latter "tends to rely heavily on argumentation" (75). Where Socrates peppered Lysis with personal questions about the actions and intentions of his closest family members in such a way that made him question the parental love he once took as given, the teacher leads Menexenus through a series of highly abstract contradictory propositions about friendship. Beginning with the seemingly straightforward question, "When someone loves a person, which of the two is it that becomes a friend?" (212a–b), Socrates ultimately sends Menexenus through a complicated maze of possible subject-in-love/object-of-love configurations that cause the argumentatively inclined boy to contradict himself, to take back the answers he at first seemed so sure of, and to doubt his own quick wit.

Even though Socrates puts Menexenus through his paces, however, he is not above appealing to the boy's intellectual vanity. And so we see clearly that

Socrates's plans for dealing with Menexenus are quite different from what they were with Lysis. And because this is *not* a lesson in how to converse with a beloved—nor does Socrates wish to seduce Menexenus—there is no danger in puffing this new interlocutor up. Socrates, for example, before he leads him through the dizzying array of questions about friendship, casts Menexenus as someone with at least some expertise: "There's a part of what I'm saying which this person here [Lysis] doesn't understand, and claims to think Menexenus knows about" (211d). A few lines later, Socrates is more direct, praising the friendship between Lysis and Menexenus and the latter's ability to "acquire this possession quickly and easily" at "such a young age" (212a). Socrates continues, "these are the very things I want to ask you about, because you're experienced in them" (212a). His ego stroked, his intellect aroused, Menexenus happily engages in Socrates's logical contest, and we see again how well Socrates is able to draw out very different kinds of interlocutors.

The result of this careful staging of multiple persuasive acts is that it allows Socrates to demonstrate (to us and to his dramatic interlocutors) that he can do all of the things Ctesippus has criticized Hippothales for not being able to do. Socrates takes steps to know his audience, and once he figures them out, he modulates his approach (including elements of invention and delivery) where necessary, appealing to each audience member in a way that is noticeably determined by that audience member's unique disposition. To return to Austin's terms, Socrates proves himself an expert at managing the distance between perlocutionary utterance and effect, largely because he attends so closely to where his perlocutionary force is directed. But the significance here is not simply that Socrates is a master rhetorician, a fact we knew already. Instead, it's that his persuasive acts are framed *as such* and for the benefit of two of Socrates's pupils. Because Plato presents Socrates's rhetorical adventures in this way, the latter's acts of persuasion become part of the dialogue's primary concern. And this encourages us to notice the way that Socrates's persuasive approach requires that he come to know well—I would even go so far as to say *possess*—the audience he targets. That is, he goes to great lengths to figure out who they are. He reads them. He renders the other he is about to encounter recognizable to himself. So interpreted, these individuals are *for* Socrates. Confined to his interpretive horizons, they become something like the "possession[s]" (211d) Socrates compares to friends in his conversation with Menexenus.

Socrates comes to possess his various audience members by identifying and then attending to their odd quirks and their particular insecurities and vanities. What's more, he makes a show of this, demonstrating first for Hippothales and then for Lysis that any good persuasive attempt will take into account the distinctiveness of the intended audience (again, we see this in Socrates's attention to Lysis's naïveté and Menexenus's propensity for debate). But the dramatic presence of these persuasive interactions is premised on their status as *models*. The conversations Socrates has here now (with Lysis and Menexenus), in other words, are presented explicitly as taking place for the future, when Hippothales and Lysis will attempt to replicate them for their own ends. Thus it would seem that the rhetorical specificity Socrates insists on is interrupted in advance by the fact that it is meant to be repeated by a different interlocutor at a different time and in a different place. By this reading, Socrates's masterful rendering-selfsame of his audience is revealed as something of an impossibility. If his capacity to attend to his audience members' singularity is given by the necessity that it be repeated, then it would seem that this singularity can never be ultimately, finally, contained. By way of its unique structure, then, the *Lysis* argues precisely this: In any act of persuasion, the orator must reduce the audience to a clearly identifiable object of cognition. At the same time, however, the dialogue exposes the impossibility of such knowledge because, in it, the seeming presence of the persuasive address is made possible by way of its repeatability. At first blush, it might seem that the *Lysis* shares a certain point a view with the *Phaedrus*. In his critique of writing and rhetoric pedagogy in that dialogue, Socrates suggests that the problem with modeling speeches of master rhetoricians is that such modeling cannot adapt to the situations and needs of singular audience members. But I think that the *Lysis*'s unique structure—its repetition of persuasive models that are to be repeated later by Socrates's eager students—suggests something further still: that the specificity or singularity of any given audience member is premised on the necessity of its repeatability, and so the unity of identity is divided in advance. In other words, maybe this to-be-identified audience member has no unified identity to be mastered. This is a difficulty that is echoed in the group's conversations on friendship, in which they consider but then dismiss the possibility of owning a friend and the possibility of one friend being "proper to" another.

SOCRATES'S FRIENDS

Taken all together, Lysis, Menexenus, Socrates, Ctesippus, and Hippothales comprise something of a strange community. Between Ctesippus and Hippothales, we see a friendly relation that is marked by complaints, sniping, and ridicule for sport. The former's willingness to embarrass the latter in front of their guest sets the dialogue in motion, and so the competitive distance between the two is accentuated by way of its structural significance as well as its vivid and humorous dramatic portrayal. The older boys' antagonism is echoed by Lysis and Menexenus, who introduce themselves to Socrates as friendly competitors. They jokingly admit that they cannot agree on the most straightforward of topics, and when Lysis beseeches Socrates to give Menexenus the same rough lesson that he has just received, we sense that Menexenus has very often applied his love for disputing to Lysis, who seems to appreciate such treatment far less than Menexenus knows. Socrates, too, has an interesting position among them. While it may be true, as Scott suggests, that Socrates ultimately encourages the younger boys to better their philosophical explorations with each other, he willingly—enthusiastically it seems—models the seduction of Lysis for Hippothales, whom he chides at the outset for loving the boy for his own selfish ends. In other words, he's implicated in all of this too, and the friendship he offers the other interlocutors isn't simply for their benefit.

The overall picture of friendship that Plato provides for us in the *Lysis*, then, has little in common with the friendship of goodness or virtue that Aristotle favors in the *Nicomachean Ethics*. Indeed, in the *Lysis*, we find none of Aristotle's commitment to loving the friend purely for the other's sake. From Aristotle's point of view,

> The complete sort of friendship is that between people who are good and are alike in virtue, since they wish for good things for one another [. . .]. And those who wish for good things for their friends for their own sake are friends most of all, since they are that way for themselves and not incidentally. (1156b)[11]

While it may be the case that by the end of the dialogue we see the seeds of this sort of friendship being planted between Socrates and the younger boys, it is certainly also true that another sort of friendship is playing out. Where Aristotle's *Rhetoric* insists that friends must be loved for their own sake—"Let *being friendly* [. . .] be [defined as] wanting for someone what one thinks are good things for him, not what one thinks benefits oneself" (2.4.2[12])—Plato's *Lysis* seems quite happy to reduce friends to their use value. In fact, a significant portion of the *Lysis* is devoted to the consideration and demonstration of what Aristotle would call, in the *Nicomachean Ethics*, utility friendship, a

---

11. Line numbers refer to Joe Sachs's translation of Aristotle's *Nicomachean Ethics*, Focus Publishing, 2002.

12. Section numbers refer to George A. Kennedy's translation of Aristotle's *On Rhetoric: A Theory of Civic Discourse*, Oxford UP, 2007.

friendship of a lesser order in which people are bound together by their usefulness to one another.[13] Socrates uses this concept to discuss friends as objects to be possessed, and it grounds several of the propositions he introduces in the *Lysis,* beginning with the argument found in Homer and Empedocles that in friendship, "like is necessarily always friend to like" (214b). Although Socrates is not entirely sold on this claim, he momentarily settles on the idea that mutually good men would indeed attract each other in friendship. He ultimately realizes, however, that friendship between (similar) good men cannot work because these good men are self-sufficient: Because they want for nothing, they do not need friends.

This leads Socrates to his next hypothesis (allegedly from Hesiod but also similar to one found in Heraclitus): "The things that are most unlike must be filled with friendship" (215d). This premise makes sense given the importance Socrates places on usefulness: "Each thing desires [. . .] not what is like it: dry desires the wet, cold hot, bitter sweet" (215e). Socrates points out, however, that this is a logical impossibility because friendship cannot be a friend to enmity, and vice versa. What makes more sense to Socrates is something of a compromise in which those who are neither good nor bad become friendly with those who are good. What is useful about friendship in this scenario is that the friend who is neither good nor bad—Socrates provides the example of the human body "compelled through sickness to embrace and love medical expertise" (217b)—can be made better by being in the presence of what is good (in this case, medicine). This is a viable scenario because the neutral friend can get what he needs from the good one and can become someone altogether different by virtue of the other's presence. So pleased is Socrates with their finding that he describes being "overjoyed, like a sort of hunter, at having adequately enough in my grasp what I was hunting for" (218c). But the demands of utility come back to thwart this hypothesis, too. The "opposites attract" argument cannot, in the end, hold because the good would have no reason to return the love of those neither good nor bad.

Of course, there is also the problem that utility friendship is primarily selfish—premised on garnering some benefit for oneself—and for this reason tends not to last. When the usefulness ebbs, so too does the friendship (1156a). And yet this is precisely the kind of friendship Socrates offers as he works to transform Lysis's conception of his closest familial relations. When Socrates questions the boy about whether his mother and father do indeed love him, all of his inquiries have to do with how *useful* Lysis is to his parents. (Near the

---

13. According to Aristotle, "Those who love one another for what is useful do not love one another for themselves, but insofar as something good comes to them from one another" (1156a).

end of their conversation, Socrates asks, for example, "Will we then be objects of love to anyone, and will anyone love us, in those things, whatever they are, in which we are of no benefit?" And Lysis responds, "Certainly not" [210c]). Socrates's aim here is not to turn Lysis into a dutiful son—indeed, he devotes the entirety of their initial conversation to making Lysis question all of the comforting things he believed about his parents. Instead, Socrates claims that if Lysis is useful to them, he will be able to do all that he wishes (208a–10d). And so, in addition to rupturing the contentedness Lysis feels about his life at home, Socrates posits here that friends are defined by how useful they are to one another. Interestingly enough, we see this utility friendship playing out in Socrates's relation to Hippothales as well. Are these two friends? One of the most compelling things about this dialogue is that it makes much of how very hard it is to answer this question, but what is clear is that Socrates's potential utility—in the form of a lesson in seduction—is what draws the young man to him.

I note the significance of utility love in the *Lysis* because Socrates uses it to accentuate another important question about the nature of friends: Are they acquisitions to be possessed and put to work for other ends? For Socrates it certainly seems so. He puts it this way to Menexenus, at least, when the boy returns to the scene after having been called away. Comparing the acquisition of friends to the acquisition of farm animals, money, and power, Socrates makes it seem as though friends are instruments to be owned and used, the means to self-interested ends:

> Since I was a boy I've actually always had a desire for a certain kind of possession, like everyone else, only it's different things for different people: one person has a desire to get horses, while for another it's dogs, for another, gold, for another, public honours; but as for me, I don't get excited about these things—what *I*'m absolutely passionate about is getting friends, and I'd wish for a good friend more than for the best example any man has of a quail or a cock, and—Zeus!—I'd wish, myself, more for that than for the best horse and dog; and I do believe—I swear by the Dog!—more than the gold of Darius I'd much sooner get me a friend, or rather, more than getting Darius himself; that's how much of a friend-lover *I* am. (211d–e)

Certainly, there's no small amount of hyperbole here, and the fact that this is part of Socrates's attempt to lure Menexenus into debate gives us reason to doubt his sincerity. But this passage is notable because in it the master conversationalist explicitly links the quality of usefulness to the capacity for being the property of another, which, like utility friendship, is an important propositional consideration for Socrates, Lysis, and Menexenus as they round out their conversation. Socrates links utility and ownership here, noting that the acquisition of friends is not unlike the acquisition of other useful items. He places a high value on such friends ("more than the gold of Darius"), but even so, friends are equated here to farm animals, they are possessed in the same way that one possesses the "best horse and dog." Socrates's discussion here—offered up with perhaps the most verve of the entire dialogue—makes explicit what he demonstrates by way of his varying persuasive addresses to Hippothales, Lysis, and Menexenus. Just as Socrates makes a show of appropriating his addressee, just as he reduces his interlocutor to a set of identifiable characteristics and quirks, so too does he reduce friends to property.

This idea comes up again in one of Socrates's more serious moments, near the end of the dialogue before the trio's conversation on friendship is cut short by the guardians who arrive to shepherd Lysis and Menexenus home. Indeed, the last positive proposal Socrates puts forth in the *Lysis* before ultimately giving up in confusion about what it means to be a friend is that one's friends can be defined as those things that belong to him: "It's what belongs (*to oikeion*) to us, then, that's actually the object of passion and friendship and desire, as it appears, Menexenus and Lysis. [. . .] The two of you, in that case, if you're friends to each other, in some way naturally belong the one to the other" (221e).[14] Although it's put a little more kindly here, the friendship Socrates ascribes to Lysis and Menexenus (to all friends, in fact) is not so different from the acquisitive one so heartily described above. Friends belong to one another, they are "proper to" or "suitable for" each other, and so they share in common some positive disposition or identity. Socrates turns this final proposition aside because, if friends "naturally belong the one to the other" (221e), then they are too much alike and so have no need of one another (222b–d)—and we have already seen refuted the notion that like is attracted to like. Seemingly frustrated by their exhaustive intellectual travels, Socrates vents:

> If neither those who are loved nor those who love nor the like nor the unlike nor the good nor those who belong nor all the other things we've gone through—for I for one don't any longer remember, there were so many of

---

14. Penner and Rowe translate *to oikeion* "what belongs to us," but *oikeion* can also mean "akin," because, as David Bolotin notes, *oikeion* is "closely related to the word oikia—'house,' 'household,' or 'home'" (56). Though Bolotin always translates *oikeion* as "akin," in his translation notes, he asks that readers keep in mind the "alternative rendering 'one's own'" (56). Liddell and Scott similarly list "in or of the house" and "of the same family or kin, related" in their definition of οἰκεῖος, although their entry also includes "friendly" and "proper to a thing, fitting, suitable, becoming" (545).

them, but anyway if none of these things is the friend, *I no longer have any idea what to say.* (222e, emphasis added)

Given that we've just witnessed Socrates's noticeably repetitive, highly staged, and so deeply accentuated persuasive displays, the fact that he now has no idea what to say comes as something of a thunderbolt. Not only has Socrates spent the better part of the dialogue demonstrating his rhetorical capacity, but he has done so by suggesting that his abilities in this area are enabled by how well he can identify and appropriate the dispositions of his various audience members. In the end, however, he is unable to define the friend that he and his interlocutors have been seeking and is left speechless.

Between the beginning and the end of the dialogue, then, we seem to have come full circle. Socrates's presence on the scene—the possibility of his discussions with Lysis and Menexenus—is owed to his promise to help Hippothales figure out a better way to address the object of his desire. But by the *Lysis*'s closing lines, Socrates and Hippothales have far more in common than we could have predicted. Like Hippothales, Socrates has no idea what to say, and the remonstrations he offered the lovestruck youth in 205d—"I said, 'Ridiculous Hippothales'"—he now applies to himself: "Now just look at us, Lysis and Menexenus! We've made ourselves ridiculous [. . .]. For these people here will say as they leave that we think that we're friends of one another—for I count myself too as one of you—but haven't yet been able to find out what the friend *is*" (223b).

In his own brief consideration of this passage, Derrida notes the "vocative élan of [Socrates's] apostrophe: we who are, *among ourselves,* friends, my friends, we who call ourselves friends, we do not know what a friend is. And we should have to imagine [. . .] that perhaps, therefore, there are none" (155). Socrates's closing address to Lysis and Menexenus, in other words, has a disruptive effect insofar as it announces *to friends* that there may be no such thing. The internal contradiction of the phrase pierces the community implied by the possessive friendship that occupies the latter part of the dialogue.

And so it would seem that for Socrates, the instrumental force of persuasion meets its limit at the ultimate unknowability of the audience to be addressed. Unable to possess the friend or to reduce him to a matter of utility, Socrates is for once—and shockingly, given his dramatically heightened persuasive function within the dialogue—unable to formulate an argument that would move his young interlocutors to action. (Indeed, Socrates's closing line is delivered as the boys turn their backs on him). But amid this aporetic frustration, something else does emerge from the text: the suggestion that the friend has no unified identity to be determined, to be returned to his possess-

or's interpretive horizon. Instead, the kind of satisfied knowing that eludes the group at the end of the dialogue signals that friendship is only ever realized when we surrender to the otherness of the friend as constitutive of the self. The proximity of the friend whom I cannot recognize, in other words, interrupts my own acquisitive subject position.

And, again, this inability to define the friend does not mean that the *Lysis* is a failure. I would even go so far as to say that it amounts to more than the typical aporetic ending in which Plato encourages readers and interlocutors alike to continue thinking through an issue on their own. Though the "friends" of the *Lysis* attempt to narcissistically identify and appropriate one another, these attempts are always interrupted. What emerges instead is a friendship (if we can call it such) that grapples with the boundless unknown of the other, a friendship (again, if there is one) that foregrounds distance instead of reciprocity and fusion. Socrates's ultimate inability "to find out what the friend *is*" (223b), furthermore, helps us reimagine persuasion's ethics. Are there friends? Socrates isn't sure. But they are addressed. And while Socrates's forms of persuasive address attempt to make his audience members identifiable objects of cognition, this objectification is interrupted—interrupted by the constitutive repeatability of the address and interrupted by way of the audience member's/friend's unknowability.

What we find as the dialogue concludes is that the best friends may in fact be Hippothales and Socrates at their most ridiculous. Because they don't know their friends—because they haven't been able to reduce them to fully *present* objects of cognition—their persuasive acts are empty, ritualized, and devoid of any meaningful connection to the ones that they target. Blinded by his passion for Lysis, Hippothales can only muster the most general praise for the boy. In the end, perhaps, the condition of being unable to speak specifically about our friends is the very condition of friendship itself.

CHAPTER 6

Derrida's Farewell

> Three days before the celebration they erect a tent in which the bones of the dead are laid out, and everyone brings to his own dead any offering which he pleases. At the time of the funeral the bones are placed in chests of cypress wood, which are conveyed in hearses; there is one chest for each tribe. They also carry a single empty litter decked with a pall for all those whose bodies are missing, and cannot be recovered after the battle. [...]
> When the remains have been laid in the earth, some man of known ability and high reputation, chosen by the city, delivers a suitable eulogy over them; after which the people depart.
>
> —THUCYDIDES 2.34

> We are speaking today less in order to say something than to assure ourselves, with voice and with music, that we are together in the same thought. We know with what difficulty one finds right and decent words at such a moment when no recourse should be had to common usage since all conventions will seem intolerable or vain.
>
> —JACQUES DERRIDA, "IN MEMORIAM: OF THE SOUL," 72

Thanks in large part to *The Work of Mourning* (2001), Pascale-Anne Brault and Michael Naas's edited collection of Derrida's memorial essays, consolatory letters, and funeral speeches for the friends and colleagues who died before him,[1] Derrida is now well known for his rhetorical expressions of mourning. This particular renown, in fact, is probably his preeminent rhetorical legacy. J. Hillis Miller, for one, names Derrida as "one of the greatest writers of such memoirs or memorials of all time" ("Derrida's Remains" 202). Despite the difficulties such speaking caused him, and the ubiquitous objections he raised about the "generality of the genre" (*Work* 95),

---

1. A version of this book was later published in French as *Chaque fois unique, la fin du monde* with two additional texts and a new foreword by Derrida.

Derrida chose to take on the staid tradition of the funeral oration, a rhetorical form known for its rote march through praise, lament, and consolation (Burgess 149–56), and a genre George A. Kennedy once derided for its penchant for "oratorical inebriation" (*Art* 157). While Derrida borrows many identifiable commonplaces from classical funeral orators before him, such as Pericles, Gorgias, and Lysias, he nonetheless does something more with the genre, and his memorials allow us to rethink one of rhetoric's emblematic forms. In delivering speeches honoring the lives and work of Roland Barthes, Michel Foucault, Gilles Deleuze, Emmanuel Levinas, and Jean-Francois Lyotard, among others, Derrida followed his own ethical injunction from *Specters of Marx*: That it is incumbent upon us to converse with the dead—not in order to "ontologize [their] remains" through recognition and identification, but to learn from them and to be transformed in the exposure to their otherness (9). Perhaps what is less well attended to, however, is Derrida's sustained interest in the highly aporetic rhetorical form of the funeral oration, the oldest and most exemplary genre of epideictic or ceremonial rhetoric. Responding as he did, again and again, to the vagaries of illness, aging, and timing, Derrida generated an oeuvre of compelling ceremonial speeches that highlight the ethical imperative inherent in even this most formalized and, in many cases rigid, of rhetorical forms. In speaking of and for the dead, that is, he demonstrates that the empty formulas of persuasion can foster a nonappropriative response to the other—and, in the case of the epideictic address, a response to the absolutely singular occasion that merits it.

That Derrida, the thinker who shows us that presence is always interrupted by *l'avenir*, the future-to-come, would cultivate an interest and expertise in the rhetorical genre most strongly associated with the present moment might come as something of a surprise. Even as he hinted at the funeral speech's capacity to forge a certain encounter with the nonpresent other, Derrida remained wary of its formulaic structure and its ceremonial (and thus repeatable) send-off of singularity:

> In its classical form, the funeral oration had a good side, especially when it permitted one to call out directly to the dead, sometimes very informally. This is of course a supplementary fiction, for it is always the dead in me, always the ones standing around the coffin whom I call out to. But because of its caricatured excess, the overstatement of this rhetoric at least pointed out that we ought not to remain among ourselves. The interactions of the living must be interrupted, the veil must be torn toward the other, the other dead *in* us though other still. (*Work* 51–52)

Recalling his observation in *Politics of Friendship* that the only "communication" possible among friends is an unanswerable call to the other who remains at an infinite remove, Derrida nonetheless highlights the primarily appropriative and ontologizing function of the classical funeral oration. It is only through the genre's "caricatured excess" and "overstatement" that the appropriative movement of recognizing the other (always a self-recognition, as he reminds us) is interrupted. In his rhetorical work of mourning, in other words, Derrida attempts to make the funeral speech otherwise. He suggests that the point of the funeral speech is not to be understood, certainly not by the dead, and not even by those gathered around the coffin. The point is to speak, not to "speak to." Not to "speak to" the dead, not to "speak to" one another, but to interrupt the illusion that a community of mourners can ever be more than a community of others, gathered in proximity but infinitely distanced from each other. Significantly, just prior to the occasion of his own death, Derrida arranged for the following to be read to his mourners: "Jacques wanted no rites and no orations. He knows what an ordeal it is for the friend who takes on this task" ("Final Words" 462). That task—of addressing the singular other in such a formulaic mode—was clearly an agonizing and disquieting rhetorical performance for Derrida. It was a rhetorical task with which he was profoundly uneasy, and one he would wish on no others. Despite all this, however, he attempted time and again to make the form otherwise—to transform that most appropriative and appropriating genre into an encounter with the event.

THEORIZING EPIDEICTIC RHETORIC

No rhetorical genre, in both its ancient and modern forms, has received as much sustained attention and critical reflection as the funeral oration. We can get a sense of its historical significance in Thucydides's introduction to Pericles's funeral oration for the Athenian soldiers who fell during the Peloponnesian War. Here the historian describes the quintessential epideictic scene: In response to the deaths of those slaughtered on the battlefield, the Athenian polis organized a public ritual to pay tribute to its dead. Finally, before an audience of mourners gathered at the ceremonial site, an eloquent leader delivered a speech in praise of their deeds. Thucydides's descriptive emphasis on the material elements of this mournful epideictic event—carefully arranged bones, offerings carried to the tent, an eerily empty litter—highlight the significance of ceremony and ritual in Pericles's rhetorical situation. Just as his famous oration goes on to extol the virtues of the fallen heroes and praise the glory of the Athenian state, it also serves as a final offering before the bier, no less palpable than a personal memento set inside a cypress box. Thucydides's historical narrative draws our attention to the importance of these ancient ritualistic conventions, and he thus characterizes the funeral oration as inseparable from the occasion that merits it.

Aristotle also recognized epideictic rhetoric's intimate relationship with its defining occasion when he theorized the ceremonial orations delivered in the ancient world. One important way he emphasized this intimacy was through his assignment of a temporal orientation to each of the three genres of rhetoric. When describing the forensic, epideictic, and deliberative genres, he explained:

> Each of these [species] has its own "time"; for the deliberative speaker, the future (for whether exhorting or dissuading he advises about future events); for the speaker in court, the past (for he always prosecutes or defends concerning what has been done); in epideictic the present is the most important. (*Rhetoric* 1.3.4)

The genre most closely linked to the occasion during which it was delivered, epideictic oratory seemed to fall neatly between the past-oriented concern of forensic rhetoric and the future- oriented concern of the deliberative genre. Theorizing temporality in this way required Aristotle to delineate the mode and purpose of each rhetorical genre, and with his usual attention to the importance of audience, he argued that it was the hearers present at each oration who determined the purpose of the speech (*Rhetoric* 1.3.4). Hearers of deliberative and forensic oratory were considered judges (*kritai*) who made decisions about courses of civic action, while hearers of epideictic oratory were considered observers (*theoroi*) who, Aristotle noted, focused simply on the orator's skill (*Rhetoric* 1.3.2). Thus, the purpose of its audience marked epideictic rhetoric off from the more useful deliberative and forensic genres.

Although this time- and audience-driven classification seems straightforward enough, Aristotle complicates his assignment of epideictic rhetoric to the temporal province of the present by stating that while ceremonial orators "praise or blame in regard to existing qualities, [. . .] they often also make use of other things, both reminding [the audience] of the past and projecting the course of the future" (*Rhetoric* 1.3.4). This explicit connection of the present to the past and future—and of the epideictic to the forensic and deliberative—hints at the complexities involved in theorizing rhetoric and temporality. For his part, Thucydides demonstrates how the eulogist is faced with a particularly complicated problem of presence. Not only is the funeral speech bound to the temporal presence of its occasion, but it must also contend with the spatial presence of bones, the eternally absent friends to whom these bones point, and the collective gathered to mourn them. From its earliest incarnation in the funeral oration, then, epideictic rhetoric has contended with a heightened problem of presence—a problem with which much modern rhetorical scholarship has had a hard time contending.

The traditional approach to this difficulty is to dismiss epideictic oratory as irrelevant and gratuitous display. Recalling Aristotle's dismissal of the *theoroi* who made up the audience, Cynthia Sheard notes that epideictic is the genre most likely to be seen as "mere rhetoric" (767). Denigrated for its highly figurative nature and its privileging of style above substance, it has been "associated with sophism and sophistry from its very beginnings [and] burdened from the start by suspicions of the speaker's self-indulgence and opportunism, his manipulation of audience sentiments and his distance from the interests of the community" (Sheard 767–68).

George Kennedy also highlights the widespread suspicion of the epideictic orator, explaining that the genre often comes across as "an indulgence of whim which has caused the works to be regarded as [. . .] playful exercises by an oratorical virtuoso" (*Art* 152). Sheard and Kennedy neatly summarize epideictic rhetoric's historical struggle for credibility: Because it has neither a tangible effect on future courses of civic action nor holds accountable any agent for his past deeds, its function is limited to poetic display meant for consumption by an audience of spectators. This emphasis on artistry over civic action led E. M. Cope to deem epideictic oratory as "inferior to [forensic and deliberative rhetoric] in extent, importance, and interest" (121). And in his classic study *Epideictic Literature,* Theodore Burgess conceded that the great value of ornamentation found in epideictic oratory often skewed speeches away from an interest in truth (94–95). Although they don't adhere to this assessment, Chaim Perelman and Lucie Olbrechts-Tyteca note how epideictic rhetoric is often opposed to deliberative and forensic:

> Unlike *political* and *legal* debates, real contests in which two opponents sought to gain the adherence [. . .] of an audience that would decide on the issue of a trial or on a course of action to be followed, epideictic speeches had nothing to do with all that. A single orator [. . .] made a speech, which no one opposed, on topics which were apparently uncontroversial and without practical consequences. [. . .] After listening to the speaker, [the audience] merely applauded and went away. (47–48)

The problem with this view, of course, is that it deems irrelevant everything associated with display, valuing rhetoric exclusively for its practical consequence. Furthermore, it is epideictic rhetoric's very grounding in the present that leads to this devaluation: Such speeches, with little significance of purpose, are at best appreciated for their ornament and at worst altogether ignored. Thus, in a field not infrequently burdened with the label "mere rhetoric," the epideictic genre, lacking a civic orientation, becomes the most "mere."[2]

Several rhetoric scholars have recognized the consequences of this approach and have attempted to "rescue" epideictic rhetoric by demonstrating its practical and civic function. Perelman and Olbrechts-Tyteca, for example, oppose the account excerpted above by suggesting that the genre actually helps put into action the decisions made by the judging audiences of deliberative and forensic speeches: "Epideictic oratory has significance and importance for *argumentation* because it strengthens the *disposition towards action* by increasing adherence to the values it lauds" (50, emphasis in original). Their account signals a significant movement away from the traditional dismissal of epideictic rhetoric through an emphasis on the important role of civic values within ceremonial speeches. Perelman and Olbrechts-Tyteca go even further to suggest that this civic emphasis has practical, future-oriented potential for persuading audiences to act. Brian Vickers shares a similar interest in the normative power of values found in epideictic rhetoric, noting that the ceremonial oratory of Plato and Isocrates worked to reinforce the society's existing values and provide the useful service of promoting civic cohesion (55).

Adopting a more sociopolitical approach to one particular form of epideictic oratory, Nicole Loraux examines the ideological effects of the *epitaphioi logoi* in fifth- and fourth-century Athens. In Loraux's analysis, the funeral oration is positioned as an ideological political genre that played an integral role

---

2. Though this modern denigration of the epideictic genre finds an influential witness in Aristotle, the attitude was not especially dominant in antiquity. George Kennedy points to an Isocratean tradition of classical rhetoric that opposes the Aristotelian tradition insofar as it "emphasizes written rather than spoken discourse, epideictic rather than deliberative or judicial speech, style rather than argument, amplification and smoothness rather than forcefulness" (*New* 49). Indeed, in his discussion of the panegyric in *Antidosis*, Isocrates argues for the superiority of epideictic speeches that had no stake in political or legal arenas. Of these display speeches he writes: "Everyone would agree that these are more like musical and rhythmical compositions than those uttered in the lawcourts. They set out events with a more poetic and complex style and seek to employ grander and more original enthymemes [. . .] The whole audience enjoys when they hear these [. . .] and many wish to study them, for they think those who are at the forefront of this kind of composition are much wiser and better and can be more useful than those who are eloquent in legal matters" (214–15).

in developing Athenian mentality and civic action. As such, the funeral speech becomes a generative institution that, in addition to creating a cohesive identity for those citizens who participated in the state-sanctioned ceremonies, went so far as to help invent the conception of Athens as an enduring democratic community. "But what is speechmaking if not an act?" (16), Loraux asks, suggesting that the funeral oration had far-reaching political implications— not only for those *theoroi* present at the ceremony, but also for generations of scholars who would study Athenian society as an early and influential enactment of democratic ideals. In the form of the funeral oration, then, epideictic rhetoric is shown by Loraux to have civic effects that span centuries.[3] Donovan Ochs similarly highlights the civic function of the epideictic genre, suggesting that the Athenian state funeral oration reinforced community values and recontextualized personal loss as a sacrifice for the greater good. Because the values of the state are lauded in the funeral oration, he writes, mourners are less likely to question the reasons their loved ones died in the wars instigated by Athens (68). And unlike the private funeral rites that also occurred in classical Greece, the state ceremonies removed divisive social markers, as the "rich/poor, aristocratic/common, urban/rural, brave/cowardly, strong/weak, etc. [. . .] are equal and equally valued in the state ceremony" (66). The funeral oration and its accompanying ceremonial practices are thus shown as symbolic actions that helped to promote social cohesion and loyalty to the Athenian state.

In these civic approaches taken by Ochs, Loraux, Vickers, and Perelman and Olbrechts-Tyteca, the move away from dismissing epideictic rhetoric is enabled by expanding its time orientation into the future. Not just praise and blame fixated on the present (*Rhetoric* 1.3.4), epideictic rhetoric has lasting effects on its hearers, effects that enable them to reach communicative resolutions through appeals to shared values. But while this trajectory of thought invests the genre with powerful political potential, it sacrifices the central role that presence plays in both Thucydides's historical narrative and Aristotle's

---

3. Loraux does not theorize the funeral oration as one form of a more broadly conceived epideictic genre, and she critiques "the tradition of the rhetoricians, inherited from Aristotle, who in the *Rhetoric* draws no distinction between epitaphios and encomium and classifies the funeral oration as an epideictic genre" (223). Loraux prefers to locate the Athenian state funeral oration within its unique historical and political situation, and she remains uninterested in theorizing the speeches rhetorically. Though my project explicitly draws on the very Aristotelian rhetorical tradition that Loraux rejects, we agree that the *way* the epideictic genre is theorized results in a devaluation of the funeral oration. From within this rhetorical tradition, however, I find her recovery of the funeral oration not unlike the reclamation projects of Vickers and Perelman and Olbrechts-Tyteca. All of these approaches share an attention to the civic that amplifies epideictic rhetoric's practical value and future-oriented effects.

rhetorical definition. Characterized as a vehicle for social change, epideictic rhetoric's defining characteristic is excised in order to make the genre more relevant, more oriented toward the future, and, in short, more deliberative. Put another way, these theorists value epideictic rhetoric only insofar as it is no longer epideictic rhetoric.[4]

There is an approach to the genre, however, that responds to those who would jettison the role of presence from epideictic oratory. Lawrence W. Rosenfield adopts a phenomenological reading of epideictic oratory that "examine[s] the condition of consciousness, the mental experiences that are presupposed in rhetorical acts" (131). Suggesting that what I have categorized as the traditional and civic approaches to epideictic rhetoric require "us to amend an ancient category in order to make it more compatible with our contemporary world" (132), Rosenfield traces the etymology of the term "epideictic" in order to theorize what Aristotle may have intended when he coined the category:

> The term epideictic comes from *epideixis* ("to shine or show forth"). Hence our translation of the word as "display" (in the sense of show *off*) is only literally correct. More precisely the word suggests an exhibiting or making apparent (in the sense of showing or highlighting) what might otherwise remain unnoticed or invisible. Its root is *epedexa*, "to exhibit as one would a specimen or paradigm." Epideictic, therefore, acts to unshroud men's notable deeds in order to let us gaze at the aura glowing from within. (135)

Rosenfield thus emphasizes epideictic rhetoric's powerful capability to foster in its audience "the recognition of what *is*" (133). In fact, he values epideictic rhetoric precisely because its audience is *not* required to impose judgment on the matters that appear in the epideictic speech:

> The epideictic auditor is not asked for a judgment of the present state of those matters, but to be a *theoros* ("witness") to the radiance emanating from

---

4. By no means do I claim to have provided an exhaustive account of the civic approach to epideictic rhetoric. Those elaborated here are examples of a particular trajectory of thought in which I see a pattern relevant to the problem of presence in epideictic rhetoric. Still other powerful reclamations of epideictic oratory remain, such as Jeffrey Walker's *Rhetoric and Poetics in Antiquity*, where the genre is theorized as a primary type of civic action: "In this view, 'epideictic' appears as that which shapes and cultivates the basic codes of value and belief by which a society or culture lives; it shapes the ideologies and imageries with which, and by which, the individual members of a community identify themselves; and, perhaps most significantly, it shapes the fundamental grounds, the 'deep' commitments and presuppositions that will underlie and ultimately determine decision and debate in particular pragmatic forums" (9).

the event itself. He is called to *see* it for what it *is* [...] rather than to impose on it some assessment (as though he were its purchaser and master) that might transform it. (140)

The category of presence, then, instead of being something that must be overcome in order to understand the epideictic genre as a significant branch of rhetoric, actually enables the rendering apparent of actions and deeds. Rosenfield furthermore links his reconfiguration of the character of presence within epideictic rhetoric to the pre-Socratic notion of luminosity, which the Greeks considered "the stimulus for mental activity" (133). Characterizing it as a stimulus, or a fluid movement that enables thought, Rosenfield extracts epideictic rhetoric from a tripartite linear time sequence. No longer is epideictic rhetoric the genre that fits cleanly between the past-oriented concern of forensic rhetoric and the future-oriented realm of deliberative. Rather, its presence is in a state of neither temporal nor spatial stasis: It is not simply there. Instead, the character of presence in epideictic oratory is an action or operation required for all perception. For this reason, Rosenfield suggests that epideictic oratory "calls upon us to join with our community in giving thought to what we witness" (133). In addition to signaling the importance of collective witnessing for epideictic rhetoric, Rosenfield's phenomenological emphasis on the "presencing" capabilities of epideictic oratory saves the genre from being cast as rhetoric's most denigrated. In fact, such a phenomenological approach goes even further, to render epideictic rhetoric the condition of possibility for both the forensic and deliberative genres. All those actions once associated with the past and future must be routed through epideictic witnessing if the orator and audience are to perceive them at all.

Having brought epideictic rhetoric into the realm of community and audience perception, Rosenfield seems to have solved the problems of presence found in both the traditional and civic approaches. In this third approach, the centrality of presence is not something that merely shows off the epideictic orator's virtuosity; rather, it allows all action to be *shown off* in the literal sense. Similarly, Rosenfield demonstrates how epideictic rhetoric need not be transformed into a utilitarian double of the deliberative genre in order to be rescued from the category of most "mere." As both Thucydides and Aristotle demonstrated, however, one of the distinctive markers of the epideictic speech is its irrevocable link to ritualistic conventions. While Rosenfield is able to demonstrate the importance of witnessing within epideictic oratory, his insights about the genre's theoretical power do not address how a single speech might adequately respond to the specificity and materiality of its unique epideictic occasion. While the *theoroi*—as spectators or observers—are not asked to judge the state of things in the present (*Rhetoric* 1.3.2), neither are they purely neutral hearers always dispassionate about what is *shown off* in the epideictic genre. Rosenfield thus casts witnessing as a universal tendency of epideictic oratory, and he does not necessarily tie this event to its occasion. By its nature, his phenomenological approach is purely theoretical, operating always on a level *above* the occasional milieu. It is Derrida, finally, who allows us to consider epideictic rhetoric as a singular response to its defining occasion and to fully understand the funeral oration as being a necessarily impossible response to the departed—an attempt to leave friends to their otherness. In Derrida's hands, the funeral speech becomes a nonrepresentational address to the other whose structure mirrors the presubjective *rapprochement* of alterity. It is, in other words, a rhetorical expression of his deconstructive ethics of affirmation.

UNREACHABLE FRIENDS

Perhaps it is unsurprising that Derrida's approach to the epideictic genre, just like his approach to ethics itself, is an aporetic one. His funerary texts always register profound hesitation before the rhetorical performance mourning, as he always signals his reluctance to write or speak *about* another—especially a friend—for fear of using the friend for his own ends. In his memorial essay for Barthes, for instance, Derrida highlights his discomfort with the presence and immediacy that haunt epideictic rhetoric:

> But what I thought impossible, indecent, and unjustifiable, what long ago and more or less secretly and resolutely I had promised myself never to do (out of concern for rigor and fidelity, if you will, and because it is in this case *too* serious) was to write *following the death*, not after, not long after the death by *returning* to it, but just following the death, *upon or on the occasion of the death*, at the commemorative gatherings and tributes, in the writings "in memory of" those who while living would have been my friends, still present enough to me that some "declaration," indeed some analysis or "study" would seem at that moment completely unbearable. (*Work* 49–50)

In the futile attempt to avoid appropriation, the traditional funeral speech— "just following the death"—makes no pretense of objectivity; in it the speaker embraces what is positive because of an unexplained but always deeply felt temporal, and even spatial, sanctity. "Upon or on the occasion of the death," when the impossibility of the deceased's response overwhelms the speaker, negative elements are either softened, disguised, or left out entirely. It is the very sanctity of this occasion that makes the funeral speech such a conventional form, one in which words can never do justice to the friend who has died. While Derrida's reservations about such immediate response might make him seem a reluctant ceremonial rhetor, these protestations foreground the ethical problems that presence poses for epideictic oratory. These thus become questions of ethical response: *What might I say that will not encroach upon the other? How might I find the words to do justice to this otherness?* Derrida seems to suggest that one way to avoid appropriating the other after his death would be to say nothing at all. If he were never to compose a speech in praise of the dead, then he would never have to commit the violent act of appropriating a friend or reducing this friend to a mere object of cognition. Rather than falling silent, however, Derrida responds: "But then what, silence? Is this not another wound, another insult?" (*Work* 50). And he uses the very conventional genre of the funeral speech to articulate the singularity of his friendship with the deceased.

As Thucydides's description of the Athenian state funeral oration makes clear, the eulogist has always been faced with particularly complicated instantiations of temporal and spatial presence. We see in his historical narrative that the bereaved individuals present at the ceremony offer gifts—personal mementos—to bones that may or may not have belonged to their own loved ones. The character of such offerings attests to the intimacy of each individual relationship even as it illustrates the impossible distance, and perhaps even anonymity, between mourned and mourner. Not unlike the famous oration delivered by Pericles in the midst of this peculiarly Athenian ritual, Derrida's funeral speeches also address the impossible relationship between the deceased and the ones who mourn them. In the address delivered at the cremation of Blanchot, he foregrounds this distance:

> I don't dare say in "*ton nom*," remembering still what Maurice Blanchot himself thought and publicly declared about such an absolute exception, this signal privilege that friendship confers, namely the *tutoiement* he says was his only once through his long-standing friendship with Emmanuel Levinas. ("Witness" 41)

Derrida's reluctance to refer to Blanchot with the "familiar you" points to the importance of leaving the deceased to his infinite otherness, and it insists on an unbridgeable distance between two who were nonetheless friends.

This is not to say that Derrida sidesteps the affective power of personal tragedy as it unfolds at the funeral. As he notes in "No Apocalypse, Not Now," the death of a friend is a deeply felt event whose catastrophic effects occur "with every individual death" (28). He adds: "There is no common measure to persuade me that a personal mourning is less serious than a nuclear war" (28). His epideictic oratory, however, also always insists on maintaining, as did Thucydides's, the impossible distance between the deceased and the mourner. Such distance is in fact required so that we do not appropriate or do violence to the one we have lost. In *Politics of Friendship*, as I mentioned in the previous chapter, Derrida emphasizes Blanchot's suggestion that it was only "*thanks to death that friendship [could] be declared*" (302). That is, only in the absolute absence of the friend, only when the friend's otherness could not possibly be recuperated, could a genuine expression of nonreciprocal friendship be proffered. The epideictic orator, then, can never claim to know the deceased, regardless of how intimate the pair was in life. In fact, the unbridgeable distance the friend now maintains in death is merely a heightened instance of the distance, of the otherness, that he kept from the speaker while living. In this way, the funeral speech dramatically illustrates something that is always the case: Advancing an argument about or staking a claim to another is an inevitable violence that we nevertheless struggle to avoid.

Thus, in his funeral speeches, Derrida highlights a type of bereavement that runs contrary to Freud, whose own work of mourning requires the interiorization, incorporation, and consumption of the other in order to move beyond his loss. While Derrida's funerary texts mobilize mourning differently, they do not deny that we "incorporate" (*Work* 159) the dead by hanging on to images and memories that keep friends with us insofar as "it is in us that their movements appear" (*Work* 159). What Derrida's funeral speeches do, however, is allow us to respond to our dead friends, now figured as collections of images that we can visualize and mobilize, while still leaving them to their infinite otherness. This is possible because the eulogist must speak as though guided by the deceased's utter inability to listen or respond. This irreconcilable distance is the enabling force of the epideictic orator's response to the death of a friend, as Derrida suggests in his text on Barthes:

> These thoughts are *for him* [. . .] meaning that I think of him and about him, not only about his work. [. . .] Yet they will no longer reach him, and this must be the starting point of my reflection; they can no longer reach him, reach all the way to him, assuming they ever could have while he was still living. [. . .] We must hold fast to this evidence, to its excessive clarity, and continually return to it as if to the simplest thing, to that alone which, while withdrawing into the impossible, still leaves us to think and gives us occasion for thought. (*Work* 35)

Derrida's epideictic oratory, therefore, is premised on the notion of a singular friendship, and this singular friendship is made possible by the "infinite distance and dissymmetry" that keeps him unreachable (*Politics* 221). From these conditions of possibility arises the notion of a nonsubjective other who cannot be appropriated or subsumed into the self. In the speech delivered at Blanchot's cremation, Derrida demonstrates how such a paradoxical notion of the simultaneously present and distant friend helps ward off this friend's appropriation. Blanchot's name, he writes, "had become [. . .] at once familiar and strange, so foreign [. . .] infinitely far from oneself, but a name, too, intimate and ancient [. . .] careful to leave you to your solitude, always mindful though to remain near you" ("Witness" 43). Thus positioned in this nonsubjective space, Blanchot, forever unable to be pinned down, is rendered "inappropriable" (49).

Given this interest in highlighting the dead friend's incomparability, it is perhaps surprising that the conventional genre of the funeral oration provides Derrida with an appropriate forum to address not only singularity, but also the impossible relation that enables it. In fact, it is through amplifying these very funerary conventions that he manages to speak. (Not, again, to speak to or for the dead, but to address the friend without assuming that these words will ever have reached the friend.) When Derrida makes reference to testimony or display in his discourse of mourning, he often speaks of the impossibility of knowing just what to say, an impossibility that enables his mourning to always be "at work" (*Work* 95). Derrida opens his funeral speech for Lyotard by highlighting his inability to express sentiments worthy of the friendship between them: "I feel at such a loss, unable to find public words for what is happening to us, for what has left speechless all those who had the good fortune to come near this great thinker" (*Work* 214). So too does he foreground this inability to speak in his oration for Paul de Man. There, he acknowledges "with what difficulty one finds right and decent words at such a moment when no recourse should be had to common usage since all conventions will either seem intolerable or in vain" (*Work* 72). And he opens the speech delivered at Louis Althusser's funeral in a similar vein: "I knew in advance that I would be unable to speak today, unable, as they say, to find the words" (*Work* 114). Time and again, Derrida ruminates on the difficulty of such speech, not just because it easily gives itself over to the appropriative version of mourning, but also because this impossibility is *owed* to the one being praised.

Derrida's admissions of his inability to speak are profuse—elements of nearly all his funerary texts. These aporetic pronouncements make death itself seem formulaic in order to prevent the text from representing or appropriating the dead friend. Furthermore, they rhetorically reenact the presubjective *rap-*

prochement, which, prior to recognition and the formation of will, engages one to another. By using such a conventional form, Derrida refrains from reducing his friends to objects of cognition, and in this way, the funeral speech creates a condition in which *what* one says has little or no meaning. Derrida emphasizes this fact by amplifying the rhetorical figure of aporia, which expresses precisely the impossibility of expression. Because it is repeated so often, and because it ruptures logical thought, this figure works to withdraw meaning from the very event of speaking. The funeral oration, then—through its accentuated reliance on aporetic pronouncement—highlights the asignifying effects of speaking, ones in which meaning is not primarily a function of presence. Rather than attempting to avoid the conventions of the funeral speech, Derrida intensifies these conventions, repeating them on the occasion of each death in order to show that the friend is entirely beyond representation.

Derrida, of course, is not the only eulogist to rely on this convention; similar words are uttered at nearly every funerary occasion, even those in antiquity. In the speech delivered before his fellow Athenians, Pericles also commented on language's inability to appropriately attend to the mournful scenario. Referencing the practice of the Athenian state ceremony, Pericles says:

> It seemed to [previous speakers] a worthy thing that such an honor should be given at their burial to the dead who have fallen on the field of battle. But I should have preferred that, when men's deeds have been brave, they should be honored in deed only, and with such an honor as this public funeral, which you are now witnessing. Then the reputation of many would not have been imperiled on the eloquence or want of eloquence of one, and their virtues believed or not as he spoke well or ill. For it is difficult to say neither too little nor too much; and even moderation is apt not to give the impression of truthfulness. (Thucydides 2.35)

Even Pericles highlights the insufficiency of speaking at the funerary occasion, no matter if the eulogist says "too little," "too much," or some balance in between. In fact, it may be that this problem of representation is one reason why stating how difficult it is to speak on the occasion of a friend's death is such a pervasive convention of the funeral speech. Through their iteration of this convention, Derrida's speeches give voice to an affirmative ethics of otherness, one that holds not only for the dead, but also applies to the living.

Through his emphasis on responsibility and iteration, we might better understand why Derrida spoke on these commemorative occasions instead of remaining silent. His orations serve as his impossible responses to the dead, responses only enabled by the impossibility of reaching the radically other who, to borrow Derrida's use of the future anterior, will have been his friend. In this tense, a signature demonstration of Derrida's concern with the present, the conditional phrasing refuses presence a static position. Instead it enacts a movement from future to past that hints towards a futurity entirely removed from linear temporality. What Derrida tells us, then, is that the function of presence in the funeral speech is always to serve as an encounter with alterity. By highlighting the impossible distance between the speaker and the deceased and by amplifying the convention of being unable to speak upon the occasion of a friend's death, Derrida suggests that presence is always other to itself. In other words, though presence seems to be a static entity, Derrida's funeral orations show that epideictic rhetoric's presence is always in response. He thus intervenes in the theoretical discussion of epideictic rhetoric by addressing the problem of presence and demonstrating how it functions as an ethics of otherness.

As I mentioned earlier in this chapter, Derrida requested that no orations be read on the occasion of his own death. In place of this ritual practice, he asked that a short note he had handwritten be read aloud and distributed to those in attendance (Vitale 185). This note instructed mourners to "smile for me [. . .] as I will have smiled for you until the end. Always prefer life and constantly affirm survival" ("Final Words" 462). These final words, in the form of a performative address, were at once a command and a reprieve. While the address spared his friends from experiencing the distress he himself had felt on many such occasions, it enacted the same nonrepresentational force that defined so many of his own funerary texts. By instructing his mourners to smile on him as he had always smiled on them, Derrida invokes an affirmative expression that communicates no signified content. That is, no content is shared—nothing from Derrida about his friends, and nothing from his friends about Derrida. Instead, each is addressed to the other in the form of an affirmative address—a nonsubjective rapport in which each other is ultimately unassimilable.

EPILOGUE

> Conclusions, among the Greeks called epilogoi, are tripartite, consisting of the Summing Up, Amplification, and Appeal to Pity.
> —RHETORIC TO HERENNIUS 2.30.47

> The starting point [of the epilogue] is to claim that one has performed what was promised, [...].
> —ARISTOTLE, RHETORIC, 3.19.4

The classical rhetorical tradition on which I have drawn throughout this book tells us in so many words that the endings of speeches—conclusions, perorations, epilogues—are meant to be exercises in persuasive evocation: brief reminders, often woven together with emotional appeals, of all that has come before. Aristotle describes a four-part epilogue aimed at "disposing the hearer favorably toward the speaker and unfavorably toward the opponent; amplifying and minimizing; moving the hearer into emotional reactions [...]; and [giving] a reminder [of the chief points in the argument]" (3.19.1). The *Rhetoric to Herennius* condenses the parts to three, glossing over Aristotle's dictate to further enhance the speaker's character and diminish the opponent's. No matter how the content is divided, however, the task is essentially the same: to lead the audience to recall what has been said and to remember how they felt about it. And since this is "an *epi-logos*, not a *logos*" (Aristotle *Rhetoric* 3.19.6)—an add-on, so to speak—these efforts to refresh the memories of the audience should be brief, or at least briefer than the central elements of the speech itself. As Michael de Brauw explains, Aristotle suggests a conclusion in proportion to the overall length of the speech, but this did not always hold: short speeches could have long epilogues and the opposite, although brevity was common (198). We can see this tendency toward the brief—even abrupt—ending most vividly in Aristotle's statement about the appropriateness of asyndeton for the epilogue. Since all that is left to do is "remind the audience of what has been said earlier" (3.19.3), even conjunctions become unnecessary: "I have spoken; you have listened, you have [the case], you judge" (3.19.6).

Given my focus in the previous chapters on texts from the classical tradition that foreground the instrumental force of persuasion, it seems natural that I look at the end to the relatively brief but still highly prescriptive classical guidelines for endings. The most common tactic prescribed for composing an effective epilogue is to remind the audience of what has been said and to develop a proof based on arguments that have already been made. Even Plato recognizes the uniformity and ubiquity of this strategy, writing through Socrates that "everyone seems to be in agreement" concerning the conclusion of discourses. To which Phaedrus replies, "You mean, summarizing everything at the end and reminding the audience of what they've heard?" (267d). The *Herennius* calls this the "Summing Up," a recapitulation that "gathers together and recalls the points we have made—briefly, that the speech may not be repeated in entirety, but that the memory of it may be refreshed" (2.30.47). Memory plays a central role, as well, in the amplification section, whose focus, according to Aristotle, is on "what has already been shown [in the proof]" (3.19.2), and in appeals to various emotions, including pity, anger, favor, and fear. While "emotional appeals are not limited to the epilogue," some are especially suited to the ending of the speech: For example, pity, the emotion felt for the innocent, worked best only after the defendant had proclaimed his innocence (de Brauw 198). The persuasive effectiveness of the epilogue, then, depends on this prescribed strategy of bringing "the hearer [. . .] back to what he remembers" (*Herennius* 2.30.47). In the end, the goal of the epilogue, as Aristotle points out in the epigraph to this chapter, is to prove that the speaker has "performed what was promised" (3.19.4). This advice is simple enough on its face, of course—all the speaker needs to do is restate what was already said—but it also requires the impossible: to confirm the completion of an act defined *essentially* by its open relation to the future.

By opening and closing *The Ethics of Persuasion* with a discussion of handbooks like the *Herennius* and the *Alexander* (and even the *Rhetoric*, although Aristotle would not care for it to be included alongside these two), I have attempted to stage one of this book's central claims: that even the most calculated attempts to produce predetermined responses in the minds of audience members involves an encounter with forces beyond the order of knowledge, and further still that the most tactical, utilitarian approaches to the art of persuasion initiate a certain unsettling experience of the impossible. In other words, the discipline of classical rhetoric, largely defined by its preoccupation with the art of persuasion as an instrument of power and control, nonetheless involves an ethical encounter in which priority is granted to the other. In Gorgias's *Encomium of Helen,* for example, the fifth-century speech that has become an emblem for the deceptive power of persuasion to exert control, we find an account of identity as given by way of its ongoing, unconditional affirmation of alterity. Such an account, I argued in Chapter 2, suggests that the presubjective *rapprochement* with an unassimilable other precedes and exceeds the instrumental force of persuasion. And in the case of the famed logographer Lysias, known equally for his willingness to write speeches for many an unsavory client and for his capacity to stylistically disappear into the speeches he composed in others' voices, we find a disrupted rhetorical identity who initiates an unsettling encounter with the event. In Chapter 3, I show how Lysias's hauntological transition from guest to host to hostage to refugee to *revenant* renders the rhetorical gun for hire a good deal less familiar than he once was and how the purity of both the Athenian state and the clean, Attic style Lysias eventually came to represent was always already contaminated.

Examples like these complicate the primarily transactional understanding of the art of persuasion as a perlocutionary endeavor. Taken from J. L. Austin's *How to Do Things with Words,* this concept (the perlocutionary speech act) refers to speech acts that produce "certain *consequential* effects upon the feelings, thoughts, or actions of the audience" (101, emphasis added); thus, the term accounts for "the use of 'language' for persuading" (103). This framework highlights the instrumental force of persuasion because it foregrounds the capacity of speech to exert asignifying force on others. Furthermore, because it installs a fully present utterance-origin as the source of the speech act, this framework casts persuasion as an activity undertaken by sovereign beings whose selfhood is uncompromised in the linguistic exchange. In Chapter 4, I argued that the coherent expressive identity assumed in this instrumental model is challenged as well by the classical rhetorical tradition's foremost humanist, Isocrates, whose famed *logon paideia* promises—on the surface at least—the moral education of the whole orator. Despite his seeming commitment to the integral self, Isocrates's pedagogical design posits an ethical subject who is performatively produced (and so transformed) in response to a radically unknowable future. And in Plato's *Lysis,* which I examined in Chapter 5, we are witness to a similar subjective dispersion when Socrates and his interlocutors encounter an impasse that thwarts their dialectical striving to comprehend both the being of friendship and the friend himself. Against this pedagogical backdrop—one that suggests, much like Isocrates, that learning is a matter of being transformed in the face of illimitable alterity—the *Lysis* suggests that calculated persuasive tactics always meet their limit at the radical unknowability of the intended audience.

I have identified the ethical components of these classical rhetorical scenes, over the course of the preceding chapters, by drawing on a specific Derridean account of ethics, which, as I describe Chapter 1, emerges in the event of an expropriating but also *affirmative* encounter with alterity in which self-identity is simultaneously invented and disturbed, enabled and interrupted. In this formulation, the other's address *precedes* self-identification; it is only in response to alterity's demand that the identity of the subject comes to "be" in the first place. Thus, the ethical encounter is characterized by an other-before-me imperative that resists the powerful tendency to appropriate difference by returning it to the realm of the selfsame. If self-identity is nothing but the ongoing activity of responding to the other, then this other cannot be violently cast out of the safe home of one's being. Ethics thus rests on a subject perpetually haunted by the other's trace, and identity is no *thing* in itself but a nonassimilating activity of living on in relation to the other.

In this sense, Derrida's idea of ethics became the analytical lens through which I reread the ancient rhetorical tradition. My hope was to identify an ethical component that would allow me to recast a discipline long known for its preoccupation with utility and instrumentality. What I found, of course, was that this rhetorical tradition had a mutually illuminating, perhaps even transformative, effect on Derrida's thought, as well. That is, given Derrida's own insistence on characterizing ethics in terms of various forms of address (affirming, speaking, listening, calling, being attentive, and saying *yes*), and given the way that he generalizes and reverses Austin's notion of the performative speech act by positing the performative structure of identity itself, Derrida's ethics, I argued, are themselves profoundly rhetorical. Their essential structure mirrors that of persuasive speech, although the focus is on an addressivity prior to empirical speech acts. We can see this rhetorical character, further, in Derrida's aporetic understanding of ethics, which takes place before and beyond the choice-making, rule-following approaches associated with normative or applied ethics. When he ties his philosophical approach to the rhetorical figure used to express doubt or to signal a necessary hesitation before moving ahead to the presumed topic at hand, Derrida emphasizes the importance of the quasi-transcendental conditions of possibility that give rise to ethical and political responsibility.

As I noted in the previous chapter, Derrida was deeply ambivalent about his role as an epideictic orator, in large part because of the strongly appropriative impulses of the funeral speech as a genre. Drawing on his considerable eloquence and artistry, he interrupted these appropriative features, often by way of a stylistic intensification that suspended the communication of representative meaning. And yet time and again he articulated the unique and deeply felt anguish associated with speaking on the occasions of his friends' deaths. In addition to suffering the loss of those he held most dear, in other words, the act of publicly addressing the dead and those gathered to mourn them seemed to cause him still further pain and desolation. In the eulogy he delivered for Jean-Francois Lyotard, for example, he hinted toward the toll such an oratorical role was beginning to take: "Upon the death of Deleuze, you asked me to attempt—that time too without delay, and in the midst of my own sorrow—a sort of testimony" (*Work* 215). And when he wrote in *Politics of Friendship* about Maurice Blanchot's funerary text for Michel Foucault, he refused to give into "the indecency of the cold reading of the rhetoritician which would uncover the sublime calculations imposed on this extraordinary declaration of friendship in mourning" (300). Despite the "indecency" of rhetoric and its associated persuasive genres, which seem to be necessarily engaged in an appropriating movement toward the addressee, there remains something ethical (pre-ethical or aporetically ethical, perhaps) on which Derrida draws as a resource. Indeed, it seems to me that there is something essentially rhetorical about Derrida's ethics, which are often formulated in the radically transformed terms of Austin's performative utterance. By his account, ethical responsibility rests on a structure of self that is given only by way of the ongoing affirmation of the other. "The self," as he has argued, "*is still to come,* not as a *future* reality but as that which will always retain the essential structure of a promise" (*Who's Afraid* 22). As I hope I have made clear by now, this promise or affirmation is a pre-performative, nonlinguistic response to the other. It precedes and exceeds the empirical speech acts that Derrida nonetheless uses to describe it. But what Derrida's thoroughgoing concern with speech acts, with genres of oratory, and with forms of address can teach us is that living on in relation to the other—"surviving" as he sometimes characterizes it—is a rhetorical relation in which self and other can never be untangled.

WORKS CITED

Airbnb. "Never a Stranger." *YouTube*, April 22, 2015.

Alter, Jonathan and Joshua Green. "Bennett: Virtue is as Virtue Does?" *Newsweek* May 8, 2003. LexisNexis.

Anderson, Nicole. *Derrida: Ethics Under Erasure*. Continuum, 2012.

Aristotle. *Nicomachean Ethics*. Translated by Joe Sachs. Focus Publishing, 2002.

———. *On Rhetoric: A Theory of Civic Discourse*. 2nd ed. Edited by George A. Kennedy. Oxford UP, 2007.

———. *Rhetoric to Alexander*. Translated by E. S. Forster. *The Complete Works of Aristotle, Vol. 2*. Edited by Jonathan Barnes. Princeton UP, 1984, pp. 2270–315.

Atkins, G. D. and Michael L. Johnson, editors. *Writing and Reading Differently: Deconstruction and the Teaching of Composition and Literature*. UP of Kansas, 1985.

Atwill, Janet. *Rhetoric Reclaimed: Aristotle and the Liberal Arts Tradition*. Cornell UP, 1998.

Austin, J. L. *How to Do Things with Words*. Edited by J. O. Urmson and Marina Sbisa. Harvard UP, 1962.

Bakewell, Geoff. "Lysias 12 and Lysias 31: Metics and Athenian Citizenship in the Aftermath of the Thirty." *Greek, Roman, and Byzantine Studies*, vol. 40, 1999, pp. 5–22.

Ballif, Michelle. "Awaiting Rhetoric's Monstrous (Be)Coming." U of South Carolina Rhetorical Theory Conference. October 2011. Columbia, SC.

———. "Historiography as Hauntology: Paranormal Investigations into the History of Rhetoric." *Theorizing Histories of Rhetoric*. Edited by Michelle Ballif. Southern Illinois UP, 2013.

———. "Regarding the Dead." *Philosophy & Rhetoric*, vol. 47, no. 4, 2014, pp. 455–71.

———. *Seduction, Sophistry, and the Woman with the Rhetorical Figure*. Southern Illinois UP, 2001.

Bateman, J.J. "Some Aspects of Lysias' Argumentation." *Phoenix*, vol. 16, no. 3, 1962, pp. 157–77.

Beardsworth, Richard. *Derrida and the Political*. Routledge, 1996.

Bennett, William J. *The Book of Virtues: A Treasury of Great Moral Stories*. Simon & Schuster, 1993.

———. "Moral Literacy and the Formation of Character." *National Association of Secondary School Principals Bulletin*, vol. 72, no. 512, December 1988, pp. 29–34.

Bennington, Geoffrey. *Interrupting Derrida*. Routledge, 2000.

———. *Legislations: The Politics of Deconstruction*. Verso, 1994.

Bernasconi, Robert. "The Trace of Levinas in Derrida." *Derrida and Différance*. Edited by David Wood and Robert Bernasconi. Northwestern UP, 1988, pp. 13–30

———. "Deconstruction and the Possibility of Ethics." *Deconstruction and Philosophy: The Texts of Jacques Derrida*. Edited by John Sallis. U of Chicago P, 1987.

Biesecker, Barbara A. "Rethinking the Rhetorical Situation from Within the Thematic of Différance." *Philosophy and Rhetoric*, vol. 22, no. 2, 1989, pp. 110–30.

Bolotin, David. *Plato's Dialogue on Friendship: A New Interpretation of the Lysis, with a New Translation*. Cornell UP, 1979.

Brown, James J. Jr. *Ethical Programs: Hospitality and the Rhetorics of Software*. U of Michigan P, 2015.

Bruss, Kristine. "Persuasive *Ethopoeia* in Dionysius's *Lysias*." *Rhetorica: A Journal of the History of Rhetoric*, vol. 31, no. 1, Winter 2013, pp. 34–57.

Burgess, Theodore C. *Epideictic Literature*. Garland Publishing, 1987.

Butman, Jeremy. "No Exit for Derrida: Jeremy Butman Interviews Simon Critchley." *Los Angeles Review of Books,* October 9, 2014, lareviewofbooks.org/article/exit-derrida#!.

Cadava, Eduardo, Peter Connor, and Jean-Luc Nancy. "'Eating Well,' Or the Calculation of the Subject: An Interview with Jacques Derrida." *Who Comes After the Subject?* Edited by Eduardo Cadava, Peter Connor, and Jean-Luc Nancy. Routledge, 1991.

Carey, C., editor. *Lysias: Selected Speeches*. Cambridge UP, 2002.

———. "Rhetorical Means of Persuasion." *Essays on Aristotle's Rhetoric*. Edited by Amelie Oksenberg Rorty. U of California P, 1996, pp. 399–415.

Cassin, Barbara. *Sophistical Practice: Toward a Consistent Relativism*. Fordham UP, 2014.

Cicero. *De Oratore*. Translated by E. W. Sutton and H. Rackham. Vol. 2, Loeb-Harvard UP, 1942.

———. "Rhetorica Ad Herennium." *Ad C. Herennium De Ratione Dicendi*. Edited by Harry Caplan. Translated by Harry Caplan. Loeb-Harvard UP, 1954.

Connolly, Joy. "The Politics of Rhetorical Education." *The Cambridge Companion to Ancient Rhetoric*. Edited by Erik Gunderson. Cambridge UP, 2009, pp.126–42.

Connors, Clare. "Derrida and the Fiction of Force." *Angelaki: Journal of the Theoretical Humanities*, vol. 12, no. 2, August 2007, pp. 9–15.

Consigny, Scott. *Gorgias: Sophist and Artist*. U of South Carolina P, 2001.

———. "The Styles of Gorgias." *Rhetoric Society Quarterly*, vol. 22, no. 3, 1992, pp. 43–53.

Cope, E. M. *An Introduction to Aristotle's Rhetoric*. Macmillan, 1867.

Critchley, Simon. *The Ethics of Deconstruction: Derrida and Levinas*. Blackwell, 1992.

———. *The Ethics of Deconstruction: Derrida and Levinas*. 2nd ed. Edinburgh UP, 1999.

———. *Ethics, Politics, Subjectivity: Essays on Derrida, Levinas and Contemporary French Thought*. Verso, 1999.

Crowley, Sharon. "Of Gorgias and Grammatology." *College Composition and Communication*, vol. 30, no. 3, 1979, pp. 279–84.

Dasenbrock, Reed W. "J. L. Austin and the Articulation of a New Rhetoric." *College Composition and Communication*, vol. 38, no. 3, 1987, pp. 291–305.

Davis, Colin. "*État Présent*: Hauntology, Spectres and Phantoms." *French Studies*, vol. 59, no. 3, 2005, pp. 373–79.

Davis, Diane. "Addressing Alterity: Rhetoric, Hermeneutics, and the Nonappropriative Relation." *Philosophy and Rhetoric*, vol. 38, no. 3, 2005, pp. 191–212.

———. *Inessential Solidarity: Rhetoric and Foreigner Relations*. U of Pittsburgh P, 2010.

———. "Performative Perfume." *Performatives After Deconstruction*. Edited by Mauro Senatore. Bloomsbury, 2013.

———. "Rhetoricity at the End of the World." *Philosophy and Rhetoric*, vol. 50, no. 4, 2017, pp. 431–51.

de Brauw, Michael. "The Parts of the Speech." *A Companion to Greek Rhetoric*. Edited by Ian Worthington. Wiley-Blackwell, 2010, pp.187–202.

de Romilly, Jacqueline. *The Great Sophists in Periclean Athens*. Translated by Janet Lloyd. Clarendon P, 2002.

Depew, David. "The Inscription of Isocrates into Aristotle's Practical Philosophy." *Isocrates and Civic Education*. Edited by Takis Poulakos and David Depew. U of Texas P, 2004, pp. 157–85.

Derrida, Jacques. *Adieu to Emmanuel Levinas*. Translated by Pascale-Anne Brault and Michael Naas. Stanford UP, 1999.

———. *Acts of Literature*. Edited by Derek Attridge. Routledge, 1992.

———. *Acts of Religion*. Translated by Gil Anidjar. Routledge, 2002.

———. *Aporias*. Translated by Thomas Dutoit. Stanford UP, 1993.

———. "A Certain Impossible Possibility of Saying the Event." Translated by Gila Walker. *Critical Inquiry*, vol. 33, 2007, pp. 441–61.

———. *Dissemination*. U of Chicago P, 1981.

———. "Final Words." Translated by Gila Walker. *Critical Inquiry*, vol. 33, no. 2, Winter 2007, p. 462.

———. "Force of Law: 'The Mystical Foundation of Authority.'" Translated by Mary Quaintance. *Deconstruction and the Possibility of Justice*. Edited by Drucilla Cornell, Michel Rosenfeld, and David Gray Carlson. Routledge, 1992, pp. 3–67.

———. "Hostipitality." Translated by Barry Stocker with Forbes Morlock. *Angelaki: Journal of the Theoretical Humanities*, vol. 5, no. 3, December 2000, pp. 3–18.

———. "How to Avoid Speaking: Denials." *Derrida and Negative Theology*. Edited by Harold Coward and Toby Foshay. SUNY P, 1992.

———. "In Memoriam: Of the Soul." Translated by Kevin Newmark. *The Work of Mourning*. Edited by Pascale-Anne Brault and Michael Naas. U of Chicago P, 2001, pp. 72–75.

———. "'Le Parjure,' Perhaps: Storytelling and Lying." *Without Alibi*. Edited by Peggy Kamuf. Stanford UP, 2002, pp. 161–201.

———. "Limited Inc a b c." Translated by Samuel Weber. *Limited Inc*. Edited by Gerald Graff. Northwestern UP, 1988, pp. 29–110.

———. *Limited Inc*. Edited by Gerald Graff. Northwestern UP, 1988.

———. *Margins of Philosophy*. Translated by Alan Bass. U of Chicago P, 1982.

———. *Memoires for Paul de Man*. Translated by Cecile Lindsay, Jonathan Culler, and Eduardo Cadava. Columbia UP, 1986.

———. "No Apocalypse, Not Now." Translated by Catherine Porter and Philip Lewis. *Diacritics*, vol. 14, no. 2, 1984, pp. 20–31.

———. *Of Grammatology*. Translated by Gayatri Chakrovorty Spivak. Johns Hopkins UP, 1997.

———. *Of Hospitality: Anne Dufourmantelle Invites Jacques Derrida to Respond*. Translated by Rachel Bowlby. Stanford UP, 2000.

———. *On Cosmopolitanism and Forgiveness*. Translated by Mark Dooley and Michael Hughes. Routledge, 1997.

———. *On the Name*. Translated by David Wood. Stanford UP, 1995.

———. *Paper Machine*. Translated by Rachel Bowlby. Stanford UP, 2005.

———. *Politics of Friendship*. Translated by George Collins. Verso, 1997.

———. *Points . . . : Interviews 1974–1994*. Edited by Elisabeth Weber. Stanford UP, 1995.

———. *Psyche: Inventions of the Other, Vol. 1*. Edited by Peggy Kamuf and Elizabeth Rottenberg. Stanford UP, 2007.

———. *Psyche: Inventions of the Other, Vol. 2*. Edited by Peggy Kamuf and Elizabeth Rottenberg. Stanford UP, 2008.

———. "Remarks on Deconstruction and Pragmatism." Simon Critchley et al. *Deconstruction and Pragmatism*. Edited by Chantal Mouffe. Routledge, 1996, pp. 77–88.

———. *Rogues: Two Essays on Reason*. Stanford UP, 2005.

———. "Signature Event Context." *Margins of Philosophy*. Translated by Alan Bass. U of Chicago P, 1982, pp. 307–30.

———. *Specters of Marx: The State of the Debt, the Work of Mourning and the New International*. Translated by Peggy Kamuf. Routledge, 1994.

———. "Ulysses Gramophone: Hear Say Yes in Joyce.'" *Acts of Literature*. Edited by Derek Attridge. Routledge, 1992, pp. 253–309.

———. "The University without Condition." *Without Alibi*. Edited by Peggy Kamuf. Stanford UP, 2000.

———. "Violence and Metaphysics." *Writing & Difference*. Translated by Alan Bass. U of Chicago P, 1978.

———. "'We Other Greeks.'" Translated by Pascale-Anne Brault and Michael Naas. *Derrida and Antiquity*. Edited by Miriam Leonard. Oxford UP, 2010.

———. *Who's Afraid of Philosophy? Right to Philosophy 1*. Translated by Jan Plug. Edited by Werner Hamacher and David E. Wellbery. Stanford UP, 2002.

———. "A Witness Forever." Translated by Charlotte Mandell. *Nowhere Without No: In Memory of Maurice Blanchot*. Edited by Michael Hart. Vagabond P, 2003, pp. 41–49.

———. *Without Alibi*. Edited and translated by Peggy Kamuf. Stanford UP, 2002.

———. *The Work of Mourning*. Edited by Pascale-Anne Brault and Michael Naas. U of Chicago P, 2001.

Derrida, Jacques, and Maurizio Ferraris. *A Taste for the Secret*. Translated by Giacomo Donis. Edited by Giacomo Donis and David Webb. Polity P, 2001.

Derrida, Jacques and Alan Montefiore. "Talking Liberties: Jacques Derrida's Interview with Alan Montefiore." *Derrida & Education*. Edited by Gert J. J. Biesta and Denise Egéa-Kuehne. Routledge, 2001, pp. 176–85.

Derrida, Jacques, Avital Ronell, and Brian Holmes. "A Number of Yes (Nombre de oui)." *Qui Parle*, vol. 2, no. 2, 1988, pp. 118–33.

Devries, William Levering. *Ethopoiia: A Rhetorical Study of the Types of Character in the Orations of Lysias*. Published Diss. Johns Hopkins UP, 1892.

Dionysius of Halicarnassus. *Dionysius of Halicarnassus: The Critical Essays Vol. 1*. Translated by Stephen Usher. Loeb Classical Library, 1974.

Doran, Robert. *The Ethics of Theory: Philosophy, History, Literature*. Bloomsbury Academic, 2016.

Dover, K. J. *Lysias and the Corpus Lysiacum*. U of California P, 1968.

Edwards, Michael. *The Attic Orators*. Bristol Classical P, 1994.

———. "Lysias and Logography." Rhetoric Society of America. San Antonio, TX. May 23, 2014. Seminar.

Edwards, Michael and Stephen Usher. *Greek Orators I: Antiphon and Lysias*. Bolchazy-Carducci Publishers, 1985.

Enos, Richard Leo. "The Epistemology of Gorgias' Rhetoric: A Re-examination." *The Southern Speech Communication Journal*, vol. 42, 1976, pp. 35–51.

Felman, Shoshanna. *The Scandal of the Speaking Body: Don Juan with J. L. Austin or Seduction in Two Languages*. Stanford UP, 2002.

Fish, Stanley. *Doing What Comes Naturally: Change, Rhetoric, and the Practice of Theory in Literary & Legal Studies*. Duke UP, 1990.

Fleming, David. "Rhetoric as a Course of Study." *College English*, vol. 61, no. 2, November 1998, pp. 169–91.

Fogelmark, Staffan. "A Troublesome Antithesis in Lysias 12.88." *Harvard Studies in Classical Philology*, no. 83, 1979, pp. 109–42.

Fritsch, Matthias. "Derrida's Democracy to Come." *Constellations*, vol. 9, no. 4, 2002, pp. 574–97.

———. "The Performative and the Normative." *Performatives After Deconstruction*. Edited by Mauro Senatore. Bloomsbury, 2013.

———. *The Promise of Memory: History and Politics in Marx, Benjamin, and Derrida*. SUNY P, 2005.

Garver, Eugene. "The Rhetoric of Friendship in Plato's *Lysis*." *Rhetorica*, vol. 24, no. 2, 2006, pp. 127–46.

Gasché, Rodolphe. *Inventions of Difference: On Jacques Derrida*. Harvard UP, 1994.

Glaser, K., "Gang und Ergebnis des Platonischen *Lysis*." *Wiener Studien*, vol. 53, 1935, pp. 47–67.

Glidden, David K. "The *Lysis* on Loving One's Own." *The Classical Quarterly*, vol. 31, no. 1, 1981, pp. 39–59.

Gorgias. *Encomium of Helen*. Translated by George Kennedy. *The Older Sophists: A Complete Translation by Several Hands of the Fragments in* Die Fragmente der Vorsokratiker *Edited by Diels–Kranz with a New Edition of Antiphon and of Euthydemus*. Edited by Rosamond Kent Sprague. U of South Carolina P, 1972, pp. 50–54.

Green, Joshua. "The Bookie of Virtue." *Washington Monthly*, June 2003, https://washingtonmonthly.com/magazine/june-2003/the-bookie-of-virtue/.

Gronbeck, Bruce E. "Gorgias on Rhetoric and Poetic: A Rehabilitation." *The Southern Speech Communication Journal*, vol. 38, Fall 1972, pp. 27–38.

Gunn, Joshua. "Mourning Humanism, or, the Idiom of Haunting." *Quarterly Journal of Speech*, vol. 92, no. 1, 2006, pp. 77–102.

Guthrie, W. K. C. *A History of Greek Philosophy, Vol. 3: The Fifth-Century Enlightenment, Part 1: The Sophists*. Cambridge UP, 1977.

———. *A History of Greek Philosophy, Vol. 4, Plato: The Man and His Dialogues: Earlier Period*. Cambridge UP, 1977.

Hawhee, Debra. *Bodily Arts: Rhetoric and Athletics in Ancient Greece*. U of Texas P, 2004.

———. "Bodily Pedagogies: Rhetoric, Athletics, and the Sophists' Three Rs." *College English*, vol. 65, no. 2, November 2002, pp. 142–62.

Howells, Christina. *Derrida: Deconstruction from Phenomenology to Ethics*. Polity P, 1999.

Howland, Jacob. "Plato's Reply to Lysias: *Republic 1* and *2* and *Against Eratosthenes*." *American Journal of Philology*, vol. 125, 2004, pp. 179–208.

Hunter, Virginia J. "Introduction: Status Distinctions in Athenian Law." *Law and Social Status in Classical Athens*. Edited by Virginia J. Hunter and J. C. Edmondson. Oxford UP, 2000, pp. 18–23.

Hägglund, Martin. *Radical Atheism: Derrida and the Time of Life*. Stanford UP, 2008.

Isocrates. *Against the Sophists*. Isocrates I. Translated by David C. Mirhady and Yun Lee Too. U of Texas P, 2000, pp. 61–66.

———. *Antidosis*. Isocrates I. Translated by David C. Mirhady and Yun Lee Too. U of Texas P, 2000, pp. 201–64.

———. *Encomium of Helen*. Isocrates I. Translated by David C. Mirhady and Yun Lee Too. U of Texas P, 2000, pp. 31–48.

———. *On the Peace*. Isocrates II. Translated by Terry L. Papillon. U of Texas P, 2004, pp. 134–66.

———. *Panathenaicus*. Isocrates II. Translated by Terry L. Papillon. U of Texas P, 2004, pp. 167–227.

———. *Panegyricus*. Isocrates II. Translated by Terry L. Papillon. U of Texas P, 2004, pp. 23–73.

———. *To Demonicus*. Isocrates I. Translated by David C. Mirhady and Yun Lee Too. U of Texas P, 2000, pp. 19–30.

Jaeger, Werner Wilhelm. *Paideia: The Ideals of Greek Culture, Vol. 3*. Translated by Gilbert Highet. Oxford UP, 1944.

Jebb, Richard C. *The Attic Orators from Lysias to Isaeos*. Macmillan and Co., 1876.

Kamen, Deborah. *Status in Classical Athens*. Princeton UP, 2013.

Kearney, Richard. *Debates in Continental Philosophy: Conversations with Contemporary Thinkers*. Fordham UP, 2004.

———. "Derrida and the Ethics of Dialogue." *Philosophy & Social Criticism*, vol. 19, no. 1, 1993, pp. 1–14.

———. "Derrida's Ethical Re-Turn." *Working through Derrida*. Edited by Gary B. Madison. Northwestern UP, 1993, pp. 28–59.

Kearney, Richard and Mark Dooley. "Hospitality, Justice, and Responsibility: A Dialogue with Jacques Derrida." *Questioning Ethics: Contemporary Debates in Continental Philosophy*. Edited by Richard Kearney and Mark Dooley. Routledge, 1999, pp. 65–83.

Kennedy, George A. *The Art of Persuasion in Greece*. Princeton UP, 1963.

———. *A New History of Classical Rhetoric*. Princeton UP, 1994.

———. "The Earliest Rhetorical Handbooks." *On Rhetoric: A Theory of Civic Discourse*. Edited by George A. Kennedy. Oxford UP, 2007, pp. 293–306.

Kennedy, Rebecca Futo. *Immigrant Women in Athens: Gender, Ethnicity, and Citizenship in the Classical City*. Routledge, 2014.

Kerferd, G. B. *The Sophistic Movement*. Cambridge UP, 1981.

Kinsley, Michael. "Bill Bennett's Bad Bet." *Slate*. May 4, 2003.

Lanham, Richard A. "The Q Question." *The Electronic Word: Democracy, Technology, and the Arts*. U of Chicago P, 1993, pp. 154–94.

Leonard, Miriam. "Introduction: 'Today, on the Eve of Platonism . . . .'" *Derrida and Antiquity*. Edited by Miriam Leonard. Oxford UP, 2010, pp. 1–16.

Levinas, Emmanuel. *Otherwise Than Being or Beyond Essence*. Translated by Alphonso Lingis. Duquesne UP, 1998.

———. *Totality and Infinity: An Essay on Exteriority*. Translated by Alphonso Lingis. Duquesne UP, 1969.

Liddell, H. G. and R. Scott. *An Intermediate Greek-English Lexicon Founded upon the Seventh Edition of Liddell and Scott's Greek-English Lexicon*. Oxford UP, 1889.

Loening, Thomas C. "The Autobiographical Speeches of Lysias and the Biographical Tradition." *Hermes*, vol. 109, 1981, pp. 280–94.

Loraux, Nicole. *The Invention of Athens: The Funeral Oration in the Classical City*. Translated by Alan Sheridan. Harvard UP, 1986.

Ludwig, Paul W. "Without Foundations: Plato's 'Lysis' and Postmodern Friendship." *The American Political Science Review*, vol. 104, no. 1, 2010, pp. 134–50.

Lysias. *Against Eratosthenes* (Lys. 12). *Lysias*. Translated by S. C. Todd. U of Texas P, 2000.

———. *Against Simon* (Lys. 3). *Lysias*. Translated by S. C. Todd. U of Texas P, 2000.

———. *For the Disabled Man* (Lys. 24). *Lysias*. Translated by S. C. Todd. U of Texas P, 2000.

———. *For Mantitheus* (Lys. 16). *Lysias*. Translated by S. C. Todd. U of Texas P, 2000.

———. *On the Death of Eratosthenes* (Lys. 1). *Lysias*. Translated by S. C. Todd. U of Texas P, 2000.

Marrou, H. I. *A History of Education in Antiquity*. Translated by George Lamb. U of Wisconsin P, 1956.

Miller, J. Hillis. "Derrida's Remains." *Mosaic*, vol. 39, no. 3, September 2006, pp. 197–211.

———. *For Derrida*. Fordham UP, 2009.

———. "Performativity as Performance/Performativity as Speech Act: Derrida's Special Theory of Performativity. *South Atlantic Quarterly*, vol. 106, no. 2, Spring 2007, pp. 219–35.

Miller, Paul A. "Ghosts in the *Politics of Friendship*." *Dead Theory: Derrida, Death, and the Afterlife of Theory*. Edited by Jeffrey R. Di Leo. Bloomsbury, 2016, pp. 111–31.

———. *Postmodern Spiritual Practices: The Construction of the Subject and the Reception of Plato in Lacan, Derrida, and Foucault*. The Ohio State UP, 2007.

Mirhady, David and Yun Lee Too. "Introduction to Isocrates." *Isocrates I*. Translated by David C. Mirhady and Yun Lee Too. U of Texas P, 2000, pp. 1–11.

Mooney, T. Brian. "Plato's Theory of Love in the 'Lysis': A Defence." *Irish Philosophical Journal*, vol. 7, no. 1–2, 1990, pp. 131–59.

Mourelatos, Alexander P. D. "Gorgias on the Function of Language." *Philosophical Topics*, vol. 25, no. 2, 1987, pp. 135–70.

Muckelbauer, John. *The Future of Invention: Rhetoric, Postmodernism, and the Problem of Change.* SUNY P, 2008.

———. *Thinking through Style: Rhetoric, Philosophy, Pedagogy.* Unpublished manuscript.

Munro, Andrew. "Reading Austin Rhetorically." *Philosophy and Rhetoric*, vol. 46, no. 1, 2013, pp. 22–43.

Murphy, Thomas M. "The Vilification of Eratosthenes and Theramenes in Lysias 12." *The American Journal of Philology*, vol. 110, no. 1, Spring 1989, pp. 40–49.

Murray, James Stuart. "Plato on Power, Moral Responsibility and the Alleged Neutrality of Gorgias' Art of Rhetoric (Gorgias 456c–457b). *Philosophy and Rhetoric*, vol. 34, no. 4, 2001, pp. 355–63.

Naas, Michael. *Derrida From Now On.* Fordham UP, 2008.

———. *Taking on the Tradition: Jacques Derrida and the Legacies of Deconstruction.* Stanford UP, 2003.

Nealon, Jeffrey T. *Alterity Politics: Ethics and Performative Subjectivity.* Duke UP, 1998.

———. "Beyond Hermeneutics: Deleuze, Derrida and Contemporary Theory." *Between Deleuze and Derrida*. Edited by Paul Patton and John Protevi. Continuum, 2003.

Neel, Jasper. *Plato, Derrida, and Writing.* Southern Illinois UP, 1988.

Nehamas, Alexander and Paul Woodruff. "Introduction." *Phaedrus.* Hackett Publishing Company, 1995.

Nichols, Mary P. *Socrates on Friendship and Community: Reflections on Plato's* Symposium, Phaedrus, *and* Lysis. Cambridge UP, 2009.

Norris, Christopher. *Derrida.* Harvard UP, 1988.

Ober, Josiah. "I, Socrates . . . The Performative Audacity of Isocrates' *Antidosis.*" *Isocrates and Civic Education*. Edited by Takis Poulakos and David Depew. U of Texas P, 2004, pp. 21–43.

Ochs, Donovan J. *Consolatory Rhetoric: Grief, Symbol, and Ritual in the Greco-Roman Era.* U of South Carolina P, 1993.

Oliver, Kelly. "Rethinking Response Ethics: A Response to Len Lawlor." *Philosophy Today*, vol. 62, no. 2, 2018, pp. 619–27.

Ortiz-Robles, Mario. "Being Jacques Derrida." *Postmodern Culture*, vol. 15, no. 3, May 2005.

Pacific Heights. Dir. John Schlesigner. Morgan Creek Productions, 1990. Film.

Patterson, Cynthia. "The Hospitality of Athenian Justice: The Metic in Court." *Law and Social Status in Classical Athens.* Edited by Virginia J. Hunter and J. C. Edmondson. Oxford UP, 2000, pp. 93–112.

Penner, Terry and Christopher Rowe. "Preface." *Plato's* Lysis. Cambridge UP, 2005, pp. ix–xiv.

Perelman, Chaim and Lucie Olbrechts-Tyteca. *The New Rhetoric: A Treatise on Argumentation.* Translated by John Wilkinson and Purcell Weaver. U of Notre Dame P, 1969.

Peters, Benoît. *Derrida: A Biography.* Translated by Andrew Brown. Polity P, 2013.

Plato. *Gorgias.* Translated by W. D. Woodhead. *Plato: The Collected Dialogues.* Edited by Edith Hamilton and Huntington Cairns. Princeton UP, 1961, pp. 229–307.

———. *Lysis.* Translated by J. Wright. *Plato: The Collected Dialogues.* Edited by Edith Hamilton and Huntington Cairns. Princeton UP, 1961, pp. 145–68.

———. *Lysis*. Translated by David Bolotin. *Plato's Dialogue on Friendship: A New Interpretation of the* Lysis, *with a New Translation*. Cornell UP, 1979.

———. *Lysis*. Edited by Terry Penner and Christopher Rowe. Cambridge UP, 2005.

———. *Phaedrus*. Translated by Alexander Nehamas and Paul Woodruff. Hackett Publishing Company, 1995.

———. *Philebus*. Translated by R. Hackforth. *Plato: The Collected Dialogues*. Edited by Edith Hamilton and Huntington Cairns. Princeton UP, 1961, pp. 1086–150.

———. *Protagoras*. Translated by W. K. C. Guthrie. *Plato: The Collected Dialogues*. Edited by Edith Hamilton and Huntington Cairns. Princeton UP, 1961, pp. 308–52.

———. *Sophist*. Translated by F. M. Cornford. *Plato: The Collected Dialogues*. Edited by Edith Hamilton and Huntington Cairns. Princeton UP, 1961, pp. 957–1017.

———. *Symposium*. Translated by Michael Joyce. *Plato: The Collected Dialogues*. Edited by Edith Hamilton and Huntington Cairns. Princeton UP, 1961, pp. 526–74.

Porter, James I. "The Seductions of Gorgias." *Classical Antiquity*, vol. 12, no. 2, October 1993, pp. 267–99.

Porter, John R. "Adultery by the Book: Lysias 1." *Attic Orators*. Edited by Edwin Carawan. Oxford UP, 2007, pp. 60–87.

Poulakos, John. "Gorgias' *Encomium to Helen* and the Defense of Rhetoric." *Rhetorica*, vol. 1, no. 2, 1983, pp. 1–15.

———. *Sophistical Rhetoric in Classical Greece*. U of South Carolina P, 1995.

Poulakos, Takis. "Isocrates' Civic Education and the Question of Doxa." *Isocrates and Civic Education*. Edited by Takis Poulakos and David Depew. U of Texas P, 2004, pp. 44–65.

———. *Speaking for the Polis: Isocrates' Rhetorical Education*. U of South Carolina P, 1997.

Poulakos, Takis and David Depew, editors. *Isocrates and Civic Education*. U of Texas P, 2004.

Raffoul, François. *The Origins of Responsibility*. Indiana UP, 2010.

Rorty, Richard. "Philosophy as a Kind of Writing: An Essay on Derrida." *New Literary History*, vol. 10, no. 1, 1978, pp. 141–60.

Rosenfeld, Michel. "Derrida's Ethical Turn and America: Looking Back from the Crossroads of Global Terrorism and the Enlightenment." *Cardozo Law Review*, vol. 27, 2006, pp. 815–45.

Rosenfield, Lawrence W. "The Practical Celebration of Epideictic." *Rhetoric in Transition*. Edited by Eugene E. White. Penn State UP, 1980, pp. 131–55.

Rosenmeyer, Thomas G. "Gorgias, Aeschylus, and Apate." *American Journal of Philology*, vol. 76, no. 3, 1955, pp. 225–60.

Saint-Amour, Paul K. "'Christmas Yet to Come': Hospitality, Futurity, the *Carol*, and 'The Dead.'" *Representations*, vol. 98, no. 1, Spring 2007, pp. 93–117.

Schiappa, Edward. "Gorgias's *Helen* Revisited." *Quarterly Journal of Speech*, vol. 81, 1995, pp. 310–24.

———. "History and Neo-Sophistic Criticism: A Reply to Poulakos." *Philosophy & Rhetoric*, vol. 23, no. 4, 1990, pp. 307–15.

Scott, Gary Alan. *Plato's Socrates as Educator*. SUNY P, 2000.

Searle, John R. "Reiterating the Differences: A Reply to Derrida." *Glyph* 2, 1977, pp. 198–208.

Seegert, Natasha. "Play of Sniffication: Coyotes Sing in the Margins." *Philosophy & Rhetoric* vol. 47, no. 2, 2014, pp. 158–78.

Segal, Charles P. "Gorgias and the Psychology of the *Logos*," *Harvard Studies in Classical Philology*, vol. 66, 1962, pp. 99–155.

Sheard, Cynthia M. "The Public Value of Epideictic Rhetoric." *College English*, vol. 58, 1996, pp. 765–94.

Sipiora, Phillip. "Introduction: The Ancient Concept of *Kairos*." *Rhetoric and Kairos: Essays in History, Theory, and Praxis*. Edited by Phillip Sipiora and James S. Baumlin. SUNY P, 2002, pp. 1–22.

Sipiora, Phillip and James S. Baumlin. *Rhetoric and Kairos: Essays in History, Theory, and Praxis*. SUNY P, 2002.

Sprague, Rosamond Kent. *The Older Sophists*. U of South Carolina P, 1972.

Steinberger, Peter J. "Who is Cephalus?" *Political Theory*, vol. 24, no. 2, May 1996, pp. 172–99.

Sullivan, Dale L. "*Kairos* and the Rhetoric of Belief." *Quarterly Journal of Speech*, vol. 78, 1992, pp. 317–32.

Thucydides. *History of the Peloponnesian War. Thucydides Translated into English, Vol. 1*. Edited by Benjamin Jowett. Clarendon P, 1900.

Timmerman, David M. and Edward Schiappa. *Classical Greek Rhetorical Theory and the Disciplining of Discourse*. Cambridge UP, 2010.

Trenkner, Sophie. *The Greek Novella in the Classical Period*. Cambridge UP, 1958.

Ulmer, Gregory L. *Applied Grammatology: Post(E)-Pedagogy from Jacques Derrida to Joseph Beuys*. Johns Hopkins UP, 1985.

Untersteiner, Mario. *The Sophists*. Translated by Kathleen Freeman. Philosophical Library, 1954.

Usher, Stephen. "Individual Characterisation in Lysias." *Eranos*, vol. 63, 1965, pp. 99–119.

———. "Lysias and His Clients." *Greek, Roman, and Byzantine Studies*, vol. 17, 1976, pp. 31–40.

Valiavitcharska, Vessela. "Correct *Logos* and Truth in Gorgias' *Encomium of Helen*." *Rhetorica: A Journal of the History of Rhetoric*, vol. 24, no. 2, 2006, pp. 147–61.

Vernant, Jean-Pierre. *The Origins of Greek Thought*. Cornell UP, 1962.

Vickers, Brian. *In Defense of Rhetoric*. Clarendon P, 1988.

Vitale, Francesco. *Biodeconstruction: Jacques Derrida and the Life Sciences*. Translated by Mauro Senatore, SUNY P, 2018.

Vitanza, Victor J. *Negation, Subjectivity, and the History of Rhetoric*. SUNY P, 1997.

Vlastos, Gregory. "The Individual as an Object of Love in Plato." *Platonic Studies*. Princeton UP, 1973, pp. 3–34.

Walker, Jeffrey. *The Genuine Teachers of This Art: Rhetorical Education in Antiquity*. U of South Carolina P, 2012.

———. *Rhetoric and Poetics in Antiquity*. Oxford UP, 2000.

Walzer, Arthur E. "Teaching 'Political Wisdom': Isocrates and the Tradition of *Dissoi Logoi*." *The Viability of the Rhetorical Tradition*. Edited by Richard Graff et al. SUNY P, 2005, pp. 113–24.

Wardy, Robert. *The Birth of Rhetoric: Gorgias, Plato and Their Successors*. Routledge, 1996.

White, Eric C. *Kaironomia: On the Will-to-Invent*. Cornell UP, 1987.

Whitehead, David. *The Ideology of the Athenian Metic*. Cambridge UP, 1977.

Wood, David. "Beyond Deconstruction?" *Contemporary French Philosophy*. Edited by A. P. Griffiths. Cambridge UP, 1987, pp. 175–94.

Wooten, Cecil W. "The Earrings of Polemarchus' Wife (Lysias 12.19)." *The Classical World*, vol. 82, no. 1, September–October 1988, pp. 29–31.

Worman, Nancy. "The Body as Argument: Helen in Four Greek Texts." *Classical Antiquity*, vol. 16, no. 1, April 1997, pp. 151–203.

Worsham, Lynn. "Moving Beyond the Logic of Sacrifice: Animal Studies, Trauma Studies, and the Path to Posthumanism." *Writing Posthumanism, Posthuman Writing*. Edited by Sidney I. Dobrin. Parlor P, 2014, 19–55.

Zlomislic, Marko. *Jacques Derrida's Aporetic Ethics*. Lexington Books, 2007.

Zuckert, Catherine H. *Plato's Philosophers: The Coherence of the Dialogues*. U of Chicago P, 2009.

INDEX

affirmation: ethics of, 25–27, 34; pre-performative force of, 55, 57–62; reproducibility of, 58

Against Eratosthenes (Lysias): about, 65–66; as advertisement for future clients, 79–80; Athens' hospitality described in, 69–70; as biography of Lysias, 69, 77, 82, 82n9; historical context for, 66n3; Lysias's transformation from guest to host to hostage to 'ghost,' 78–88; performative force of, 66; and Pericles's invitation to Lysias's family, 80–81; prose style in, 89; rhetorical skill exhibited in, 78–80, 87; as turning point in Lysias's career, 88

Alter, Jonathan, 131, 132

alterity: affirmation compared to speech act performativity, 43; and calls for responses, 27; and function of funeral speeches, 175; of ghostwriters, 98; and introductions, 17–18, 19–22; as necessary to identity, 57–58, 129; and transformation in learning, 13. *See also* otherness; self-presence

Althusser, Louis, funeral speech for, 173

Anderson, Nicole, 34, 40–41n11

antifoundationalist epistemology, 47, 49, 53

aporia: concept of, 33; in Derrida's ethics, 11, 138; in funerary texts, 14–15, 174; in hospitality, 71

arche-writing, and performativity, 9

Aristophanes of Byzantium, 67

Aristotle, 37; criticism of rhetorical handbooks, 5, 24; on epideictic rhetoric, 164, 166n2, 167–68, 169; on epilogues, 177–78; as epitome of civic education, 108; ethos, 92; and friendship, 140; on introductions, 19–21; *Nicomachean Ethics*, 154; *Rhetoric*, 91, 154, 177; rhetoric's relationship with ethics, 109; types of speeches described by, 106–7; on utility friendship, 155n13

asignification: in funeral speeches, 174; in introductions, 23; meaning of, 4; in speech act theory, 38, 179

Athenian exceptionalism, 68, 102, 102n2

Athens: hospitality toward foreigners in, 70–71; love of oratory in, 94n18; Lysias as interpreter of life in, 99; metics in, 67–68; school of rhetoric in, 102

athletic training, rhetorical training compared to, 120

Atkins, G. Douglas, 8

Attic literary tradition, 70, 87, 89–90, 99, 101, 179
audiences: appeals to emotions of, 4; as beyond our control and comprehension, 16; and epideictic rhetoric, 164, 166n2, 168–69; knowledge of, 14, 44; molding of, 12, 19, 23, 48, 62; possession of, 152–53; and receptivity, 1, 4–5, 20; use of varying rhetorical strategies on, 149–53
Austin, J. L.: *How to Do Things with Words*, 39–40, 179; influence on Derrida's work, 7, 40; and notion of promises, 113, 114; and perlocutionary force, 4; on promises, 114n19. *See also* perlocutionary force; speech act theory

Bakewell, Geoff, 78–79
Ballif, Michelle, 8–9, 50, 52, 55, 59, 96
Barthes, Roland, funeral speech for, 162, 170, 172
Bateman, J. J., 79
being: as contaminated, 35–36; disappearance in, 94–95; disruption of, 2, 11, 13, 16, 130, 149–51; education to transform nature of, 104; as initiated by the other, 43; and responsibility of 'yes,' 57–58; vulnerability in, 60. *See also* identity
Bennett, William J., 111n13, 130–32; *Book of Virtues*, 108–9, 111; and "The Bookie of Virtue," 131
Bennington, Geoffrey, 28, 28n1, 31
Bernasconi, Robert, 28, 29
Biesecker, Barbara A., 7n4, 8
Blanchot, Maurice: friendship with Foucault, 142, 181; memorial speech for, 171
Bolotin, David, 157n14
Brault, Pascale-Anne, 161
Brauw, Michael de, 177
Bruss, Kristine, 92n16
Burgess, Theodore, *Epideictic Literature*, 165

Carey, Christopher, 80, 88, 90–91, 94, 94n18
Cassin, Barbara, 39
character, development of, 104–6, 109, 111n13, 116, 118–19. *See also* ethopoeia
Cicero, 24
civic education, 108–9, 111
civic virtue, Isocrates's concern for, 13, 103–5. *See also* Isocrates

communication, meaning and performativity in, 38, 41
conclusions and epilogues, 177
Connolly, Joy, 112
Connors, Clare, 93
Consigny, Scott, 47, 51, 54–55
Cope, E. M., 165
Critchley, Simon, 3, 29n5, 31n9; *The Ethics of Deconstruction*, 30–31
Crowley, Sharon, 8n5, 53; "Of Gorgias and Grammatology," 8

Dasenbrock, Reed Way, 39
Davis, Colin, 96
Davis, Diane, 37, 45, 75, 76, 82, 114–15; *Inessential Solidarity*, 7, 8
de Man, Paul, 29, 29n5, 113, 173
decisions, 128–29, 131
deconstruction: concept of, 10–11, 25; Derrida on, 27–28; and *différance*, 7n4; ethical structure of, 30–33; importance of 'yes' in, 57–58; and otherness, 3; use of speech terminology in, 43; vocabulary for, 2
Deleuze, Gilles, 162
deliberation: and *kairos*, 127–28; toward decisions, 128–29
deliberative rhetoric, 106–8, 124–25, 164, 165, 169
Depew, David, 108–9
Derrida, Jacques: on decision making, 128–29, 131; on deconstruction, 25, 27; "ethical turn" of, 29–30, 29n5; on friendship, 158; and Greek philosophical tradition, 9–11; on hospitality, 71–76, 82; influence of Austin, 40, 42; learning from the dead, 162; notion of identity, 44; open-endedness of intellectual traditions, 16; on promises, 101, 113–15, 116, 125–26; on specters, 95–96, 98; unanticipatable alterity in, 6; 'yes' in performativity, 55, 57. *See also* alterity; aporia; decisions; deconstruction; Derridean ethics; friendship; hospitality; identity; performativity; promises; responsibility; speech act theory
Derrida, Jacques, funerary texts of: for after his own death, 175; and alterity, 170; for Althusser, 173; aporia in mourning friends, 14–15; for Barthes, 170, 172; for Blanchot, 171, 173; for de Man, 173; Derrida's discomfort with, 170–71, 181; Der-

rida's thoughts about, 162–63; difficulty of speaking, 173–74; for Lyotard, 173, 181; preserving distance between the dead and mourners, 171–72; and rhetorical legacy, 161

Derrida, Jacques, works by: *Acts of Literature*, 43; *Acts of Religion*, 72–74, 84, 99; *Adieu*, 83; *Aporias*, 73; "A Certain Impossible Possibility of Saying the Event," 101; *Dissemination*, 1, 17, 17n6, 44, 65, 68, 325; "Final Words," 163, 175; "Force of Law," 33; "Hostipitality," 71; "How to Avoid Speaking: Denials," 114, 114n19; "In Memoriam: Of the Soul," 161; "Limited Inc a b c," 38, 45, 93; *Margins of Philosophy*, 2; *Memoires for Paul de Man*, 113; "No Apocalypse, Not Now," 171–72; *Of Grammatology*, 27; *Of Hospitality*, 70, 72, 74–76, 82; *On Cosmopolitanism and Forgiveness*, 73; *On the Name*, 25, 27, 34; *Paper Machine*, 76; 'Le Parjure,' *Perhaps*, 115, 121; "Plato's Pharmacy," 35; *Points*, 32–34; *Politics of Friendship*, 33, 133, 135, 140–41, 163, 181; *Psyche: The Inventions of the Other*, 3; "Remarks on Deconstruction and Pragmatism," 47; *Rogues*, 9; "Signature Event Context," 40, 41; *Specters of Marx*, 66, 88, 98, 129, 162; *Taste for the Secret*, 34; "Ulysses Gramophone," 55, 57; "The University without Condition," 43; "Violence and Metaphysics," 32; "We Other Greeks," 10; *Who's Afraid of Philosophy?*, 181; *Without Alibi*, 113n18; *Work of Mourning*, 161

Derridean ethics: aporetic conception of, 33–35; and ethical responsibility, 36–38; as ethics of affirmation, 25–27, 34; as ethics of ethics, 27, 32–33; importance of performativity to, 40–41, 40–41n11; overview of, 2–3, 9; priority of the other in, 34; rhetorical qualities of, 11, 181; scholarly responses to, 29–30, 31; summary of, 180

Derridean hauntology, 8–9, 43, 87, 96, 115

Devries, William, 94

différance: concept of, 3, 7n4; ethical subject as effect of, 33; as reimagination of Austin's notion of performativity, 40; and responsibility, 7; and Socrates's dialogues, 14

Diogenes Laertes, 140

Dionysius of Halicarnassus, 89–90, 91n14, 92n16, 94; *The Critical Essays*, 65

Dover, K. J., 66n3, 67

Edwards, Michael, 89, 89n13

emotional appeals, 178

Encomium of Helen (Gorgias): and affirmation of identity, 179; complexity of ethical interpretation in, 52–55; notions of acquiescence and responsibility in, 55–62, 63; power of persuasion in, 12, 47, 51, 62–63; praise of *logos* in, 50, 62

ephodos, 1, 4–5, 23

epideictic rhetoric: about, 106; civic function of, 166–68, 167n3, 168n4; Derrida as practitioner of, 14; etymology of, 168; historical significance of, 163–64; in Isocrates's pedagogy, 111, 117; phenomenological approach to, 169–70; problem of presence in, 164–65, 167–69, 168n4, 171; theorizing about, 163–70. *See also* Derrida, Jacques, funerary texts

Eroticus, authorship of, 96n19

ethics: of affirmation, 25–27, 34; deconstruction of, 27–28, 28n1; definition and use of term, 2–3, 26; of ethics, 32–33; exclusion and alterity, 6n3, 35–36. *See also* Derridean ethics; friendship; hospitality; responsibility

ethopoeia, 89, 90–93, 91nn14–15, 92n16

Felman, Shoshanna, 39

Fish, Stanley, 53

Fleming, David, 106

Fogelmark, Staffan, 87

forensic rhetoric, 106, 164, 165, 169

Foucault, Michel, funerary text for, 142, 162, 181

Frazer, James George, 35–36

free will: formation of, 55, 57–58; and pre-performative 'yes,' 61

Freud, Sigmund, 172

friendship: as analogous to philosophical experience, 136; and foundations (metaphysics), 137, 137n5; and funerary texts, 171, 173, 181; of goodness or virtue, 154, 155n13; impossibility of, 140–42, 143, 144, 155; inability to define the friend, 158–59; and performativity, 26, 140–41; and political theory, 137–38; possession as concept of, 156–57, 157n14; rhetorical problem of, 139; utility friendships, 154–56. *See also Lysis* (Plato)

Fritsch, Matthias, 31, 43, 114n20

funeral speeches and memorials: Derrida's discomfort with, 170–71; Derrida's rhetoric and thought on, 161–63; and difficulty of speaking, 173; problem of temporality and presence in, 162–63, 164–65, 171, 175; as rhetorical genre, 163, 167n3. *See also* Derrida, Jacques, funerary texts

future: and deliberative oratory, 107; in epideictic oratory, 167; and the future-to-come, 126–27; and promises, 115–16; and reading texts (*see* introductions); and reproducibility of rhetorical skill, 153; responding to, 121–30, 132–33; and results of rhetorical education, 120–21

Garver, Eugene, 139, 143, 144–45, 147
Gasché, Rodolphe, 31
ghostwriting, 65, 94
Gorgias of Leontini (500–392 BCE): antifoundationalist epistemology of, 47, 49; critiques of, 52–53; and dangerous capacities of rhetoric, 47–51, 48n5, 62; Isocrates as pupil of, 102n3; *On the Non-Existent, or On Nature*, 49; perspectives on persuasion, 2; praise of speech by, 62; unanticipatable alterity in, 6, 63. See also *Encomium of Helen* (Gorgias)
great books and higher education, 108, 111
Green, Joshua, 131, 132
Gronbeck, Bruce E., 53
Grote, George, 52
Guthrie, W. K. C., 49, 50

Hägglund, Martin, *Radical Atheism*, 31–32
Harrison, Jane Ellen, 35–36
Hawhee, Debra, 117, 120, 125
Hegel, G. W. F., 52
Heidegger affair, 29, 29n5
higher education, Isocrates's contribution to, 13, 108, 111
historiography, 9, 52
home, vulnerability of, 82, 85
hospitality: conditional hospitality, 28, 75–76, 82–83; denied in death, 86n11; as double-edged sword, 71–72; hospitality by right, 70–71; impossibility of, 75–76; Latin etymology of term, 71; mutual need of conditional and unconditional laws of, 75–77; performativity and, 26; and transformation of host, 99; unconditional welcoming in, 28–29, 73–75; vulnerability of home, 82

hostage, role in hospitality, 66, 74–75, 76, 82, 83
hosts: as hostages, 74–75; and unexpected guests, 73–74
Howells, Christina, 31, 33, 37
Howland, Jacob, 79
humanist scholarship, 105
Hunter, Virginia, 68

identity: challenges to, 2–3, 93; as effect, 52; and hospitality by right, 72–73; and invisibility in speechwriting, 94; necessity of alterity to, 57; and priority of the other, 180; and promises, 114–15, 114n20; self-identity as fiction, 35–36; and singularity, 83; structuring of, 43; transformation through persuasion, 44–45; and unknowable future 'I,' 126–27
illocutionary utterances, 39, 42
introductions: differing types of, 17–18n6; as interruptions, 21–22; power of, 1; as problematical rhetorical form, 17–19; retroactive movement of, 22–23; threatening nature of, 19, 20–21
Isocrates: affinity with Bennett, 130–31; ceremonial rhetoric of, 166; and civic education, 108–9, 109–10n10; classism in, 111–12; conservatism of moral ethos of, 111–13; critique of Gorgias's *Encomium of Helen*, 62; educational promise of, 105–8, 110, 116–17, 125–27, 179; as gambler, 132–33; and *kairos*, 123–27, 133; and natural ability, 111–12, 112n15, 116; pedagogical approach of, 117–18; pedagogy and the future, 13; perspectives on persuasion, 2; unanticipatable alterity in, 6; vision of rhetorical education, 103–6, 106n8, 119–21
Isocrates, works by: *Against the Sophists*, 112n15, 117–18, 122–24, 132; *Antidosis*, 104, 110–11, 116, 132, 166n2; *To Demonicus*, 112, 132; *On the Peace*, 121; *Panathenaicus*, 105, 111n12, 119; *Panegyricus*, 101, 102n2, 106, 107
Isocrates and Civic Education (Poulakos and Depew), 108–9

Jaeger, Werner, 102n3, 103
Jebb, Richard C., 67; *The Attic Orators*, 99

Johnson, Michael L., 8
justice, 29, 29n4, 106n8, 129–30, 133

kairos: concept of, 123–24; effect on self-presence, 126–27; and Isocrates's educational promise, 124–26, 133
Kamen, Deborah, 69
Kearney, Richard, 27, 31
Kennedy, George A., 50n7, 91–92, 162, 165, 166n2
Kennedy, Rebecca, 68
Kerferd, G. B., 52
Kinsley, Michael, 131

Lanham, Richard, 109–10n10
learning: importance of process in, 118–19; as risk-taking activity, 135; as transformation, 13, 102, 179
Leonard, Miriam, 10
Levinas, Emmanuel, 30, 31, 32, 32n10, 83, 162
Liddell, H. G., 157n14
Loening, Thomas C., 66n3
logographers, 65, 89n13, 90, 94, 94n18, 96
logos: meaning of, 50n7; powers of, 50; and public deliberation, 107; vulnerability of, 53
Loraux, Nicole, 166–67, 167n3
Ludwig, Paul W., 137n5, 144; "Without Foundations," 137–38
Lyotard, Jean-Francois, funeral speech for, 162, 173, 181
Lysias: Attic prose of, 70, 87, 89–90, 99; contributions to Greek oratory, 89; escape from imprisonment, 85–86; *For the Disabled Man*, 91–92; as ghostwriter, 94–97, 99, 101; as haunter of Athenian democracy, 66–67, 70, 86–88, 99, 101; as host to Athenian citizens, 81; as hostage after arrest, 82–85; and invisibility as speechwriter, 88–89, 94, 179; ontological instability of, 88; otherness of, 12–13; perspectives on persuasion, 2; as privileged metic, 67–68, 69–70, 77, 81, 83–84, 101; prose style of, 89–90; spectral qualities of, 96–97; theorization of, 95–96; unanticipatable alterity in, 6. *See also* hospitality
Lysis (Plato): aporetic approach in, 138–39; critiques of, 135–38; model of friendship in, 141–42; nature of friendships among characters in, 153–54; opening dialogue of, 143–44; and opposites attract argument for friendship, 155; overview of, 13–14; on pedagogy, 137; persuasion in, 143, 144; on persuasion's ethical force, 139–40; persuasive strategies in, 148–53; rhetorical failure in, 135–36, 144–45, 147; Socrates as rhetorical coach in, 145–48, 150–51; Socrates's inability to define friendship in, 158–59; thematic content of, 142–43; unanticipatable alterity in, 6; unknowability of friendship in, 179; utility friendships in, 154–57

Marrou, H. I., 103, 104, 117
metics (resident aliens): about, 67, 67n4; Athens' hospitality toward, 70–71, 76–77; *isoteleia* status, 69, 69n5; legal and political vulnerability of, 68–69; rights and responsibilities of, 68
Miller, J. Hillis, 40n11, 114n19, 161
Miller, Paul Allen, 9–10, 142
Montefiore, Alan, "Talking Liberties," interview with Derrida, 25, 26, 57
moral education, 110–13, 111n13, 130–32, 179
Mourelatos, Alexander P. D., 50
Muckelbauer, John, 4, 11
Munro, Andrew, 39
Murphy, Thomas M., 79
Murray, James Stuart, 49

Naas, Michael, 10–11, 28–29, 29n2, 75, 77, 140, 161
Nealon, Jeffrey T., 31, 33, 42n12
Neel, Jasper, 8
Nehamas, Alexander, 96n19
Nichols, Mary P., *Socrates on Friendship and Community*, 136–37, 136n4

Ober, Josiah, 104
Ochs, Donovan, 167
oikeion, 157n14
oikeiotes (suitability), 141
Olbrechts-Tyteca, Lucie, 165, 166, 167, 167n3
Oliver, Kelly, 32
Ortiz-Robles, Mario, 113
otherness: asserted by promises, 115–16; of the dead, 171; ethics of, 110; impossibility of defining, 16; and responsibility, 3; the

self's surrender to, 129; transformation into dramatic characters, 92. *See also* alterity; identity; Lysias; metics (resident aliens)

Patterson, Cynthia, 68, 71, 84, 84n10
Penner, Terry, 136, 149, 149n10, 150, 157n14
Perelman, Chaim, 165, 166, 167, 167n3
performative utterances, 42, 44–45, 57, 58, 114, 181
performativity: and *arche*-writing, 9; in communication, 38 (*see also* speech act theory); Derrida's notion of, 7, 11, 26, 40–41; importance to Derridean ethics, 45; and pre-performative forces, 42–43; in promises, 114; 'yes' in, 55, 56, 57, 58. *See also* friendship
Pericles's funeral oration, 15, 163–64, 174
perlocutionary force: and alterity, 11, 63; concept of, 4; as demonstrated by Lysias, 80; persuasion and, 11; Socrates and, 152
perlocutionary speech acts: concept of, 39; ethical significance of, 39
persuasion: components of classical paradigm of, 26; conditions of possibility for, 2; ethics of alterity in, 24; interaction of forces in, 44–45; openness to, 7; pernicious capacities of, 48, 62; as *rapprochement* with the other, 44, 178–79; as transformative encounter with otherness, 3; understanding the art of, 15. *See also* conclusions and epilogues; Derridean ethics; introductions; otherness; rhetoric; rhetorical education; rhetorical techniques and strategies; speech act theory
Peters, Benoît, 29n5
Phaedrus (Plato): authorship of *Eroticus* in, 96n19; critique of, 35; critique of Lysias's ghostwriting in, 79, 96–97; Lysias's presence and absence in, 97, 98; and modeling master rhetoricians, 153; Phaedrus's integrity in, 97–98; rhetoric in, 139, 142; on sophists and philosophy in, 49; tension of hospitality and spectrality in, 98–99; transformation of Lysias in, 88–89
pharmakoi, burning of, 35–36
Philebus (Plato), 48
philosophia, views of, 104

Plato: Academy of, 103; ceremonial rhetoric of, 166; and civic education, 108, 109, 109–10n10; on conclusions, 178; friendship and persuasion, 13–14; on Gorgias, 48; on Lysias, 12, 79; perspectives on persuasion, 2; rhetoric's relationship with ethics, 109; view of rhetoric, 48n5, 49. *See also* friendship; *Lysis* (Plato); *Phaedrus* (Plato)
Plato, works by: *Gorgias*, 48–49, 139, 142–43; *Philebus*, 48; *Protagoras*, 13, 49, 142–43; *Republic*, 79, 81n8; *Sophist*, 13, 49, 142–43; *Symposium*, 135. See also *Lysis* (Plato); *Phaedrus* (Plato)
Plato's Lysis (Penner and Rowe), 136
political theory and friendship, 137–38
Porter, James I., 49, 51, 53, 59
postmodernism, 138
Poulakos, John, 52, 54, 59, 102
Poulakos, Takis, 103, 107, 108–9, 119
pre-performative forces, 12, 55, 57, 181. See also *Encomium of Helen*; performativity; promises
progymnasmata, 117
promises: about, 101, 113; as haunted, 125; and the self, 181; and time, 115–16. *See also* Isocrates
prooimion: about, 1, 4; benefit of, 20; composed after the fact, 22; in Derrida's work, 18n6; direct opening as problematical rhetorical form, 17–21; as disruptive text, 23
public life, contribution to, 103, 105–6, 111n12
purity, loss of, 35–36

Raffoul, François, 33
reading, ethics of, 35
reproducibility of affirmation, 58
responsibility: and affirmation of the other, 181; concept of ethical responsibility, 34; and conditions of possibility, 180; contamination of self as basis for, 36–37; enabled by ethics, 32; and funeral oration, 174–75; and openness to change, 130; to the other, 27, 37, 84, 128; rupture of self as requirement to developing, 121; and spectral presence, 96; to victims, 87. See also *Encomium of Helen* (Gorgias)
rhetoric: artistry in, 165–66, 166n2; bad reputation of, 47 (*see also* Gorgias of Leontini (500–392 BCE)); and civic education,

109–10n10 (*see also* Isocrates); classical tradition of, 15, 24, 180; instrumentality of, 3–5, 24, 179; as means of power and control, 48–49 (*see also* Lysias). *See also* Aristotle; persuasion; Plato; speech act theory

Rhetoric to Alexander, 1, 4–5, 19

Rhetoric to Herennius, 1, 4–5, 19, 23, 177, 178

rhetorical education: codes and rules in, 119–20, 122–23, 129–30, 130; competing visions of, 103–4; Isocrates's vision of, 104–5; pedagogical approaches to, 8, 8n5, 102, 102n3, 148–53; purpose of, 119–21; and responses to an unknowable future, 121–30, 132–33; under Isocrates, 103. *See also* Aristotle; Isocrates; *Lysis* (Plato); Plato

rhetorical handbooks, 5, 18n6, 23–24. *See also Rhetoric to Alexander*; *Rhetoric to Herennius*

rhetorical techniques and strategies, 4, 148–53, 178. *See also* conclusions and epilogues; introductions

Romilly, Jacqueline de, 52

Rosenfield, Lawrence W., 168, 169–70

Rosenmeyer, Thomas G., 50

Rowe, Christopher, 136, 149, 149n10, 150, 157n14

Schiappa, Edward, 48n5, 52, 104

scholarship, Derrida's impact on, 8, 29–30, 31

Scott, Gary, 147, 150, 151

Scott, R., 157n14

Segal, Charles P., 50

self-presence: decentering of, 149–50, 151; effect of *kairos* on, 126–27; interruption of, 2, 11, 13, 16, 34–35, 37. *See also* hospitality; identity

Sheard, Cynthia, 165

Sicilian Expedition, 47, 47n2

sight, pre-performative force of, 61

Sipiora, Phillip, 123

Socrates, persuasive force of, 139–40

sophistic education, 102n3

sophistry, 49, 51, 52, 165

sophists, 12, 38, 52. *See also* Gorgias of Leontini (500–392 BCE); logographers

specters: on boundaries of presence and absence, 95; virtuality of, 96

speech: interrupting the influence of, 51–52, 62–63; pharmaceutical effects of, 60; as political tool, 4

speech act theory: asignification in, 38; in Derridean thought, 11, 26; effects of language on audiences, 179; performativity and meaning, 41–42, 57–58

speeches: elements of, 19n7; Isocrates's distinction of good speeches, 124

speechwriting, professional, 97. *See also* logographers

Steinberger, Peter J., 81n8

Thirty Tyrants, 65, 66, 66n3, 78, 82, 86

Thucydides, 161, 163–65, 167–68, 169, 171

Timmerman, David M., 104

truth: Gorgias's antifoundationalist thinking on, 47–48n3, 49; and *logos*, 50; and philosophy, 136n4, 137; and rhetoric, 5, 12

Ulmer, Gregory L., 8

Usher, Stephen, 80, 89, 91, 93, 96n19

utterance-origin, 39, 40, 42

Valiavitcharska, Vessela, 54

Vernant, Jean-Pierre, 4, 6

Vickers, Brian, 166, 167, 167n3

virtue: as disrupted by ethics, 110; and Isocrates's educational vision, 13, 103–5, 131

Vitanza, Victor, 53

Walker, Jeffrey, 105, 108, 117–18; *Rhetoric and Poetics in Antiquity*, 168n4

Walzer, Arthur E., 106n8

Wardy, Robert, 62

Western metaphysics, 9–11, 27

White, Eric Charles, 124

Whitehead, David, 67, 67n4, 69, 69n5, 70–71

Woodruff, Paul, 96n19

Wooten, Cecil W., 79

The Work of Mourning (Pascale-Anne and Naas), 161, 161n1

Worman, Nancy, 59

writing process, 8n5; assumptions about, 8

Zuckert, Catherine H., 136; *Plato's Philosophers*, 137

CLASSICAL MEMORIES/MODERN IDENTITIES
Paul Allen Miller and Richard H. Armstrong, Series Editors

Classical antiquity has bequeathed a body of values and a "cultural koine" that later Western cultures have appropriated and adapted as their own. However, the transmission of ancient culture was and remains a malleable and contested process. This series explores how the classical world has been variously interpreted, transformed, and appropriated to forge a usable past and a livable present. Books published in this series detail both the positive and negative aspects of classical reception and take an expansive view of the topic. Thus it includes works that examine the function of translations, adaptations, invocations, and classical scholarship in the formation of personal, cultural, national, sexual, and racial formations.

The Ethics of Persuasion: Derrida's Rhetorical Legacies
BROOKE ROLLINS

*Arms and the Woman: Classical Tradition and
Women Writers in the Venetian Renaissance*
FRANCESCA D'ALESSANDRO BEHR

Hip Sublime: Beat Writers and the Classical Tradition
EDITED BY SHEILA MURNAGHAN AND RALPH M. ROSEN

Ancient Sex: New Essays
EDITED BY RUBY BLONDELL AND KIRK ORMAND

Odyssean Identities in Modern Cultures: The Journey Home
EDITED BY HUNTER GARDNER AND SHEILA MURNAGHAN

Virginia Woolf, Jane Ellen Harrison, and the Spirit of Modernist Classicism
JEAN MILLS

Humanism and Classical Crisis: Anxiety, Intertexts, and the Miltonic Memory
JACOB BLEVINS

Tragic Effects: Ethics and Tragedy in the Age of Translation
THERESE AUGST

Reflections of Romanity: Discourses of Subjectivity in Imperial Rome
RICHARD ALSTON AND EFROSSINI SPENTZOU

Philology and Its Histories
EDITED BY SEAN GURD

*Postmodern Spiritual Practices: The Construction of the Subject and
the Reception of Plato in Lacan, Derrida, and Foucault*
PAUL ALLEN MILLER